THE GLOBAL 1920S

The 1920s is often recognised as a decade of fascism, flappers and film. Covering the political, economic and social developments of the 1920s throughout the world, *The Global 1920s* takes an international and cross-cultural perspective on the critical changes and conditions that prevailed from roughly 1919 to 1930.

With twelve chapters on themes including international diplomacy and the imperial powers, film and music, art and literature, women and society, democracy, fascism, and science and technology, this book explores both the 'big' questions of capitalism, class and communism on the one hand and the everyday experience of citizens around the globe on the other. Utilising archival sources throughout, it concludes with an extensive discussion of the circumstances surrounding the 1929 stock market crash and the onset of the Great Depression, the effects of which were felt worldwide.

Covering topics from the oil boom in South America to the start of civil war in China, employment advances and setbacks for women across the globe, and the advent of radio and air travel, the authors provide a concise yet comprehensive overview of this turbulent decade. Containing illustrations and a selection of discussion questions at the end of each chapter, this book is valuable reading for students of the 1920s in global history.

Richard Carr is a lecturer at Anglia Ruskin University, UK. He has written several books on political history including *Veteran MPs and Conservative Politics in the Aftermath of the Great War: The Memory of All That*. He is currently authoring a biography of Charlie Chaplin for Routledge.

Bradley W. Hart is an assistant professor at California State University, Fresno, USA. His previous works include *George Pitt-Rivers and the Nazis*, a biography of a prominent British anthropologist and fascist sympathiser, along with the co-edited volume *The Foundations of the British Conservative Party*.

DECADES IN GLOBAL HISTORY

This series takes a fresh view of decades in history, discussing each period from a truly global perspective and interrogating the traditional trope of a decade. In asking questions about what each decade actually represents throughout the wider world and exploring the transnational connections that shaped its course, this global approach allows the reader to see the great events of each decade as intricately bound into and moulded by international forces.

Titles in the series:

The Global 1920s
Richard Carr and Bradley W. Hart

Forthcoming titles:

The Global 1970s
Duco Hellema

The Global 1980s
Jonathan Davis

The Global 1930s
Susan Kingsley Kent and Marc Matera

THE GLOBAL 1920S

Politics, economics and society

Richard Carr and Bradley W. Hart

Routledge
Taylor & Francis Group

LONDON AND NEW YORK

First published 2016
by Routledge
2 Park Square, Milton Park, Abingdon, Oxon OX14 4RN

and by Routledge
711 Third Avenue, New York, NY 10017

Routledge is an imprint of the Taylor & Francis Group, an informa business

British Library Cataloguing in Publication Data
A catalogue record for this book is available from the British Library

Library of Congress Cataloging in Publication Data
Carr, Richard, 1985- author.
The global 1920s : politics, economics and society / Richard Carr and Bradley W. Hart.
pages cm. -- (Decades in global history)
Includes bibliographical references and index.
ISBN 978-1-138-77478-0 (hardback : alk. paper) -- ISBN 978-1-138-77479-7 (pbk. : alk. paper) -- ISBN 978-1-315-64072-3 (ebook) 1. Nineteen twenties. I. Hart, Bradley W., author. II. Title.
D720.C36 2016
909.82'2--dc23
2015032886

ISBN: 978-1-138-77478-0 (hbk)
ISBN: 978-1-138-77479-7 (pbk)
ISBN: 978-1-315-64072-3 (ebk)

Typeset in Bembo
by Taylor & Francis Books

CONTENTS

FIGURES

ACKNOWLEDGEMENTS

This book would not have been possible without the assistance of a number of individuals who deserve recognition. Firstly, we are grateful to Amy Welmers and the staff at Routledge for making this project possible and bearing with us through several delays in the writing process. Eve Setch was tremendously encouraging in commissioning the work in the first place. In addition, we are grateful to the anonymous peer reviewers who made a number of helpful suggestions throughout the project.

During the research and writing process itself, we have been fortunate to draw on the assistance of a number of current and former students who showed a keen interest in the project and will undoubtedly soon be writing books of their own. In California we received the valuable and extraordinary assistance of Gavin Baird, Isa Chancey and Megi Hakobjanyan, all of whom brought their unique skills and insights to the project. In Egypt, we were fortunate to have the help of Sumaya Attia, and in Cambridge we received the research and statistical support of Josh Younespour.

Teaching with Lucy Bland, Jon Davis, Sean Lang and Rohan McWilliam on various modules at Anglia Ruskin (ARU) which intersect with this period certainly helped sharpen some of the chapters. Alison Ainley has always been a model of kindness and help as Head of Department for Humanities and Social Sciences at ARU. In addition, the faculty of California State University, Fresno, provided important support throughout the writing process. Our students, past and present, provided many valuable questions and insights which have added to this work in innumerable ways.

Finally, we would be remiss to not include a word of thanks to the Master and fellows of Churchill College, Cambridge, for all the support rendered during the research and writing process of this book, among other projects. Specifically, Allen Packwood and his staff at the Churchill Archives Centre, Cambridge, have always been immensely helpful and hospitable. We offer our sincere thanks for all their support.

INTRODUCTION

Chaos broke out on New York City's Wall Street on the afternoon of 29 October 1929. Sweat-drenched men flooded out of the stock exchange, some heading for the church at the end of the block where they huddled together regardless of their faith (or lack of it). Others prayed and wept on the edges of the trading floor in scenes replicated across New York and beyond. Entire fortunes were wiped out that afternoon, symbolically marking the beginning of the period remembered today as the Great Depression, and many more would be lost in the months to come. Rumours began to spread around the country of businessmen committing suicide in the days and weeks that followed the crash and, while sometimes exaggerated, there were documented cases of people taking their own lives rather than face life after being ruined. The dream of the 'Roaring Twenties' had crashed to an abrupt halt on the streets of New York, and the pain would soon spread around the globe. Two years after the crash, the British government would be forced to abandon the gold standard amidst a run on the country's gold reserves, humiliating the country's government and further rupturing the interwar world financial system. At the same time, the German government stood on the brink of collapse in the face of skyrocketing unemployment. In 1933, Adolf Hitler would become the country's Chancellor and bring an end to the democratic experiment of the Weimar Republic.

For many, this seemed to come out of nowhere. Indeed, in many countries the twenties were seen as a period of nearly boundless optimism in the aftermath of the First World War. Technology increasingly made the world a smaller place, women received new rights in the United States and Europe, and new forms of entertainment cut through the drudgery of work. Wages rose for many workers, and a small minority became extremely wealthy through their investment portfolios and entrepreneurial activities. One need only to glance over the pages of today's most famous novel from the era, F. Scott Fitzgerald's *The Great Gatsby*, to get a sense of how the upper echelons of the rich lived, at least in Europe and the United States.

On the other hand, this high-on-the-hog living was far from a universal experience. While a few got very rich in the West and elsewhere, the vast majority saw their lot improve only modestly. Racial discrimination was still commonplace across the globe, and vast stretches of Africa and Asia remained under the colonial control of imperialist countries thousands of miles away. For the over 400 million Chinese seeing their nation undergo a lengthy civil war and struggle against the continued yoke of foreign domination, there was not much sign that the twenties were 'roaring'. Nor in Western countries like Canada, France or the United States, did the 1920s always see an increase in the level of income enjoyed by the less wealthy. This was not an era of universal progress.

For everyone, however, the 1920s were much like the cover photo of this book: a brief dance on the edge of a precipice. Regardless of where one lived, the following decade and a half would almost certainly be considerably worse than any given point in the 1920s, with a few notable exceptions. This book tells the story of why that was the case, and highlights the disastrous consequences of the events that took place at the end of the decade.

Structure of the book

To provide a comprehensive and accessible account of the 1920s on a global scale – a considerable task, given the diversity of human experience – this book has been divided into thematic sections. The first part, comprising chapters 1–3, examines the world of the 1920s, specifically the political and social factors that drove and affected events. Chapter 1 explores the consequences of the 1919 Treaty of Versailles and other diplomatic agreements that literally redrew the world map in the early 1920s. Amid the ashes of the Austro-Hungarian Empire, an array of new countries were created in Central and Eastern Europe, the borders of which would remain contentious for years. In the Middle East, the dismantlement of the Ottoman Empire gave France and Britain control over wide swathes of the region, several parts of which would soon become notable for a good that would exercise increased importance as the century continued: oil. At the same time, managing these new colonial possessions immediately changed the nature of both empires, as the British would quickly discover in Egypt, and Italy would begin to emerge as a power late to the imperial great game, but eager to acquire new territories for its new fascist regime.

Building upon our first chapter, chapter 2 examines the class and race issues that citizens around the world faced throughout the decade. As will be seen, even in lands of seeming opportunity, social and economic progress were not always dependent on the actions of individuals but often on factors beyond their control. The twenties were far from an egalitarian world. Along similar lines, chapter 3 explores the technological and scientific changes that took place in the decade. Some of these made the world a 'smaller' place – notably the automobile, airplane and radio – by bringing people together both physically and with common cultural bonds. Radio had the additional effect of making news travel at a breakneck speed, and heroes like Charles Lindbergh immediately became household names for millions of people in the United States and elsewhere. Not all aspects of scientific progress were positive, however, and a perverted interpretation of evolutionary theory was used to justify racial prejudice, immigration restriction and even sexual sterilisation throughout the decade. While millions had their lives improved by new innovations, scientific progress was also responsible for significant human rights abuses and a new version of racial prejudice that was cloaked in the guise of rationality despite its horrific outcomes. The Janus-faced nature of this decade will indeed be a perennial refrain throughout this volume.

Part II turns to examine culture and gender in the 1920s, and chapter 4 explores the most quintessential of 1920s leisure activities: the cinema. Hollywood films conquered the world in the twenties, and celebrities like Charlie Chaplin became internationally recognised. In the sporting world, the increasing internationalisation of football (soccer) brought fans together in (mostly) peaceful rivalry, while in the United States baseball stars like Babe Ruth became heroes to millions of young Americans, thanks again to the power of radio. As we will see, the twenties were a great time to be entertained, and one increasingly did not have to even leave the house. Chapter 5 discusses the authors who similarly captivated the reading world throughout the decade, including the circle of expatriates in Paris that included Ernest Hemingway, before turning to examine the visual arts, music and evolutions in patterns of thought which could have profound political consequences from Mexico City to Tokyo. Chapter 6 shifts gear to examine the changing role of women in societies around the world in the twenties. The decade saw women first gain the right to vote in the Unites States and elsewhere, and it also saw a limited liberalisation of sexual mores in some areas. As with many aspects of this book however, there was significant regional divergence on this issue.

Part III then turns the focus to the politics and political ideologies of the twenties. Chapter 7 explores the often-difficult route that the world's democracies were forced to tread. There was certainly no assurance that democracy as a form of government would survive the decade or beyond, and it indeed failed in several countries. Here we look at the cases of Britain, France, Turkey and the United States, as well as consider how this affected dependent states such as Fiji, India and Liberia. Chapter 8 then explores one of the major non-democratic ideologies that captivated millions: communism. Following the 1917 Russian Revolution, the Bolsheviks, led by Vladimir Lenin, solidified their hold on power and turned their gaze toward instigating communist revolution in other countries. This was not a far-fetched possibility in many states, and a series of failed uprisings struck Europe in the early years of the decade. In the United States and Britain, concern over communist infiltration gave anti-communist politicians a useful weapon against their opponents and, in the US, led to police raids on leftist organisations and the deportation of 'radicals'. By the end of the decade, no further major communist revolutions had (yet) been successful and the new leader of the Soviet Union was himself ready to abandon the idea of worldwide revolution, at least for now. Still, it is worth considering developments in China and South-east Asia as we look to events later in the century and this section offers some insight into the 1920s experience of both. Chapter 9 turns the focus to the alternative ideology of the decade, fascism, and the fascination it also held for millions around the world. Beginning with Benito Mussolini's March on Rome, fascism seemed to be initially successful in Italy and soon sparked imitators around the world. If a country was likely to go in a non-democratic direction in the twenties, communism and fascism offered the most likely alternatives. The origins and travails of German National Socialism will also be considered here with a view to the decade that followed, and we will briefly consider fascism's effect in states from France to Brazil and Argentina.

Part IV ends our study with a discussion of the economic conditions of the 1920s and the dramatic events of late 1929. Chapter 10 examines the state of the world economy throughout the decade, particularly debates over the gold standard and the discovery of oil in the Middle East and Latin America that permanently changed the political status of those regions. At the same time, Germany was obligated to pay vast sums of money in war reparations to the allies, harming the German economy severely. The early years of the decade were marked by staggering levels of hyperinflation that virtually brought the entire country to a halt before stabilisation took place. The most successful economic example was the United States, which was itself owed vast sums of money by its First World War allies and experienced a period of rapid growth in the second half of the decade. All that would come to a crashing stop in October 1929, however, when the US stock market plummeted across multiple days – most dramatically on what became known as 'Black Tuesday'. Previous crashes and downturns had taken place and recovery had always come, but this crash, both in scale and sheer sense of shock, was different. Chapter 11 examines the events of the crash itself and its proximate consequences, while Chapter 12 explores how countries around the world responded to the economic conditions of the early 1930s. The main figure explored here is John Maynard Keynes, a British economist who proposed vast amounts of government spending to put the economy on the road to recovery (though he was not the only economist of the era to do so). While Keynes' advice was initially ignored by most, it eventually gained credibility with governments around the world into the 1930s and beyond. This chapter examines the range of economic options available to policy makers at the time and asks readers to consider the consequences and possible benefits of each.

These sections collectively paint a picture of life for both the elite and the average citizen in the 1920s, along with the challenges and choices they faced in the period. Throughout them, we have deliberately tried to overturn common preconceptions about the period – that every American woman was a 'flapper' and drank bootlegged liquor, to give an extreme example – in favour of a more accurate representation of the decade. We have also presented our sections on political ideology relatively impartially, as people at the time would have viewed them. The horrors of the Second World War and the Holocaust were still far in the future when Mussolini seized power in Rome, and it is important to understand the interest and optimism that fascism represented at the time, despite its obvious discrediting in the

1940s. Similarly, many of the crimes of Stalin had not yet taken place at the end of the twenties, and the horrendous bloodshed of the Russian Civil War was actively defended (or simply ignored) by the regime's supporters abroad. In no way does this convey any sympathy for those ideologies or an effort to ignore their horrific human costs but, as historians, we must represent the past as it was, not as we may wish it to be.

To be clear from the outset, this is a deliberately populist book. It utilises all the major tools of historical analysis – as well as archival material from Cambridge to California and beyond – but our aim is to broaden understanding of the period, not necessarily pander to the common room. We suitably reference where needed, yet the intention is not to impress the reader with reams of footnotes – indeed we eschew footnotes here for additional up-front readability – but to provide a manageable, concise set of information on some complex questions. Thus, our account attempts to offer the casual reader a series of insights into a decade they may never have considered before, or at least not on a global scale. It aims to provide bite-sized chunks of some key themes of an important era in our (relatively) recent past. As such, it is intended to be readable both cover to cover, but also for those who wish to dip in and out of – or assign students to read – individual chapters. For the student looking for international comparisons for a domestic-focused university module, the reader just interested in skimming a punchy account of a vital period, or an academic expert on one of our chapter topics looking for the broader contemporary context, this is intended to provide a useful survey.

This book also hopes to engage the reader on an active basis by offering tools for additional reflection and research. Each chapter includes a 'recommended further reading' list that contains both primary and secondary sources that amplify the themes and issues discussed. In addition, each chapter contains a series of questions that may be used to spark further discussion and research. Some answers to these questions may be found in the text itself, but all would benefit from further research. Many of these would be suitable as the basis for classroom discussion or essay-length assignments. All ask the reader to reflect on their own personal views in light of the evidence and issues presented in the main text.

Finally, it is important to note that this work is by no means a completely comprehensive account of all events in every place during the 1920s. With a global population of two billion by 1930 and a volume of around 114,000 words, to do so each word in this book would have to somehow cater to the experience of around 17,500 people. Inevitably, therefore, we have had to make many difficult decisions about aspects to include and which we were forced to omit for reasons of brevity. This should not suggest that those events are in some way less important than those included here, and we encourage all readers to conduct their own research into aspects of the decade that we have explored less extensively in the present pages.

Of course, all books written on such a large scale have to make such calls. For one, Adam Tooze's recent book on *The Deluge* – often referenced in what follows – is a magisterial account of America's rise to global hegemony throughout the long 1920s. But even it has to make its selections. On the one hand, the South American oil boom is not covered in that volume but is in the present book. On the other, this volume discusses Japanese literature but spends less time on its politics than Tooze (2014) does. Suffice it to say, this book is not the end of the story. Consider the similar case of Emily Rosenberg's 2012 transnational study *A World Connecting*, which tops the scales at over 1,100 pages (detailing the 1870 to 1945 period) but which does not, for example, mention Charlie Chaplin at all (Rosenberg 2012: passim). Daniel Gorman's *The Emergence of International Society in the 1920s* is an extremely valuable addition too, but, by its own admission, concentrates on 'the internationalization of the British Empire ... and the active role played by individual Anglo-Americans' (Gorman 2012: 10). There is nothing wrong with this – indeed, the current book gives Anglophone dialogue much emphasis – and there are always trade-offs to be made. But what we can do, hopefully, is to provide an entrée into the key dilemmas faced by policy makers and ordinary people alike, and give the reader the tools to explore such questions from there.

Elements of this account may be deemed top-down rather than bottom-up, and the view from Paris, London and Washington is indeed discussed at length. Partly this is about availability of sources and creating a cohesive work. But it is important to contextualise this. By the mid-1920s the French and British Empires ruled over 550 million people – in excess of a quarter of the earth's population. In 1929 the combined Gross Domestic Products (GDPs) of Western Europe and the United States exceeded the total of China, India and Brazil combined by four to one. The West did predominate in this era, and the effects of this – both in the West and beyond – are worth telling. That is not to say that this was a universally positive phenomenon, but it was a present one. In any case, this volume sets out several global stories. Whether it be the growth of nationalism in the Middle East, the origins and opening skirmishes of the Chinese Civil War, or the global travels of the young Ho Chi Minh, this work has much for those interested in the developing world.

A transnational element to this book is of course its very rationale. Key works such as Mark Mazower's (1998) *Dark Continent* have offered a European perspective on the gamut of the twentieth century. Particular nations have had their experiences of the 1920s analysed by Richard J. Evans (2004), Richard Bosworth (2005), Richard Overy (2009) and others (all cited in what follows). Monographs on particular themes – communism, Nazism, culture, gender and so forth – of such nations are of course legion and referenced below. But a comparative survey volume of the globe which takes in politics, society, culture and economics throughout this turbulent decade was rather lacking from the literature. For all its acknowledged limitations, this book steps into this space. If what follows helps people explore, discuss and understand a decade that took the world from the aftermath of one world war to laying the groundwork necessary for another, it will have served its purpose.

Works cited

Bosworth, R.J.B. (2005), *Mussolini's Italy*, London: Allen Lane.
Evans, R.J. (2004), *The Coming of the Third Reich*, London: Allen Lane.

Gorman, D. (2012), *The Emergence of International Society in the 1920s*, Cambridge: Cambridge University Press.

Mazower, M. (1998), *Dark Continent: Europe's Twentieth Century*, London: Allen Lane.

Overy, R. (2009), *The Morbid Age: Britain Between the Wars*, London: Allen Lane.

Rosenberg, E.S. (2012), *A World Connecting: 1870–1945*, Cambridge, MA: Harvard University Press.

Tooze, A. (2014), *The Deluge: The Great War and the Remaking of Global Order*, London: Allen Lane.

PART I

1

EMPIRES AND THE AFTERMATH OF VERSAILLES

In January 1919, delegates from 24 nations began meeting in Paris to negotiate a treaty that would profoundly alter not only the lines of the world map but also the lives of millions of people. The Treaty of Versailles, as the document that the talks eventually produced would be known, was the source of immediate controversy and remains disputed by historians to the present day. For its detractors, the treaty was a misguided attempt to punish Germany that eventually sowed the seeds for the rise of Adolf Hitler and the Second World War, while more sympathetic commentators have viewed it as a flawed but workable document that was ultimately destroyed by the onset of a Great Depression that many could not foresee, coupled with the political extremism that came to pass in its wake. Historians today remain divided, with an increasing number recognising that the treaty was probably the most pragmatic compromise that could be reached under both difficult circumstances and pressing time constraints, despite some acknowledged flaws (Boemeke *et al.* 1998: 3). As Adam Tooze has recently argued, the fact that 'it took a second dramatic crisis, the Great Depression' to unleash the forces of anti-Versailles and anti-liberal political insurgency in many nations means mistakes must have lain beyond the cartography of 1919 at the very least (Tooze 2014: 18).

That said, it is undeniable that in many ways the Treaty of Versailles shaped the political direction of the 1920s, and had consequences far beyond the drawing of borders on maps and reparations payments between governments. As this volume's final chapters note, the debate over the economic impact of the Treaty began immediately – particularly over the question of German reparations and more generally what future the country that many, and indeed the treaty, stated had caused a war that had ended in the deaths of over 17 million people. To address such issues, this chapter considers first the terms of the Treaty of Versailles itself, along with the objectives that the allied governments whose representatives authored its terms were hoping to accomplish, before turning to the effects of the treaty around the globe. These were most directly felt in Europe, which saw the creation of a number of new states out of the ruins of defeated empires, and in the colonial regions of Africa and the Middle East. Such changes would have long-term ramifications, as we will note.

Beyond altering the world map, the Treaty also created a new body – the League of Nations – tasked with providing collective security and preventing future wars. The League had first been called for by President Woodrow Wilson in his wartime Fourteen Points which had been drawn up during the conflict to provide an exit strategy through which combatants could emerge with honour intact. Yet, ironically, the United States would never join the organisation it had provided the inspiration for and indeed refused to sign the Treaty itself. The League would thus be created without the emerging world power of the 1920s being part of its deliberations, circumscribing its influence significantly. At the same time, however, the League retained importance throughout the decade, particularly in areas that had been cleaved off from former imperial states. Finally, this chapter concludes with an examination of the diplomacy that followed the Treaty of Versailles and continued throughout the decade. On the one hand, many of these efforts were designed to address the problems that had already emerged with various clauses of the treaty only a few years after its signing, particularly involving German war reparations and territorial claims. The fear in many allied governments was that if harsh terms remained in place, German resentment against its terms would grow, in addition to the economic destruction that might be suffered by all if the country were to collapse. The crippling of the German economy – as a major importer and exporter of Western goods – also could potentially undermine the GDPs and balance of payments positions of victorious powers. It was a tricky balancing act to get right. By the late 1920s optimists in Britain and France believed that the major complaints had been suitably addressed, while the sceptics still feared what might come next.

In contrast to these pragmatic negotiations to preserve the post-war order, the 1920s saw a number of efforts to secure the conditions for a lasting world peace. The Washington Naval Conference of 1921–2, for instance, resulted in a series of agreements to limit naval armaments and prevent future arms races. The world's traditional naval power of Great Britain and the new global force of the United States naturally secured the highest tonnage limits for new ship construction, while lower limits were imposed on Japan, Italy and France. In 1928, signatories to the Kellogg–Briand Pact agreed to 'condemn recourse to war for the solution of international controversies, and renounce it, as an instrument of national policy in their relations with one another'. The United States, France, Britain and Germany were among the first to sign, theoretically outlawing the possibility of future war between them or any of the other dozens of countries that soon signed on as well. More pragmatically, the 1925 Geneva Protocol outlawed 'the use in war of asphyxiating, poisonous or other gases, and of all analogous liquids, materials or devices', and while the United States would not ratify it until 1975, it was widely seen as an important step forward in the effort to prevent a recurrence of the widespread use of poison gas that had taken place in the First World War (UN 1925: passim). On paper and to some degree in deed, the 1920s was a period of general disarmament and deliberate attempts to reduce international tensions. By the mid-1930s, many would look back and view disarmament as naïve or foolish, but in the immediate aftermath of Versailles there was optimism that the 'war to end all wars' might have actually produced major steps to do so. With a multi-lateral Treaty of Versailles in place and further bi-lateral agreements through the decade to bolster it, this was not the naïve suggestion it may appear.

The Treaty and the European powers

The Versailles peacemakers in 1919 were faced with an overwhelming number of immediate concerns. Millions of soldiers were still at arms in the field, European economies lay in shambles, and there was widespread starvation in Germany. Weighed against this was the fact that the German army appeared to have not been crushingly defeated (and certainly Germany itself was unoccupied) and thus, while the Germans were severely weakened, a resumption of hostilities was possible. Equally, the Russian Civil War was waging in the East at the cost of hundreds of thousands of lives, and the question of how much of the former Russian Empire the Bolsheviks would manage to conquer was a pressing one, as they might end up with a border on Germany itself and thus have a direct route into Central Europe. The negotiations at Versailles were thus not conducted in a vacuum but were a response to pressing, life-and-death considerations. Importantly, the Treaty of Versailles was between the allied nations and Germany alone: peace with Austria–Hungary and Germany's other allies would have to be agreed separately, placing the negotiations within an even wider context. Zara Steiner has noted that in 1919 'there was no possible return to the old order. The disruptions were too many and the effects too widespread. It was a changed world in which the rulers of Europe now operated' (Steiner 2005: 11). This is no doubt true, but it is important to acknowledge that Europe had both changed and was still *changing* as the delegates gathered.

The dominant players at Versailles were the 'Big Four': US President Woodrow Wilson, whose Fourteen Points had become the framework around which nego-tiations would at least initially proceed; British Prime Minister David Lloyd George; Georges Clemenceau, Prime Minister of France; and Italian Prime Minister Vittorio Emanuele Orlando. All of these came into the conference with differing objectives: Wilson sought the ideals of the Fourteen Points, including a prohibition on secret treaties (as had taken place before the outbreak of the First World War), free trade, freedom of the seas (rejected immediately by the British on the grounds that it would preclude blockades against hostile countries), 'a free, open-minded, and absolutely impartial adjustment of all colonial claims', and the creation of an international organisation (the League of Nations) to mediate future disputes before they became war. For Tooze, this was an 'anti-militarist, post-imperialist agenda for a country convinced of the global influence that it would exercise at arm's length through the means of soft power – economics and ideology' (Tooze 2014: 16).

Evidence of this growing influence can be gleaned from the fact that the liberal-minded and internationalist Fourteen Points had been disseminated by the US government without consulting the British or the French and, as Winston Churchill later recounted, both Lloyd George and Clemenceau were immediately sceptical of their implications (Churchill 1929: 103–4). At the same time, when the German army began to collapse in late 1918, the initial diplomatic outreach from its government was directed at Wilson in the hopes that the Fourteen Points might provide the basis for a more favourable peace than might be expected under other circumstances (Churchill 1929: 99). Wilson's January 1917 call – prior to America entering the war – for a 'peace without victory' suddenly sounded very appealing to the Germans (Boemeke 1998: 609).

The French and the British were far less willing to grant the Germans the favourable terms they sought, however, and they were not about to give up the notion that they had won what had proved to be a nightmarish conflict and thus deserved significant compensation. The French, having suffered horrific casualties and material damage from years of warfare that had often taken place in French territory, were committed to not only smashing German military might and claiming German territory, but also extracting as much money in reparations as possible. These efforts would soon bring them into conflict with the other allies. As American commentator Herbert Adams Gibbons put it in 1923, 'from the moment the war ended down to the present time the French attitude has been that the victors were amply justified in whatever steps they took because, had Germany been victorious, she would have done the same' (Gibbons 1923: 29–30). The French defended themselves in simple terms: as future Prime Minister (and Versailles delegate) André Tardieu wrote, 'To make certain her safety was the first duty of France. To secure reparation was her second ... Germany was doubly responsible for the destruction caused by the war; due first to her premeditated aggression and then made worse by her systematic savagery' (Tardieu 1921: 280). At this time there were not many doves in the Elysée.

Lloyd George's view was in broad terms similar but rather more moderate, and he vowed in December 1918 that his objectives were to secure a criminal trial for the now-deposed German Kaiser, the punishment of German war criminals, and financial reparations for the costs of the war ('Make them pay' was a much repeated slogan) (Gibbons 1923: 32–3; Churchill 1929: 154). The Italians, having entered the war on the side of the allies late, hoped to obtain modest territorial gains, described later in this book. Despite Russia having fought on the side of the allies for most of the war only to sign a separate peace (the Treaty of Brest-Litovsk) with the Germans after the overthrow of the Tsar, the Russian Bolshevik government was not invited to take part in the negotiations. The Germans were also not invited, raising the immediate concern that any treaty the country was forced to sign would be seen as a 'dictated' peace rather than a negotiated one.

The Treaty of Versailles was signed in late June 1919 following months of negotiations that Wilson himself had travelled from the United States to attend – becoming the first President to leave the country during his tenure. The final agreement was lengthy and complicated, with a US State Department printing of the text with commentary stretching more than 700 pages (US Department of State 1947: passim). The map of Europe would henceforth look rather different: the country of Poland, to Germany's East, would be recreated after centuries of being ruled by other powers; the Rhineland region of Germany, on the border with France, would be demilitarised; the territory of Alsace–Lorraine was returned to France; the German city of Danzig, now lying in Polish territory, would become a 'free city'; and a new, multi-national state, Czechoslovakia, would be carved out of former parts of Germany and the Austro-Hungarian Empire. Later treaties would separate Austria and Hungary themselves, and carve the southern portions of their former empire into a series of states that would become Yugoslavia. While Germany would not be dismantled completely, as Austria–Hungary would be, the country would lose approximately 13 per cent of her territory, much of which was heavily industrial and economically significant. She was also forbidden any Anschluss, or union, with the new rump Austrian state (Lamb 1989: 6). And, further, Germany was stripped of her overseas colonies, including a series of islands in the Pacific Ocean that eventually were delivered to Japan and, in addition, the German military's strength would be reduced to a set number of 100,000 soldiers (US Department of State 1947: 278). The spectre of pre-war Prussian militarism was to be extinguished, or so the peacemakers hoped.

But as A.J.P. Taylor noted in his famously strident anti-German tract *The Course of German History* – written during the Second World War – these territorial shifts created a shift in mentality amongst the German elites. 'Before 1914', Taylor argued,

> Prussian landowners regarded the separation of Austria from Germany as [nineteenth-century leader Otto von] Bismarck's greatest achievement, the guarantee of their own position. Now, resisting the loss of their Polish lands [at Versailles], they were prepared to resist the loss of Austria also. The Treaty of Versailles was a defeat both for conservative German nationalism and for demagogic German nationalism; therefore it united them as never before and ensured that all parties in Germany would combine to overthrow it the moment that the army leaders gave them permission to do so.
>
> *(Taylor 1945: 218)*

The debate over whether Versailles was doomed from the outset has, as mentioned, exercised historians ever since. Certainly, as our ninth chapter notes, the degree to which elites elevated fascist parties into power is an issue which unites Italy in the early 1920s and Germany a decade later.

Equally if not more important than these territorial concerns surrounding Germany's frontiers, however, was the question of reparations. Both Clemenceau and Lloyd George had agreed that Germany should be made to pay financial compensation for the destruction caused by the First World War. Article 231 of the Treaty, commonly known as the 'War Guilt Clause', specified explicitly that Germany accepts the responsibility of Germany and her allies for causing all the loss and damage to which the Allied and Associated Governments and their nationals have been subjected as a consequence of the war imposed upon them by the aggression of Germany and her allies.

(US Department of State 1947: 413)

The notion that Germany bore *sole* responsibility for the outbreak of the First World War was to many questionable at best, and to many Germans it would be outright risible. German political scientist Max Weber was among those who were so outraged by the War Guilt Clause and the prospect of paying potentially ruinous reparations that they thought Germany should risk an allied invasion and occupation rather than acceding to such disgraceful terms. Yet the War Guilt Clause remained in the treaty, the German delegation signed it under protest, and the legal basis for German reparations had been established.

Reparations would be the source of much controversy throughout the 1920s, as this volume's chapter on economics before the 1929 Wall Street crash will discuss. Interestingly, as Niall Ferguson points out, 'it is well known that at Versailles the decision was taken to make Germany liable for the costs not just of war damage but also of wartime pensions and separation allowances; hence the huge scale of the reparations bill subsequently presented'. Yet, as he notes,

> it is less well known – because the British later tried to blame the French – that this was largely done at the insistence of the Australian Prime Minister William 'Billy' M. Hughes, who discerned that his country would gain nothing if a narrow definition of reparations were adopted.
>
> *(Ferguson 2003: 316)*

There was something of an imperial parable here: Hughes (born in London to Welsh parents and who had only emigrated to Australia aged 22) was dictating to the old world the price demanded by the new for the blood it had shed coming to the mother country's aid. With so many cooks mixing the broth, a concrete, permanent settlement was certainly hard to broker. But with only the victors at the negotiating table moderation was always in danger of being a casualty of any discussions.

Indeed, the reparations system agreed to at Versailles came under immediate attack, most notably by British economist John Maynard Keynes, who had been the Treasury representative of the British delegation at the peace talks but left in protest at the direction the negotiations were taking. In *The Economic Consequences of the Peace* (1920), he argued in print that the reparations system established in the Treaty would lead Germany and ultimately Europe to economic ruin because there was simply no way the Germans would be able to pay the amount of reparations required without seeking loans from the United States (to which Britain and France themselves owed massive war debts). Further, he provocatively accused the French of exaggerating the financial cost of wartime damage to inflate the amount – a charge he would repeat and defend three years later in *A Revision of the Treaty*

(Keynes 1922: 106–7). Keynes' criticism was influential on both sides of the Atlantic, leading many to question whether the treaty was flawed from the beginning.

Regardless of Keynes' criticism, the reparations aspect of the treaty remained intact. Keynes suggested at the end of the war that the allies should demand no more than 20 billion marks in reparations, and this was the figure that had also been discussed in German economic circles. The question of how the reparations would be paid was left unfinished at Versailles pending further negotiations, and in January 1921 the allies agreed to demand a startling 226 billion marks. The Germans were outraged and counter-offered 30 billion marks, which was rejected, and in April the allies reduced their demand to 132 billion marks (about $33 billion), with the first 1 billion payable by September, and the remainder broken into three classes of bonds with differing maturity dates. Germany's quarterly payments would thus amount to around 2 billion marks, plus 26 per cent of the value of the country's exports. Failure to pay would result in the occupation of the Ruhr, as specified in the Treaty as the penalty for non-compliance. As Ferguson has observed, Germany made great efforts to make these payments in the early years of the 1920s, turning over between 4 and 7 per cent of national income to the allies. From 1920 to 1923, more than 50 per cent of the country's revenue was used to pay reparations alone, driving up the budget deficit and making the financial situation increasingly untenable (Ferguson 1998: 409–10, 424–5). The financial demands of the allies would soon have the effect Keynes had feared. The economic effect of the reparations system will be considered in the final chapters of this book. Suffice to say, by 1923 the system had begun to break down, leading first to the occupation of the Ruhr and eventually to revisions to the plan.

Hanging over these discussions was the spectre of the massive war debt owed by Britain, France and the other allies to the United States. Keynes argued that these debts were so large and economically damaging that they were practically uncollectable, and if the United States actually attempted to collect them the international financial situation would become 'intolerable' (Keynes 1922: 176). Even if the US government had wanted to forgive or even modify the debt however, public opinion would have been firmly against the decision. A Gallup poll as late as 1936 found that 53 per cent of the American public wanted the government to demand full payment from the countries that owed it money, 37 per cent were willing to consider a reduction in the amount to collect at least something, and only 9 per cent were willing to accept full forgiveness. A full 80 per cent were against loaning any more money to the allies (Gallup). In 1923, Britain agreed to a plan to pay back $4.6 billion to the US government over the next 62 years, though payments were eventually suspended in the 1930s and the debt technically exists to the present day (Cashman 1998: 249). One long-term consequence of Versailles was certainly economic thrift and a depressed trade cycle.

The Middle East and North Africa

Just as the end of the First World War had been responsible for re-drawing the contours of Eastern Europe, so too it was responsible for dramatically changing the map of the Middle East. For centuries, most of the Middle East had been under the domination of the Ottoman Empire, colloquially referred to as the 'sick man of Europe' since the late nineteenth century. The Ottomans had allied themselves with the Central Powers and were defeated in 1918. As discussed later, the Ottomans had engaged in a number of particularly horrendous crimes against their own population over the course of the war, including the Armenian Genocide that killed more than a million people and numerous other massacres of non-Muslim groups. The country had been ruled by a political group known as the Young Turks in the early twentieth century, and eventually this body was expelled in a coup by three leaders, known as the 'Three Pashas', who maintained their grip on power until the end of the war. More bloodshed followed, and the nation of Turkey emerged in Anatolia under the leadership of Kemal Atatürk, a First World War hero.

The British had expended significant blood and treasure fighting against the Ottomans during the First World War. In spring 1915, the British landed thousands of troops on the Gallipoli peninsula in an effort to secure a naval passage to take the Ottoman capital of Constantinople and knock the Empire out of the war in a single fell swoop. The Ottomans were prepared for the assault, however, and pinned the British and ANZAC (Australia and New Zealand Army Corps) soldiers on the beaches. After suffering nearly 250,000 casualties, the British withdrew in defeat. The following year, however, a new opportunity presented itself when Sharif Hussein bin Ali, the Emir of Mecca, revolted against Ottoman rule. Hussein had long been on friendly terms with the British, and in his revolt he relied heavily on British support to maintain his support among the Arab tribes and Bedouin he relied on. The British not only provided a brilliant military commander in the form of T.E. Lawrence ('Lawrence of Arabia') but also logistical support (and gold) for the rebellion. Despite early setbacks, in 1917 the British managed to capture the Holy City – Jerusalem – and Hussein's son Faisal captured the city of Aqaba and, eventually, Damascus. In his victories and battlefield presence, Faisal had become the figure around which Arab nationalist hopes were coalescing, and his government in Damascus began to advocate a pan-Arab identity and a single political entity that stretched from Damascus to Baghdad to Mecca. In January 1919, Faisal agreed in principle to the terms of the Balfour Declaration, in which Britain had committed itself to the development of a future Jewish state in Palestine (Dawisha 2005: 39–40; Teitelbaum 2001: 74–8).

At the end of the First World War, Hussein and his family were sitting in the dominant position in the Middle East, but only with British support. It was this reliance on European support that would begin to be the undoing of the arrangement. In early 1916, a French diplomat and a British counterpart had drawn up a plan for the division of the Middle East at the end of the war. The French would be given Syria, while the British would be given Iraq. Palestine would be jointly administered, while the rest of the region would be left more or less independent and presumably become European client states. The Sykes–Picot Agreement, as it was called, was a cynical arrangement designed, as Scott Anderson has observed, to keep the Anglo-French allies on good terms rather than set up a viable policy for the region. Furthermore, there was a good argument to be made that the British had already promised the valuable lands in Syria to Hussein at the end of the war (Anderson

FIGURE 1.1 King Faisal – pictured here with Abdulaziz (Ibn Saud) of Saudi Arabia –
maintained high hopes for a Pan Arab state.

2013: 161–2). Faisal travelled to Versailles in an effort to secure an expansive Arab
state in Syria and the wider region, but was rebuffed. In March 1920, he launched
an outright rebellion against the French but was defeated (Anderson 2013: 490–1).

In 1920, rebellion also broke out in Iraq, precipitating a crisis for the British.
Winston Churchill was appointed Secretary of State to the Colonial Office and
convened a conference in Cairo to resolve the wider situation in the Middle East.
The conclusion was that Faisal should be made King of Iraq in view of his 'very
special qualifications for the post'. His brother Abdullah, who was massing an army
to attack the French in Syria, was offered a new state – Transjordan – of which he
became king (Churchill 1929: 492–4). This arrangement naturally meant that
Britain would in effect provide for Iraq's stability. In 1921, the British army had 32
battalions in Iraq to maintain law and order, being gradually reduced over the
decade, along with overall expenditure. Churchill was pleased with the results:

It is worth recording that this striking reduction of military strength (with corresponding financial retrenchment) has been carried through without a hitch and without any resultant disturbance in Iraq. When the nature of the country is considered, its vast distances, the unsettled nature of many of its inhabitants and its huge desert frontier, over which really effective control is impossible, it may fairly be claimed that the results achieved have been astonishing.

(Churchill 1929: 495)

Astonishing, perhaps, but also very expensive. As Ferguson has observed, the First World War had taken a heavy financial toll on the British Empire already. In 1921, the approximately £23 million spent in Iraq alone was larger than the entire UK health budget. This imposed an increasing burden: 'Before 1914, the benefits of Empire had seemed to most people on balance to outweigh the costs', Ferguson argues. 'After the war the costs suddenly, inescapably, outweighed the benefits' (Ferguson 2003: 317).

While Churchill might have been pleased with the result in Iraq and Transjordan, Hussein himself was not long for his own rule. In 1924, in the midst of a brief and bizarre bid to establish a Caliphate following that institution's abolition by Atatürk (discussed later), Hussein's capital was surrounded by forces under rival Arab leader Ibn Saud, who had the support of the conservative Wahhabi movement. With the frustrated British unwilling to intervene on his behalf, Hussein fled into exile in Cyprus. Ibn Saud was now in possession of Islam's holy cities of Mecca and Medina, and there was no chance that he would accede to his former rival becoming Caliph and he therefore refused to even discuss the question when it came up (Nafi 1998: 100). Now deprived of both his kingdom and the title of Caliph, Hussein died in Amman in 1931. His sons would remain on the thrones of their respective kingdoms for years, and his descendants remain on the Jordanian throne to the present day (Teitelbaum 2001: 282–4). For his own part, T.E. Lawrence took the political failure to secure Syria for Arab rule hard, telling a correspondent in 1920, 'I'm afraid I can't ever come to Syria again. Because I failed' (Brown 1980: 174).

The British would not only have Iraq and the Transjordan to manage but also Palestine and Egypt, and both would prove more troublesome throughout the decade. Egypt had been seized from the Ottoman Empire in 1882, and during the First World War it had been an important base for military operations in the region. The Suez Canal, linking the Mediterranean Sea to the Red Sea and hence the Indian Ocean (and India itself), was a primary strategic consideration for the British government and was seen as an absolutely non-negotiable interest. Egypt's political prospects were effectively circumscribed by its strategic significance to the British Empire. At the end of the war, however, the British faced new questions about Egypt's future. Unlike many areas of the Middle East, after centuries of direct and indirect colonialism Egyptian cultural identity was by now a mixture of both Islamic tradition and Western elite practices. Decades of domination by the British had only heightened this dichotomy and created a potentially explosive situation at the end of the conflict (Dawisha 2005: 98–9).

In 1919, the Egyptian situation reached a breaking point. The key figure who emerged amidst the unrest was Saad Zaghloul, a popular legislator who soon became an icon. Born to a middle-class family living on the Nile Delta, Zaghloul was educated at Al-Azhar University and received a law degree from the Egyptian School of Law. After his marriage to Sufeya Zaghloul, daughter of the Prime Minister and one of Egypt's most recognisable feminists, Zaghloul was appointed the Minister of Justice in 1910. After the First World War, Zaghloul and his supporters formed a liberal nationalist group, known as the Wafd ('Delegation'), and began to appeal for the British to end the protectorate and recognise the independence of Egypt and Sudan. (At that time, both countries were united as one nation under the rule of the Ottoman Pasha Muhammad Ali) (Cook 2011: passim).

In 1919, therefore, Zaghloul petitioned to travel to the Versailles peace talks to negotiate for Egyptian self-determination on the basis of Wilson's Fourteen Points. However, this was denied and the final version of the Treaty fully acknowledged British control of Egypt and forced the Germans to concede all past claims to the country (US Department of State 1947: 268; Manela 2007: 71). Rather than allow the letters and petitions produced by the Wafd to be discussed at Versailles, the British simply convinced the Versailles secretariat to file them away rather than send them on the peace conference delegates (Manela 2007: 74). Zaghloul and his associates were subsequently exiled to Malta as the result of their political activities. The decision quickly turned catastrophic for the British, who had underestimated Zaghloul's increasing appeal as a national hero (Watikiotis 1991: passim). Disorder and rebellion broke out almost immediately after he was arrested, and quickly escalated across Egypt.

This was the beginning of a distinct cultural identity in the country. One of the most profound concepts that came out of Egypt during this time was the concise and proactive way the Egyptians organised themselves against the British (La Revue de Paris 1922: passim). The Egyptians had never previously displayed this level of patriotic fury. The Egyptians were organised, self-sufficient and angry. Combined with discipline and resolve, the Egyptians achieved what other Arab nations could not: political independence through collective state pressure (La Revue de Paris 1922: passim). This indicated to Egyptians that their capabilities were not limited to government-enforced policies or laws, and this spirit of revolution ultimately carried into the downfall of their modern government after the fall of Hosni Mubarak in 2011 (Lang 2013: passim).

The 1919 revolution was in many ways a turning point for Egypt, both politically and culturally. During street protests, Egyptian women marched alongside men in the streets wearing veils. Traditionally, Egyptian women had remained out of public life, and even upper-class women were still generally a part of the traditional harem system and had few to no rights. On the other hand, under British rule it had become considered genteel for women to adopt classic English mannerisms and duties that dictated a very specific female identity in the home. The higher the social status, the less involved politically women traditionally had been. The presence of women protesting on the streets of Egyptian cities made a widespread impact, and in 1922, Huda Sha'rawi would lead the first feminist movement in Egypt by forming an organisation called 'Al Itihiad al Nisa al Masri' (The Egyptian Feminist Union).

In the end, the 1919 rebellion resulted in a compromise between the British government and the Egyptian nationalists. In late 1919, the government dispatched a delegation known as the Milner Mission to examine the political situation. Prior to its dispatch, the diplomatic correspondent of *The Times* reported that he had been briefed on the mission by an official who contemptuously 'said what children the Egyptians were', indicating the general mentality of the Foreign Office toward the rebellion (Kennedy 1919–20, 5 November 1919).

The mission reported that the status quo was unsustainable, and as a result the British government formally granted Egypt independence in early 1922. This was not complete autonomy, however, as the British retained control over military matters and foreign affairs. The result was another awkward situation in which Egyptian authorities were effectively in the power of British officials. A king, Fuad I, was appointed, though his power was clearly circumscribed by the British who not only held his ultimate fate in their hands but also were the only force that could protect him from the constant parliamentary push to remove his power and privilege. Indeed, the British had a vested interest in keeping the maximum amount of power in the hands of the king rather than the more unpredictable parliamentarians (Nafi 1998: 154). As Tooze has therefore written, 'a new order had been created in the Middle East, anchored on nominally independent Egypt and Iraq, but in fact based on a wilful disregard for political legitimacy, a lack that in turn rebounded on the moral foundation of the British Empire as a whole' (Tooze 2014: 381).

Nominal independence in 1922 did not mean full equality for the women who had protested in 1919, nor did it mean that Egypt would embrace the Arab nationalist dreams of Hussein bin Ali. Despite the 1923 constitution asserting that all Egyptians were to be treated equally, a few weeks later, an electoral law clarified that these rights only applied to Egyptian men. Though women were recognised to be an instrumental part of helping achieve autonomy through the nationalist movements, they were still not able to garner enough control to attain the same political rights themselves (Pollard 2005: passim). More widely, post-1919 Egyptian cultural identity was far from clear. The British were a heavy influence, and women began taking off the burka while men adopted more Westernised clothing. Arts, music and education adopted British systems as well as marriage and home life. British goods were now being sold widely in stores, and women in Egypt were increasingly subscribing to British customs. The biggest visual transition was in fashion, where the issue of the veil was heavily debated. There was no longer a solid definition of what the veil represented, as it was prevalent as the face of female revolutionaries, yet was still seen as a relic from the Ottoman past (Baron 1989: passim). The higher the social class, the more varied the wearing of the veil became. Women were usually wrapped in a thick shawl with their heads and faces covered, but women in the upper class increasingly wore hats or very thin veils where the features of their face were still visible (Baron 1989: passim). This slowly eased into the complete removal of the veil, as was taking place simultaneously in Atatürk's Turkey.

These changes increasingly set Egypt apart from the Arab world. In 1925, Zaghloul scoffed at the idea that the Arab world could ever be profitably united, and an Arab rebellion against French rule in Syria that same year was met with statements of solidarity, some minor fundraising efforts on behalf of the victims and little else (Dawisha 2005: 103). That being said, both the Arabic language and the common religion of Islam intractably drew some elements of Egyptian society into events in the wider region. As will be discussed in later chapters, the birth and expansion of the Muslim Brotherhood under the leadership of Hasan al-Banna in the last years of the decade marked the emergence of a political movement with interests that went far beyond Egypt's borders (Dawisha 2005: 102). King Fuad donated funds for the restoration of the significant al-Aqsa Mosque in Jerusalem, but otherwise showed relatively little interest in either Jerusalem or the wider Arab world (Nafi 1998: 154).

While the unrest in Egypt had begun to settle by the mid-1920s, and the status quo there would remain in place until after the Second World War, a far more delicate situation was emerging in Palestine, the most contested and turbulent area of the region. Containing the sacred city of Jerusalem, Palestine had been the site of vicious warfare for millennia, most recently between the British and the Ottoman Empire. After capturing the city in late 1917 from the retreating Ottomans, British General Edmund Allenby dismounted his horse and entered the city on foot in a show of personal humility. In 1920, the League of Nations delivered a Mandate for Palestine to the British government, giving it authority to govern the region with the understanding that it would pursue, in accordance with the Balfour Declaration, 'the establishment in Palestine of a national home for the Jewish people, it being clearly understood that nothing shall be done which may prejudice the civil and religious rights of existing non-Jewish communities in Palestine, or the rights and political status enjoyed by Jews in any other country' (US Department of State 1947: 95). Negotiations between the British government and Zionist leader Chaim Weizmann had begun during the First World War and continued after its end, with Weizmann predicting that 70 to 80 thousand Jews would migrate to Palestine each year and, when sufficient numbers were reached, would be ready to form their own state (Laqueur 1972: 452).

The British administration was thus left in a position of governing a multi-religious, multi-ethnic region of the world that also contained a sacred city for three major religions. Jerusalem naturally became the centre of tensions between the groups, and in 1929 the situation began to boil over after the city's Arab community complained about Jewish modifications to the area around the Wailing Wall (the lower side of the ancient Temple Mount, sacred to Judaism, the top of which had since become the location of the Dome of the Rock and the al-Aqsa Mosque, both sacred Islamic sites). Peaceful protests escalated into mob violence and the stabbing of a Jewish youth, leading to a week of rioting. More than 100 Jews were killed or wounded in the violence, including 40 who were killed in the city of

Hebron. The British High Commissioner denounced the violence, while Zionists increasingly feared what might come next. Throughout the coming decade, the political situation in Palestine would deteriorate further, with a series of Arab revolts shaking the fragile stability of the region and increasingly creating a crisis for the British (Laqueur 1972: 254–6). The Balfour Declaration and the British Mandate had set into motion the events that would eventually culminate with the creation of the State of Israel in 1948 with Weizmann as its first president, but this was still far in the future as the 1920s came to an end. Jewish immigration to the region continued, tensions on both sides continued to rise and by the mid-1930s there would be widespread violence throughout the Mandate.

We deal with Mussolini in chapter 9's analysis of fascism, but amidst the above turmoil it is worth briefly dwelling on his attempt to meddle in the wider region. In the early 1920s the Italian fascist regime had sporadically made noises about transferring the British or French (mostly the latter) Mandates in the Middle East to his nation. In 1927 and again in 1929 the fascist-sympathising British press magnate Lord Rothermere had proposed that Palestine or Iraq would be best suited for this purpose, which briefly aroused much attention in the Italian government. Once it became clear that there were legal difficulties in doing so (the League had, after all, Mandated these territories to Britain and France for a reason) Mussolini promptly began supporting the creation of independent states in the Middle East that he could slowly bring under direct or informal Italian influence. To aid this process he began dispatching doctors and technical experts to Yemen to ostensibly provide medical aid and communications advice to what was still a fledgling nation. This was far from pure benevolence however – both doctors and technical experts fed back intelligence from the country about the British intentions in the area. In December 1929, Mussolini even consented to the formal occupation of the dis-puted islands of Hanish and Jabal Zuqar in the Red Sea (following a much more discussed illegal occupation of the Greek island of Corfu earlier in the decade). In part there was an element of *Flucht nach vorn* to all this – to distract from their own need to 're-conquer Libya' throughout the 1920s and the negative coverage this received in the Islamic press, it was useful to talk of freedom for other Arabs. The Arab copyists of Italian fascism – 'Young Egypt', the Syrian Steel Shirts and the *Futuwwah* in Iraq – provided something of a pro-Mussolini presence, even if one not likely to take power anytime soon (Arielli 2010: 20–38).

In any event, Mussolini was fighting an uphill struggle. By the end of the 1920s the former Ottoman Empire had been parcelled out amongst the victorious allies, and Italy had not secured a major share of the winnings (a source of anger only topped by their European ambitions on the Dalmatian coastline not being met either). Britain had received Mandates for Iraq, Palestine and Egypt, with the latter quickly being given nominal independence. The French were given the profitable region of Syria, from which they partitioned Lebanon. These outcomes stood in stark contrast to what Britain had promised its Arab allies in the middle stages of the First World War, and Hussein bin Ali's ambitions to rule a large Arab state that spanned the region were thwarted at Versailles. The two kingdoms that his sons were given as a form of compensation – Iraq and Transjordan (later Jordan) – would be more enduring, but the former would be overthrown in a bloody military coup after the Second World War and ultimately fall under the dictatorship of Saddam Hussein. Ibn Saud, for his part, consolidated his holdings on the Arabian Peninsula and declared a new kingdom – Saudi Arabia – in 1932. The discovery of oil reserves soon made the kingdom immensely wealthy, and, at the time of writing, one of Ibn Saud's numerous sons remains on the throne. The Middle East as it exists at the beginning of the twenty-first century has its origins in the compromises and betrayals that took place in the 1920s.

The League of Nations

The international body that was tasked with overseeing these changes to the world map was the League of Nations, which Woodrow Wilson had called for in his Fourteen Points. As will be discussed, the great irony was that the United States never ratified the Treaty of Versailles or joined the League of Nations due to Republican opposition in the US Senate, but the institution had been created regardless. Based in Geneva, the League was given a wide range of issues to consider: it was responsible for administering plebiscites in various parts of Europe to gauge whether the local population sought their own states or wished to be a part of other nations; it was asked to formalise the Mandate system that affected not only the Middle East but former German colonies around the world; and it was given responsibility for holding conventions on arms reduction, disease prevention, and a whole host of other issues. In essence, it was an experiment in widespread inter-national governance and theoretically had the final say on conflicts arising from the terms of the Treaty of Versailles and other matters. It formed, as Bruno Cabanes has recently noted, part of the 'transnational turn' and move toward greater humanitarianism that marked the period after the conflict (Cabanes 2014: 1).

In construction the League was incredibly complex. As Susan Pedersen has shown,

> the League cannot be treated as if it were a state, possessed of a clear decision-making structure and coercive power. Instead it is better understood as a force field, one made up of shifting alliances, networks and institutions, which a host of actors entered and sought to exploit.
>
> *(Pedersen 2015: 5)*

Three distinct forces were involved in this process. Firstly, the 50-plus members of the League Assembly – a number kept relatively low by the size of European empires – which met every September. Here the great nations exercised much indirect influence, though the most obvious signs of throwing one's weight around were exhibited by leaders of smaller nations such as Eduard Benes of Czechoslovakia or Belgium's Paul Hymans. By being part of grandiose international schemes – and just as importantly being seen to be a part of them – middle-ranking powers or lower could improve both their own international standing and the domestic popularity of their leader. Secondly, there was the case of the League Council where the great powers had permanent status and others had to jockey for position. Brazil was so affronted at German membership of this body over and above itself that it walked out of the League in the late 1920s. Poland managed to hold onto membership of this exclusive club throughout the lifetime of the League, though it did not do it much good during the road to 1939. And, lastly, in terms of the League's organs, there was a secretariat of officials who would administer the various plebiscites the League was set up to oversee and thereby provide a generic level of diplomatic expertise that many sovereign states did not themselves enjoy (Pedersen 2015: 1–10). It was in this functional form – administering the fate of peoples from Teschen to the Aland Islands – that the League had perhaps its most direct impact in the 1920s.

That said, the biggest problem was not what constituted the League but who was allowed to join. Most famously Germany was excluded from membership at the insistence of France, and Russia was excluded because of its Bolshevik government and ongoing civil war. The impact of these exclusions was obvious to most informed observers: Gibbons, for instance, remarked darkly that,

> no student of world affairs believes that the League of Nations can become anything else than the subservient tool of the Entente powers [the allies], unable to move in anything against their interests or wishes, unless Germany and Russia are permanent members of the Council [of the League].

> *(Gibbons 1923: 75–6)*

FIGURE 1.2 The League of Nations instigated several transnational initiatives during its ill-fated existence. Here the Malaria Commission meets in Geneva, 1928.

Winston Churchill would later write that the body provided 'a frail and unsure bulwark against stormy seas and sullen clouds' when they began to descend in 1922, as the inevitable crisis, discussed later, over German reparations arrived (Churchill 1929: 484).

With the United States excluding itself from the League, the body's legitimacy increasingly lay with Britain and France's continued support. The British establishment was itself split, with some, like Lloyd George, sceptical of its ultimate efficacy but optimistic that it might provide a stabilising force in Europe (Cohrs 2008: 65). Others, including diplomat Philip Noel-Baker, the assistant to Lord Robert Cecil, the British delegation's leader, were 'fanatical' in their belief that the League was the only way to secure disarmament and lasting peace (Lamb 1989: 29). In Britain itself, the League of Nations Union (LNU) pressured policy makers in a number of ways. With over 250,000 members in the mid-1920s and more than 400,000 by 1931, the LNU was powerful pressure group for the internationalist agenda within what was the earth's largest multi-national empire. Though largely aligned to the declining Liberal Party (the first President of the LNU was the former Liberal Foreign Secretary Lord Grey), the LNU pursued a cross-party strategy to try and align Conservative thinkers to the cause. Churchill's scepticism aside, the debate within the Conservative Party as to the plausibility of the League raged throughout the 1920s and into the 1930s. Younger, more liberal-minded Tories could indeed take a pro-LNU and pro-League position. Up and coming Conservative MPs such as John Loder and Victor Cazalet had active involvement with the LNU in the 1920s and another, the future Secretary of State for War Alfred Duff Cooper, moved from a position of 'sceptical benevolence' towards the LNU to 'a belief that either the League of Nations must triumph or there must be another war' (Carr 2011: 36).

The ambivalence many of the European democratic right showed towards the new body stemmed from the fact that its rationale – and that of Wilsonian liberalism per se – had a set of long-term consequences that were ambiguous for their country's future fortunes. We discuss Gandhi and the Indian National Congress in chapters 5 and 6, but it is worth noting up-front that – as with Palestine – the British had committed themselves during the strife of war to a situation (in India the realisation of self-government) that they were not particularly keen on expediting. In the case of the so-called Montagu Declaration of 1917 there was at least some wiggle-room – the British remained 'the judges of the time and measure of each advance' in that direction – but the direction of travel on India was clear, and this worried many. Self-determination might well be desirable for the 'faraway peoples of whom we know nothing' – to paraphrase Neville Chamberlain's later remark on Czechoslovakia – but for Britain or France's colonies it was a different matter. This was made even more difficult by the post-war problems in Britain's closest de facto colony of Ireland where, following an abortive attempt at Home Rule before the First World War and the Easter Rising against British rule during it, the Irish Republican Army soon began a campaign of sustained attacks on British garrisons in 1919 and 1920 in an effort to pressure London into creating an independent

Irish nation. Over the summer of 1920 over 500 Irishmen resigned from the Royal Irish Constabulary – the British-run police force – to be replaced by 800 so-called 'Black and Tans'. These new paramilitaries – named after the uniform they wore – carried out reprisals for IRA violence that involved murder and pillage. In one famous incident – the so-called 'Sack of Balbriggan' – over 50 houses were destroyed, an act which attracted international press coverage due to the number of journalists then stationed in nearby Dublin covering the matter. Irish-American opinion, and indeed the Labour Party in Britain, were vehemently against such action. Interestingly however, younger ex-servicemen politicians on Britain's traditional right denounced the violence too. As Richard Carr notes, 'war veterans did not condemn the violence primarily because it was unacceptable in a traditionally moral sense … but because it was unacceptable to the type of chivalrous war they believed themselves to have fought a few years earlier' (Carr 2013: 149). Gandhi – through non-violent means – would challenge such liberal assumptions about 'decency' in India too. How foreign policy should be executed in the 1920s – in the wake of global conflict – was a fluid question for many. For their part, the Irish won so-called 'Free State' status in 1921 – independence in all but name – and finally left the last vestige of British influence, the Commonwealth, in the 1940s. The 1921 partition of the island of Ireland into Catholic South (the twenty-six counties of the Irish Republic) and Protestant North (the six counties of Northern Ireland) remains to the present day.

Other than the vague assertions about self-determination, the League (heavily British influenced, after all) had little impact on the Irish question. But British diplomats under its auspices were certainly prepared to exercise influence elsewhere. Indeed, the long-time Labour Party MP Phillip Noel-Baker's unwavering belief in the League may have played a role in one of its first major tests that was not related to German reparations and the colonial mandate system. In 1923, the country of Abyssinia, in Eastern Africa, applied for membership in the League, much to the consternation of the Foreign Office, which believed that the French had inspired the application so the country could sell arms and ammunition in the region and possibly damage British influence. The Italians were also said to be privately opposed, but would not act unless the British also objected to the application. Cecil was in favour of admitting Abyssinia, but the Foreign Secretary, Lord Curzon, was opposed. When the issue was raised, Curzon instructed Cecil to take steps to prevent the application's success on the grounds that Abyssinia still maintained the institution of slavery and was home to a burgeoning arms trade. However, Cecil claimed to not have received the Foreign Office instructions to coordinate opposition effort with the Italians in time – the allegation was later made that Noel-Baker deliberately misplaced the telegram instructing him to do so – and by the time he was directly contacted it was too late to publicly act without losing face. Abyssinia was admitted to the League in October 1923, setting the stage for one of the League's greatest crises when Italian dictator Benito Mussolini invaded the country in 1935 and disregarded the organisation's attempts at peacemaking (Lamb 1989: 27–31). Despite the eventual tensions the Abyssinia issue would generate, in the short term a major issue seemed resolved when following the Locarno Treaty, discussed later, Germany itself was finally admitted to the League of Nations in 1926.

For all the League's much-discussed failures, it is worth ending this section on something of a success. On 29 October 1919 the first meeting of the International Labour Office (later Organization) took place in Washington D.C. and introduced a series of recommendations concerning the introduction of greater social reform and worker's rights which were known as the Washington Convention. This new body, under the auspices of the League of Nations, had been created under Part XIII of the Treaty of Versailles. There Article 427 of the Treaty asserted that the new ILO would be tasked with producing 'methods and principles for labour conditions which all industrial communities should endeavour to apply, so far as their special circumstances will permit'. Here then there was some wiggle room in the language. But the broad principles which shaped the ILO were clear enough: 'labour should not be regarded merely as a commodity', countries should deliver 'the payment to the employed of a wage adequate to maintain a reasonable standard of living', and the 'adoption of an eight hours day or a forty-eight hours week as the standard' should be 'aimed at where it has not already been attained'. This had significant impact throughout the globe. When the twelfth conference of the ILO met in Geneva in 1929, it was able to boast that countries such as Argentina and Venezuela had moved towards virtual adoption of the Washington Convention vis-à-vis the eight-hour working day. Generally the Benelux countries of North-west Europe were the most far advanced along meeting the ILO's demands throughout the 1920s – but the general point was that an international pressure group had been created to push governments toward concrete action on labour matters. Laissez-faire was fighting a losing battle throughout the 1920s and that was partly the League of Nations' doing (ILO n.d.: passim).

Arms control

When it became clear that the United States would not be joining the League of Nations, the entire premise of the organisation's existence was called into question. How could there be substantial progress toward international peace, and collective security, when the world's emergent power, to which virtually all of the First World War's victors owed money, would not be at the table? Despite staunch opposition in his own party to the League, Republican President Warren G. Harding was aware of the implications of his country's absence from the organisation. As a result, in 1921 the United States convened a peace conference of its own to discuss a wide range of international issues. The Washington Naval Conference, as it was known, would both mark a step forward in the process of international disarmament but also exacerbate the rift with the United States' key allies.

A number of countries took part in the 1921–2 conference, but the key players were the United States, Britain, France, Italy and Japan. The American delegates had several objectives in mind: firstly, to limit the number of ships being built by the participants to avoid a costly and dangerous naval arms race along the lines of what had taken place in Europe in the late nineteenth century and, secondly, to repair declining relations with Japan, which technically still had an alliance with Britain dating back to 1902. The treaty that was eventually reached at the conference put a hard limit on battleship construction for all five countries over the next decade, with Britain and the United States given the largest construction allowances (525,000 tonnes each) and Japan (315,000), France (175,000) and Italy (175,000) awarded more modest limits – the latter two, in effect, being downgraded from global to regional power status. In addition, there would be limits on the maximum tonnage of each ship, and a total tonnage that could not be exceeded. Furthermore, a larger nine-country agreement guaranteed the territorial integrity of China, which had fallen under threat from Japan and other powers (Cashman 1998: 247–8).

By 1924, the signatory powers had begun to chafe under the yoke of the Washington system. British commentators lamented that the agreement, coupled with the massive debts owed to the United States, had ruined British naval supremacy forever. Conservative British writer William Ralph Inge, Dean of St Paul's Cathedral and nicknamed 'the Gloomy Dean' for his pessimistic pontifications, bemoaned in 1926 that:

> British naval supremacy is at an end, and with it the instrument by which we built up and maintained our Empire. Naval strength depends mainly on national wealth. We are no longer rich enough to build ships against all possible rivals; and the Americans, by insisting on our repayment of the vast debt, incurred for the sake of France … have secured that we shall remain permanently tributary to themselves, and unable to challenge them on the water. Our Government had practically to choose between accepting Wilson's 'point' about the freedom of the seas, conceived in an unfriendly spirit to Britain, and agreeing to a numerical equality between the British and American fleets. They wisely accepted the latter, since the unlimited resources of the United States would make effective competition impossible. Our position as a world-power is thus permanently altered for the worse.
>
> *(Inge 1926: 150)*

Ironically, the American public and the Republican Party increasingly complained about the opposite. Both the British and the Japanese began to build new battleships in 1924, and in the general election that year the Democrats attacked Calvin Coolidge's Administration (Harding had died in 1923) for signing up to a treaty that restricted American military might. The US Navy then began to build new ships of its own, while the Republicans played the only political card possible and blamed the British (rather than their own party) for making a mockery of the treaty (Moser 1999: 48–9). Following the failure of a naval reduction conference in Geneva in 1927, the US Navy began to discuss the construction of new heavy cruisers, but Congress was unwilling to fund the project until it was dramatically revealed that the British and the French had made a secret agreement to support one another's military expenditures in the face of German and American opposition. American public opinion was outraged, Congress passed the money for the cruisers, and hot-headed voices in the United States began to discuss the possibility of war with Britain. This ludicrous notion never came close to reality, but it is telling that relations between the countries had dipped so low so quickly after the end of the First World War (Moser 1999: 53–60).

This woeful episode played out concurrently with the last great disarmament conference of the 1920s: the Pact of Paris or, as it was more commonly known, the Kellogg–Briand Pact. The Pact explicitly renounced the use of warfare to achieve national aims in order make it, as Patrick O. Cohrs has put it, 'an instrument for the promotion of peaceful change, not *status quo* preservation' (Cohrs 2008: 461). In essence, the world's countries were now obligated to resolve disputes by non-violent means rather than resorting to war. Specifically, the Pact was designed to reduce tensions between France and Germany in the hopes that future conflict would be avoided. Sensitive to isolationist sentiment, the Republican Party argued that the treaty did not commit the United States to a future role in European affairs and, with polls showing 95 per cent public support for ratification, the US Senate approved the treaty with only one vote against it (Moser 1999: 61). It was a startling reversal from only a few years earlier when the Senate had tied itself into knots over the Treaty of Versailles and ultimately rejected it, and, as Cohrs has argued, Kellogg–Briand 'would mark the greatest extent of US engagement on behalf of war prevention – not only in the 1920s, but, essentially, before Hitler's challenge to the international order in the 1930s and the postwar planning of the 1940s' (Cohrs 2008: 472).

Conclusion

The world, in short, had changed a great deal since the comforting days of 1914. One witness to all this was Aubrey Leo Kennedy, known as Leo, a diplomatic correspondent for *The Times* of London. Born in 1885, Kennedy had the textbook background of a well-to-do British man of his era. After education at the prestigious Harrow School and Magdalen College, Oxford, he served bravely during the war (winning the Military Cross) with the Scots Guards. In 1919 he returned to his old job at *The Times* and tried to make sense of the new world around him. Travelling around Europe interviewing the key politicians of the day, he jotted down his private thoughts in a series of journals that survive at Churchill College, Cambridge. These reveal much about the hopes and fears held by those in power.

In November 1919 Kennedy was in Paris and met

Monsieur Benes the Czechoslovak Foreign Minister, who had arrived that morning from Prague but looked as fresh as possible. [He] is an alert nice little man, quick honest and to the point in his replies. He spoke eagerly of his idea that Prague should be the centre of central Europe instead of Vienna – traffic, rolling stock, communications are the trouble at present, and hamper Bohemia's development. Speaking of the name Czecho-Slovakia, he explained that it is a

programme necessary to keep not yet fused races together. – it may disappear
and give way to the more civilised Bohemia.

(Kennedy 1919–20, 16 November 1919)

Here then we can see that the 1920s were about to begin in several interesting
ways. Firstly, to some degree, with real optimism. Benes believed that his Prague
could overtake Vienna – and a city at the periphery of the old Austro-Hungarian
Empire, in other words, could carve itself a new more prominent identity in a new
country. Re-drawing the map could mean recasting places at the stroke of a pen.
But Benes was also clearly worried, and not just about the temporary infrastructure
problems he mentioned. Hitler's later comment that Czechoslovakia was the 'bastard
child of Versailles' may in part have referred to its continued existence as a democratic
state when others in the region (including Hungary and Poland) swiftly fell to
totalitarian or at least militaristic regimes. But Benes' point about the 'not yet fused
races' and the possible need to rebrand the country as 'Bohemia' – asserting the
Czech dominance over the Slovaks – meant that the Wilsonian order of self-
determination had indeed led to some ambiguities. How, in short, could the trade-off
between representing different ethnic groups and actually having a viable state that
could defend itself be managed?

Moving through Germany and Poland in the summer of 1920, Kennedy then
encountered various further challenges. In June he was moved to write that despite
notions of pre-war pan-Slavism having drawn Russian into the global conflict, 'slav
linguistic unity is … not a very active vital force – they have differed just enough
not to understand each other, and politically some of them hate each other (e.g.
Poles, Russians and Czechs)' (Kennedy 1919–20, 1 June 1920). The most obvious
manifestation of this was the Russo-Polish war, which lasted from February 1919
to March 1921. With Polish leader Jozef Pilsudski looking to expand Poland's
borders to create a bulwark against the emergence of a newly aggressive Germany, the
territories of the Ukraine and Belarus – historically part of the old Polish–Lithuanian
Commonwealth in the eighteenth century – were high on his cartographical wish
list. Similarly, as Lenin and the USSR looked to formalise the re-annexation of
territories temporarily lost to the Germans at the Treaty of Brest-Litovsk, they too
were looking westwards into such areas. A conflagration soon occurred which
eventually resulted in a partition of the disputed territories at the Treaty of Riga.

But, particularly given the potential for communist expansion this volume later
explores, it is worth giving light to another of Kennedy's conversations during this
summer. Certainly the Bolsheviks in Moscow were looking, where possible, to
expand. But so too were the generals in Warsaw. In June, Kennedy had an

> interesting talk with Gen[eral] Rozwadowski, who took me about in his
> motor-car most of the morning, as he had engagements and so the only time
> he could talk to me was in between. He developed fully his ideas for the
> commercial exploitation of the Ukraine with the help of England and
> France – we should help economically, France politically and possibly he

hoped with colonial troops … He spoke in the ancient conquering spirit of old Poland and referred to the Ukrainians themselves as dogs. This is all v[ery] well but Poland hasn't got Ukraine yet, and doesn't look like getting it.

(Kennedy 1919–20, 23 June 1920)

Here again, then, we must draw limitations over the notion of a co-operative, liberal Europe that was only split asunder by economic depression. Nor were Germany or Italy the only powers with territorial grievances. On the Eastern Front, the First World War had been far more mobile and fluid than that seen in the West, and much of this marked the later drawing (and re-drawing) of borders. The reason for this could be seen in Kennedy's later visit to the disputed town of Teschen in July 1920: 'We entered the plebiscite area just south of Biala … This is an attractive little German town – absolutely German, with just a sprinkling of Poles and Jews – Poles in all the country round' (Kennedy 1919–20, 5 July 1920). This territory was eventually divided between Czechoslovakia and Poland (again after brief military skirmishes), and would be one of the areas Poland would annex from the Czechs as Hitler settled the Sudetenland question in 1938.

The 1920s began, in other words, with several question marks over what the future map of Europe would look like, and by the end of the decade those questions had not yet been convincingly answered in the minds of many. While various treaties, pacts and borders existed on paper, the uneasy status quo would be called into question by Hitler in the decade to come. Less than a decade after the signing of the Kellogg–Briand pact renouncing warfare, Europe would once again be preparing for a likely widespread conflict. Notably, Hitler's complaints against the European order established by Versailles were based not only on these territorial adjustments but also the disastrous reparations system that will be discussed in the final chapters of this book.

The political situation was hardly better in the Middle East, where the British and the French had made huge territorial gains from the ruins of the Ottoman Empire but were now faced with the prospect of actually governing those areas. As noted, following initial uncertainty Iraq and Transjordan became comparatively stable British-backed monarchies, and Egypt, always an exception to the wider conditions of the region, was given its nominal independence but remained very much under the British heel. The 1919 revolution had begun to sweep away the vestiges of the Ottoman past – seeking new roles for women, for instance – but progress remained generally piecemeal. Egypt quickly became divided between those who sought to be Westernised in education, language and clothing and those who sought an Islamic or pan-Arabic identity.

It was not just Europe and the Middle East that found themselves enthralled by Wilson's vision of national self-determination. During the Versailles negotiations, Wilson received hundreds of letters, petitions and other documents from groups and individuals around the world who hoped that the principle of 'national self-determination' would be applied to them. Very few such documents actually made it to the President's desk, and even fewer received serious consideration, but it is clear that the Fourteen Points had become a major inspiration to millions who hoped that their lot would soon be improved. In China, nationalists argued that their long subjugation to Western and Japanese power should be brought to an end (China had declared war on Germany in the final months of the war in an effort to gain a seat at the victor's table) (Manela 2007: 5, 107). The Treaty eventually gave Japan rather than China control over the German-held area of Shandong, sparking protests that involved future communist premier Zhou Enlai. In early 1920 Zhou was arrested for his anti-government activities and sent to prison, where he moved intellectually closer to the tenets of Marxism. He would later embrace communism during a European sojourn that followed his release (Jian 2014: 149–50). Zhou's path to communism lay at least partially in the disappointments of Versailles.

Similarly, many Koreans hoped that Wilson and Versailles would prove able to right the wrongs that decades of Japanese domination had produced. The hopes of both the Chinese and the Korean delegations at Versailles came to nothing beyond empty words, but regardless it was the first time that these grievances had been given consideration by the international community. In the event, however, it would not be until after the Second World War that East Asia would begin to break free of the colonial yoke. Similarly, the British had managed to almost completely bury the protestations of the Egyptian nationalists, all but guaranteeing further unrest throughout the 1920s. Zaghloul himself returned to Egypt as Prime Minister in the middle years of the decade and was remembered as 'father of the nation' on his death in 1927 (Manela 2007: 216–18).

These changes to the world map after Versailles were all nominally supervised by the League of Nations, a body in which few world statesmen had more than scant confidence. By 1923, when Abyssinia was admitted, the body had already failed to resolve important questions related to the situation in Europe, and the ground had been laid for its eventual humiliation at the hands of Mussolini. While the admission of Germany in the middle years of the decade was a major step toward the country's rehabilitation in the international sphere, just a few years later, Hitler would withdraw the country's membership.

With the United States remaining outside the League, diplomacy had to be conducted beyond its auspices to have real significance. The Washington Naval Treaties were a major effort to avoid an arms build-up that might easily turn against the United States (particularly in the unlikely event that Japan were to invoke its treaty with Britain). As with many a compromise, no one was happy with the result and nearly everyone complained. By the end of the decade, all countries were looking to escape the Treaties' strictures, and while American anger had initially been directed at the British it was increasingly clear that it was the Japanese naval build-up that would soon be the more important issue.

By the end of the 1920s, political reality had changed for millions of people who now lived under a new imperial power or in a country that had not even existed in 1914. The British and the French had seen their empires expand into new areas as they claimed the 'spoils' of the First World War, but the cracks in this new order had already begun to show. The Soviets had managed to solidify their own state, discussed in chapter 9, and Lenin had given way to Stalin. Germany had survived the worst of the economic crisis described, but the Weimar Republic remained weak. Japan continued to build up its naval power, while the United States struggled between its isolationist core and the seemingly inexorable push toward a permanent role in world affairs. As the remaining chapters of this book will make clear, these questions and their implications were at the core of what the 1920s represented for those who lived through them and, in the West at least, many frequently looked back on them in the 1930s as a shining moment of hope amidst an increasingly gathering storm.

Questions

- Was the Treaty of Versailles a failure? Why or why not?
- Was the Treaty of Versailles fair or unfair to Germany? Why or why not?
- Why were the European powers so willing to ignore their previous promises to Arab leaders in the Middle East?
- What factors made the League of Nations so weak in handling the big issues of the 1920s?
- Why did so many treaties and pacts made in the 1920s result in ultimate failure?

Recommended further reading

Cabanes, B. (2014), *The Great War and the Origins of Humanitarianism, 1918–1924*, Cambridge: Cambridge University Press.

Cohrs, P.O. (2008), *The Unfinished Peace after World War I: America, Britain and the Stabilisation of Europe, 1919–1932*, Cambridge: Cambridge University Press.

Jian, C. (2014), 'Zhou Enlai and China's "Prolonged Rise"', in Guha, R. (ed.), *Makers of Modern Asia*, Cambridge, MA: Harvard University Press, pp. 147–171.

Lamb, R. (1989), *The Drift to War, 1922–1939*, New York: St Martin's Press.

Manela, E. (2007), *The Wilsonian Moment: Self-Determination and the International Origins of Anticolonial Nationalism*, Oxford: Oxford University Press.

Pedersen, S. (2015), *The Guardians: The League of Nations and the Crisis of Empire*, Oxford: Oxford University Press.

Steiner, Z. (2005), *The Lights that Failed: European International History 1919–1933*, Oxford: Oxford University Press.

Tooze, A. (2014), *The Deluge: The Great War and the Remaking of Global Order*, London: Allen Lane.

Works cited

Anderson, S. (2013), *Lawrence in Arabia: War, Deceit, Imperial Folly and the Making of the Modern Middle East*, New York: Doubleday.

Arielli, N. (2010), *Fascist Italy and the Middle East, 1933–40*, London: Palgrave.

Baron, B. (1989). 'Unveiling in Early 20th Century Egypt, Practical and Symbolic Considerations', *Middle Eastern Studies*, 25/3, 370–386.

Boemeke, M.F. (1998), 'Woodrow Wilson's Image of Germany, the War-Guilt Question, and the Treaty of Versailles', in Boemeke, M.F., Feldman, G.B. and Glaser, E. (eds), *The Treaty of Versailles: A Reassessment after 75 Years*, Cambridge: Cambridge University Press, pp. 603–614.

Boemeke, M.F., Feldman, G.B. and Glaser, E. (eds) (1998), *The Treaty of Versailles: A Reassessment after 75 Years*, Cambridge: Cambridge University Press.

Brown, M. (ed.) (1980), *T.E. Lawrence: The Selected Letters*, New York: W.W. Norton & Company.

Cabanes, B. (2014), *The Great War and the Origins of Humanitarianism, 1918–1924*, Cambridge: Cambridge University Press.

Carr, R. (2011), 'Veterans of the First World War and Conservative Anti-Appeasement', *Twentieth Century British History*, 22/1, 28–51.

Carr, R. (2013), *Veteran MPs and Conservative Politics in the Aftermath of the Great War*, Farnham: Ashgate.

Cashman, S.D. (1998), *America Ascendant: From Theodore Roosevelt to FDR in the Century of American Power, 1901–1945*, New York: New York University Press.

Churchill, W.S. (1929), *The Aftermath: The World Crisis, 1918–1928*, New York: Charles Scribner's Sons.

Cohrs, P.O. (2008), *The Unfinished Peace after World War I: America, Britain and the Stabilisation of Europe, 1919–1932*, Cambridge: Cambridge University Press.

Cook, S.A. (2011), *The Struggle for Egypt: From Nasser to Tahrir Square*, Oxford: Oxford University Press.

Dawisha, A. (2005), *Arab Nationalism in the Twentieth Century*, Princeton: Princeton University Press.

Ferguson, N. (1998), 'The Balance of Payments Question: Versailles and After', in Boemeke, M.F., Feldman, G.B. and Glaser, E. (eds), *The Treaty of Versailles: A Reassessment after 75 Years*, Cambridge: Cambridge University Press, pp. 401–440.

Ferguson, N. (2003), *Empire: How Britain Made the Modern World*, London: Penguin.

Gibbons, H.A. (1923), *Europe since 1918*, New York: The Century Co.

ILO (n.d.), International Labour Organization, online archive via www.ilo.org/century/research/keydocuments/lang–en/index.htm

Inge, W.R. (1926), *England*, New York: Charles Scribner's Sons.

Jian, C. (2014), 'Zhou Enlai and China's "Prolonged Rise"', in Guha, R. (ed.) *Makers of Modern Asia*, Cambridge, MA: Harvard University Press, pp. 147–171.

Kennedy, L. (1919–20), Journals held at the Churchill Archives Centre, Cambridge, LKEN 1/1.

Keynes, J.M. (1920), *The Economic Consequences of the Peace*, New York: Harcourt, Brace and Howe.

Keynes, J.M. (1922), *A Revision of the Treaty: Being a Sequel to The Economic Consequences of the Peace*, New York: Harcourt, Brace and Company.

La Revue de Paris (1922), 'The Present Status of Egypt', April 1 (Independent Political and Literary Semi-Monthly). *The Living Age (1897–1941), American Periodicals*, p. 441.

Lamb, R. (1989), *The Drift to War, 1922–1939*, New York: St Martin's Press.

Lang, A. (2013), 'From Revolutions to Constitutions: The Case of Egypt', *International Affairs*, 89/2, 345–363.

Laqueur, W. (1972), *A History of Zionism*, New York: Holt, Rinehart and Winston.

Manela, E. (2007), *The Wilsonian Moment: Self-Determination and the International Origins of Anticolonial Nationalism*, Oxford: Oxford University Press.

Moser, J.E. (1999), *Twisting the Lion's Tail: American Anglophobia between the World Wars*, New York: New York University Press.

Nafi, B.M. (1998), *Arabism, Islamism and the Palestine Question 1908–1941: A Political History*, Ithaca: Ithaca Press.

Pedersen, S. (2015), *The Guardians: The League of Nations and the Crisis of Empire*, Oxford: Oxford University Press.

Pollard, L. (2005), *Nurturing the Nation, the Family Politics of Modernizing, Colonizing, and Liberating Egypt*, Berkeley: University of California Press.

Steiner, Z. (2005), *The Lights that Failed: European International History 1919–1933*, Oxford: Oxford University Press.

Tardieu, A. (1921), *The Truth About the Treaty*, Indianapolis: The Bobbs-Merrill Company.

Taylor, A.J.P. (1945), *The Course of German History*, London: Methuen and Co.

Teitelbaum, J. (2001), *The Rise and Fall of the Hashemite Kingdom of Arabia*, New York: New York University Press.

Tooze, A. (2014), *The Deluge: The Great War and the Remaking of Global Order*, London: Allen Lane.

UN (United Nations) (1925), Geneva Protocol, via http://www.un.org/disarmament/WMD/Bio/pdf/Status_Protocol.pdf

US Department of State (1947), 'The Treaty of Versailles and After: Annotations of the Text of the Treaty', Washington: US Government Printing Office.

Watikiotis, P.J. (1991), *The History of Modern Egypt*, London: Weidenfeld & Nicolson.

2

EQUALITY, CLASS, RACE AND GENERAL LIVING

The nineteenth century saw the politicisation of class across the globe. In Europe, Karl Marx wrote of the inevitable clash between the industrialised and urban proletariat and the bourgeois elites who enslaved them, both economically and spiritually. Telling the workers they had nothing to lose but their chains, he and Friedrich Engels helped codify an ideology that although it would have to bend to particular national circumstance (and eventually come to power in one of Europe's least urbanised nations, Russia) would go on to profoundly affect the course of the twentieth century. Indeed, before the First World War even capitalist America saw the rise of its own socialist party, and its candidate Eugene V. Debs managed to poll a respectable 900,000 votes in the 1912 Presidential Election. Elsewhere in the Anglophone world, British politicians had long spoken of the ills of 'two nations' – a phrase associated with the Conservative Benjamin Disraeli – and the tales Charles Dickens weaved of a sharp divide between rich and poor were by no means merely fiction. Concrete expression would be given to this through the creation of the Labour Representation Committee (later Party) in 1900. Due to such shifts in the way, location, and length of time people lived, class was clearly on the agenda as the twentieth century began in many an advanced nation and beyond.

The years that followed the First World War in many cases swept aside old orders without quite making clear what was to follow. Whilst civil war raged in Russia, abortive left-wing revolutions failed in Bavaria and Hungary, and the debate waged between left-leaning forces attempting to play up class struggle and those of the right or centre-right attempting to downplay the importance of such considerations. The nation, or presumptive national interest, was lifted above such petty concerns by politicians from Stanley Baldwin to Calvin Coolidge, in part for their own political gain. And yet, beneath the surface, tensions clearly rumbled throughout the globe. As we will see, particularly through the perspective of the British left and the output of both the Fabian Society pressure group and the historian R.H. Tawney, nations tackled and debated the issue of inequality in various manners.

Race was an issue that clearly affected millions across the globe too. As the 1920s began there were still large swathes of people in only their forties or fifties who had been slaves in their youth in a number of territories from Brazil to Borneo. Sylvester Magee (1841–1971, disputed), the last living American slave and Cudjoe Lewis (1840–1935), the last American slave to have been born on African soil, were both very much alive throughout this decade too, as were thousands of American Civil War veterans. And yet even with the abolition of slavery decades old in most countries clear inequalities surrounding race remained. From D.W. Griffith's film *Birth of a Nation* (1917) and its depiction of black 'savagery' during the Reconstruction era to concrete legislative changes that were not only in force but often extended during this period, the treatment of white and non-white citizens in most facets of 1920s life remained divergent.

It is important to dig beneath these trends and view the period as about more than its most glamorous and famous leading lights. Certainly, the 1920s was a decade of big name personalities and new, epoch defining -isms. But the world, for all their efforts, was bigger than Charlie Chaplin, Mussolini or Stalin, and neither fascism nor communism succeeded in conquering the globe. Instead, this complicated period saw intersections of class, race and gender in various forms. The latter we consider in chapter 6. The first two find their primary discussion in the pages that follow.

Class

Class was a live issue in most countries in the 1920s. As mentioned, in part this was a natural consequence of communism's rise and long-run trends going back to the European-wide (albeit mostly unsuccessful) revolutions of 1848. If Marx's theoretical aim had been to awaken the proletariat from its slumber, the Soviet Union now provided a ready-made example (good and bad, certainly dramatic) of what communism could look like in practice. With the Communist International (Comintern) seeking to spread the gospel of class consciousness across the globe, and unemployment rising sharply after the end of the First World War in many nations, the divide between 'rich' and 'poor' was again thrown into sharp relief. In the nation perhaps least likely to go communist – though experiencing its own 'Red Scare' – American unemployment rose from 1.4 per cent in 1919 to 11.7 per cent just two years later. Post-war economic booms were commonplace as soldiers returned home with disposable incomes and wartime regulations were relaxed, but they often did not last: Weimar Germany was the tip of an economic iceberg that many nations felt throughout the decade and which exacerbated the plight of the poor. Although the middle and upper class lost their savings (turning in some cases to National Socialism to fix the economy), at least they had savings to draw upon. In eroding the value of the mark, however, it is true that hyperinflation seemed something of a leveller, at least in its early stages.

Despite such economic difficulties, paradoxically, the 1920s was also a decade of glamour, excess and debauchery. This phenomenon was at once venerated and derided. Charlie Chaplin's first completely non-comedic film, *A Woman of Paris* (1923), portrayed members of the Parisian aristocracy as indulging in a hedonistic lifestyle (voyeurism, drinking) whilst at the same time being utterly detached from normal human emotions. The fictional town of West Egg on Long Island served as a similar means through which F. Scott Fitzgerald's 1925 *The Great Gatsby* could highlight class division, bourgeois extra-marital affairs and the effects of 1920s American capitalism. This was a widespread problem: as R.H. Tawney observed from Oxford, England, 'the admiration of society is directed towards those who get; not towards those who give'. The 1920s *Acquisitive Society*, whose 'whole tendency and interest and pre-occupation is to promote the acquisition of wealth' was for the religious and ethically minded Tawney, a social ill (Tawney 1920: 36 and 29).

Although many Americans and Europeans would grow to venerate the Jazz Age it was argued by others – such as the British Conservative MP Reginald Banks – to be a 'plague from abroad' akin 'to Russian influenza' (Banks 1929: 18, 57). And thus whilst black musicians and entertainers like Paul Robeson – who gave up his legal career in large part due to the racism he encountered – were permitted to enter social establishments for the purposes of entertaining whites, they would often have been barred from the same locations had they tried to enter them as customers. Another famous example was the trumpeter Louis Armstrong who moved to New York in 1924 to play with the African-American Fletcher Henderson Orchestra. There he played regularly in all-white venues such as the Roseland Ballroom. The Ballroom, which moved to Broadway from Philadelphia in 1919, was described as a 'whites only' dance club which offered 'refined dancing'. The fact that such 'refined dancing' was often facilitated by Armstrong, Duke Ellington and other black musicians was a continual irony of the period.

Race we explore later in this chapter (and indeed in others), but for most people there was an economic hierarchy of one form or another. Patronage was of course a big part of this and familial, scholarly or regimental connections clearly still mattered to those who managed to make their way to the top in the West. In 1930, Robert T. Nightingale conducted a prosopographical study for the Fabian Society of leading British diplomats since the 1880s. Nightingale analysed the 87 men to hold the highest ranks in both the Foreign Office and Diplomatic Service. He concluded that of this number, 50 were the children of aristocrats or rentiers, 12 of civil servants and 19 of professionals. Thirty-eight had attended the prestigious school of Eton and 49 had attended Oxford or Cambridge universities. To get on in Britain in the 1920s class still mattered intensely, and this was not necessarily ideal for the national interest. As Nightingale observed:

> Men who have been nurtured in the British upper class have lived in a world secluded from the common people ... Those so reared and so trained are imbued with the peculiar prejudices of their walk of life. They are far too removed from the common people to comprehend their point of view ... The successful

diplomatist needs in this age the capacity to mix with men of all classes and standpoints.

(Nightingale 1930: 16)

In an empire that was already beginning to crack, there may be much in that. Generally however, the leaders – mostly, though not exclusively on the right – could be myopic to such ills. Though enlightened Conservatives were beginning to see the light, such types often knew little of the poverty in their homeland, let alone the wider world. One witness to such poverty in the West was Malcolm MacDonald, son of Britain's first Labour Party Prime Minister and a Cabinet Minister in his own right in the 1930s. Writing on the world of the 1900s, he remarked that 'the contrast between the extremely opulent manner of living of those well-to-do families and the miserable destitution of their slum-dwelling fellow countrymen in London's East End and elsewhere was extreme. A score of years later it still remained appalling, as I got to know from personal experience' (MacDonald n.d.: 8). This personal experience was garnered early in his political career as a local councillor in 1920s Limehouse. There, rather than hold the usual surgeries where constituents met him in a town hall or local community centre, he would often have to go to his constituents' homes. And this, as he noted, was not because they were ill,

> it was because at the time they had no clothes to wear for an appointment out-of-doors … I would find my constituent lying on a bed covered in a blanket. He or she apologised for causing me the trouble of journeying to their hovel, and explained that the members of their family had only two or three suits fit for grown-up males and two or three dresses fit for adult females to wear, and that these had been donned that evening by sons or daughters.
>
> (MacDonald n.d.: 9)

All this was taking place in the capital city of the largest empire on earth. The 1920s, even in London, were not all bathwater cocktails and American jazz.

The statistics of equality

Two considerations directly affected the lives of millions of people in the 1920s: did their country's economy increase in size across the board, and did individuals at the lower end of the income scale see their slice of the cake grow as a result? On the first point it is clear that, prior to the great crash which ended the decade, most economies around the world grew throughout the 1920s. Using the purchasing power parity measure of gross domestic product (how much a given country is producing with the fluctuations in currency evened out), there was a relatively uniform development of most leading economies throughout the decade. After a post-war trough, nations such as Canada, France, the United States and Britain experienced a period of more or less steady growth from 1921 to 1929. For Britain and France, in particular, the large empires they still enjoyed in Africa, Asia and elsewhere provided a ready-made market for goods and a source of raw materials that provided a degree of economic stability despite external factors. There were of course regional differences and these nations all experienced a small downturn at one stage or another (such as France in 1924–5 and 1926–7, and the UK in 1925–6), but the general pattern was positive. Give or take, most advanced economies expanded by about a fifth over the 1920s.

The two major deviations from this overall trend were Italy and Germany, which both suffered the massive political upheavals outlined elsewhere in this volume. Whilst the German economy increased by almost a third between 1919 and 1922, it then suffered a dip of about a fifth over 1922–3 before once again accelerating to over $4bn by 1928 – $1.2bn bigger than it had been when the French entered the Ruhr in January 1923. Italy likewise experienced a collapse from $3.4bn in 1918 to $2.5bn in 1921. Benito Mussolini's Fascist government saw years of stagnation (1923–4, 1925–6) and even recession (1926–7) but it engendered something of a recovery through the 1920s, taking Italy from $2.6bn in 1922 to $3.1bn by 1929. Fascist Italy also rode out the effects of the Wall Street Crash rather better than many leading democratic nations, principally because of the autarkic economic model Mussolini was pursuing. Between 1929 and 1931 the Italian economy declined by about 7 per cent. This was marginally worse than the 6.7 per cent seen in the UK during the same period. It did, however, far exceed the experience of the United States (31 per cent decline between 1929 and 1933), Australia (17.3 per cent decline between 1929 and 1931) and the Germany about to experience its own National Socialist takeover (17 per cent drop between 1929 and 1932) (Gapminder n.d.: passim). Exposure to the global economy we cover in chapters 10 through 12.

In Latin America, several nations experienced economic stagnation throughout the 1920s – arguably including Brazil (whose GDP experienced a 'Western' style 15 per cent increase but from a much lower base and without the impact of the Great War to contend with) and Mexico (which had actually dipped about 4 per cent from its 1920 level even before the 1929 Wall Street Crash took hold). The Brazilian economy was particularly aided by a dramatic increase in coffee consumption in the United States and Europe throughout the decade. A concerted advertising campaign in the United States, funded partially by Brazilian growers themselves, touted the supposed health benefits of coffee to Americans and funded scientific research that concluded that the beverage was not only safe but also carried health benefits. The fact that alcohol consumption was banned in the United States by Prohibition helped make coffee the era-defining drink of the decade as coffee houses sprang up across the country, bean prices soared and brands like Hills Brothers and Maxwell House became household names. Brazilian growers, American distributors and independent coffee shop owners all benefitted from the explosion of interest in a caffeinated beverage that was rapidly replacing alcohol as the nation's social drink of choice (Pendergrast 2010, 143–63).

Along similar lines, two more Latin American success stories of the decade were Argentina (whose per capita GDP exceeded Germany's throughout the 1920s) and

Venezuela (whose economy trebled in size throughout the decade). The latter was almost entirely oil driven. In 1918, an oil well at Barrosso blew a 200 foot spout that produced almost 100,000 barrels worth of product a day. By 1929, Venezuela was the world's leading exporter of oil. As the automobile took off, so too did Venezuela's economy. It was in many ways the surprise global success story of the decade.

The second question, however, was whether this increased output led to increased equality. Did a rising tide lift all boats, or just the yachts? Generally, it seems, all the watercraft managed to rise, at least a little. According to the World Top Incomes Database (a treasure trove of data pertaining to such matters – Alvaredo *et al.* n.d.), the 1920s was a decade of increasing equality across the globe. If the political goal was re-distribution, in short, the 1920s worked. As George Bernard Shaw wrote,

> the war of 1914–18 affected [the goals of equality] favourably by compelling the Government to supersede private commercial enterprise in several directions by direct control ... The unprecedented taxation and super-taxation of property for the support of the war was also in [this] line.
>
> *(Shaw 1930: 18)*

This trend panned out in most leading economies throughout the 1920s, and not just in terms of taxes on property. In Thomas Piketty's prominent recent analysis of the effect of *Capital in the Twenty-First Century*, he observes that

> the shocks that buffeted the economy in the period 1914–45 – World War I, the Bolshevik Revolution of 1917 ... and the consequent advent of new regulatory and tax policies along with controls on capital – reduced capital's share of income to historically low levels.
>
> *(Piketty 2014: 41)*

The war, in short, levelled many domestic playing fields.

The numbers in what follows are somewhat technical, but the overall point matters. In terms of the marginal tax rate the richest paid on their income, there were substantial advances throughout the 1920s that would set the stage for later developments. From the United States and France levying no income tax before the war (or 1913 in the American case), France increased their top rate to above 70 per cent under the *Cartel des gauches* in the mid-1920s, with the United States adopting a similar rate in the early-1920s before successive Republican administrations cut the top rate back to a low of 25 per cent under Herbert Hoover in the final years of the decade. Germany (c.4 per cent) and the UK (c.8 per cent) had at least maintained (new) higher rates before the war, but these too were steadily increased to 40 per cent and 60 per cent respectively. In terms of inheritance levies, the UK leapt from a top rate of 15 per cent to 40 per cent in the 1920s, Germany and the United States from no tax whatsoever pre-war to 35 per cent and 40 per cent respectively, and France from 7 per cent before the conflict to around 30 per cent in the mid-1920s (Piketty 2014: 503). Other nations, including Canada and

Sweden, introduced progressive taxation as a result of the war (even for partially defensive reasons, since Sweden stayed out of both the twentieth century's global conflicts).

We can see the effect of these measures through analysing the incomes of the richest global citizens. Using the aforementioned incomes database, it is evident that in Europe there was a general decline in the percentage of income taken home by the 10 per cent highest-remunerated citizens. The richest, in other words, took home a slightly smaller slice of the cake in 1930 than they had ten years earlier. In Denmark the total take of this group fell from 41.1 per cent of all income to 40 per cent during the 1920s, and in the Netherlands the equivalent decline was 46.2 per cent to 43 per cent. Between 1919 and 1928 the top German decile experienced a fall in their relative share from 38 per cent to 32.2 per cent, and the top 10 per cent of Swedes saw a fall in their share from 41.9 per cent to 38.4 per cent. The pattern was of an elite taking home slightly less than they had a decade or two earlier. This was hardly communism, but it does help explain why such nations managed to resist that fate.

France – despite advances in its tax system – was a great exception, with a rise in the incomes of the top decile from 39.6 per cent in 1920 to 41.1 per cent by 1930. In part this represented a stock market boom with the value of the French *Bourse* moving from 1.7 times its 1913 level in 1920 to five times the pre-war level by the time events took their toll in New York at the end of the decade. Similarly, across the Atlantic the richest decile of Americans took home more and more of national income, with an increase from 38.1 per cent to 43.1 per cent over the 1920s – partially a result of later tax cuts, but again due to stock market speculation. Across the globe, for every dollar generated in national income by advanced nations in the 1920s, the richest tenth of the population would take about 40 cents. In the early twenty-first century, for comparison, it is generally between about 28 and 42 cents for leading European economies and 47 cents for the United States. Generally speaking, wealthy individuals in the 1920s made about the same share of the national income as they do today, with the American rich today actually taking home more than they did in the days of the *Great Gatsby*.

That was the extremely wealthy, but there is also specific data for the 'hyper-wealthy'. Drilling down further, the income share of the richest 1 per cent dropped in many places in the 1920s as well – though here again the trend was not universal. On the one hand, the wealthiest 1 per cent of Australians in 1921 were taking in 11.6 per cent of national income, compared to a lower figure of 9.8 per cent by 1930. The top 1 per cent of their New Zealand neighbours experienced a similar drop from 11.3 per cent to 10.6 per cent. Such declining trends could be observed in distant Japan (17.1 per cent to 16.8 per cent between 1920 and 1930) and Sweden (16.3 per cent in 1919 to 13.7 per cent by 1930). The figures for South Africa – the African state for which we have the most reliable data in this period – remained relatively stable at a fifth of all income (20.3 per cent to 20.5 per cent).

But there was clear divergence within other nations. In the United States, the top 1 per cent saw their income share rise from 14.5 per cent in 1920 to 16.4 per cent by 1930. Their Canadian equivalents experienced a similar increase, from 14.4 per cent to 16.1 per cent over the same period. Japan's drop notwithstanding, other Asian nations' top earners saw a North American type rise, including an increase in India for the top 1 per cent from 12.7 per cent to 14.5 per cent (1922 to 1930) and Indonesia (11.8 per cent in 1921 to 16.6 per cent in 1930).

For the masses – which we may define as the bottom 90 per cent of earners – average incomes (in nominal cash terms) rose in most European states between 1920 and 1930 – in Denmark by 8.8 per cent, France 14.8 per cent and the Netherlands 25.7 per cent. In the United States, again, incomes stagnated during the decade and by 1930 – with the impact of the Wall Street Crash – stood at about 1 per cent below 1920 levels. By 1933, the bottom 90 per cent of Americans would experience a further 29 per cent drop. Things were not about to get any better soon – as the inhabitants of slum 'Hoovervilles' would experience first-hand.

The two reasons for this increasing inequality have already been hinted at. Firstly, more redistributive systems of taxation involved substantial transference from rich to poor (or at least to government, the efficacy and redistributive nature of such spending of course depended on who was in power). The demand of the left was to go further. As Tawney noted,

> if the peers and millionaires who are preaching the duty of production to miners and dock labourers desire that more wealth, not more waste, should be produced, the simplest way in which they can achieve their aim is to transfer to the public their whole incomes over (say) $5,000 a year, in order that it may be spent in setting to work, not gardeners, chauffeurs, domestic servants and shopkeepers in the West End of London, but builders, mechanics and teachers.
>
> *(Tawney 1920: 38–9)*

It would take another global conflict, but the highest rate of British taxation during the Second World War indeed all but achieved this, with the Churchill Coalition confiscating 99.25 per cent of marginal incomes of the richest. For all their limitations, the 1920s were clearly far more advanced than the Victorian or Edwardian era in almost every state in this regard.

The second great equaliser was the gradual collapse of European influence. With returns on capital investment in colonies and dependencies decreasing after the First World War, the rich saw their usual forms of investment income diminish (returns on foreign investment had long been stupendously high for European, particularly British, investors, to the extent that return on overseas investments amounted to a full 7 per cent of British GDP before the First World War) (Frieden 2006: 50). The decline of investment return meant that those affected had to either undertake more (increasingly higher taxed) work at home, sell domestic assets (again subject to taxation and redistribution) such as the country estate, or simply put up with smaller returns. In Piketty's analysis of the rate of returns on capital investment (r) having historically exceeded those of national income/wages (g), the interwar period generally at least saw the gap between r and g narrow, and this was to the benefit of broad equality. As Tawney noted at the time,

> the real economic cleavage is not, as is often said, between employers and the employed, but between all who do constructive work, from scientist to laborer, on the one hand, and all whose main interest is the preservation of existing proprietary rights upon the other, irrespective of whether they contribute to constructive work or not.
>
> *(Tawney 1920: 79)*

Arguably, it was ever thus.

Whether in Europe or beyond, historians are rightly wary of the alleged benefits of 'trickle-down' economics that claim widespread public benefits from increasing the resources (and incomes) of the wealthy. The 1920s saw severe limitations in this regard. But to some degree a wealthier world did mean benefits on the ground. In sub-Saharan Africa, North Africa and the Middle East, fewer than one in five children were enrolled in secondary education in the 1920s. The equivalent figure for South America was fewer than four in ten, though this was a rise from around three in ten at the beginning of the decade. Literacy remained poor in several states with fewer than one in five Egyptians and black South Africans able to read by 1930 and with fewer than one in ten Indians literate. On the positive side, the 1920s saw a great leap forward of at least 10 per cent in Latin American nations such as Cuba (62 per cent to 72 per cent), Chile (63 per cent to 75 per cent) and Colombia (44 per cent to 54 per cent) (UNESCO 2006). Though data is patchy for the first of these nations, for the latter two this trend appears tied into a clearly improving economic performance generally – with per capita GDP rising by 17.6 per cent in Colombia and 19.9 per cent in Chile throughout the 1920s (World Economics n.d.). Trickle-down economics could be unreliable, but there were clearly effects in particular instances.

The debate over equality

The statistics delineated above were not available to all at the time, but the debate they touch upon – the need for greater equality amidst a world of stark divides between the West and the rest, and even within individual nations – was understood and articulated by many. In a 1929 speech to the Bombay Presidency of Muslim Educational Conference, Sir Fazli Hussein, Local Government Minister in the Punjab, talked of the 'present grave economic inequalities' potentially producing a 'deprivation of the means of the intellectual well-being of the next generation' (*Times of India*, 23 October 1929). Likewise, visiting India in 1924, a Westerner, Dr Harry Ward, had given a series of lectures on social problems. Ward's thesis was heavily tied to the problems of alcohol: 'he maintained that social workers the world over found drink at the bottom of the trouble, the main cause leading to poverty, disease, bad tenements, and such waste of human energies'. At the same time however, Ward noted that our modern economic system was both false and sinful. Our industrial morals and life must change so much that there could be no accumulation of wealth in a few hands with millions dying in their struggle for existence in all our large cities.

Acknowledging his audience, he remarked that 'India could well afford to learn a lesson from the West in that connection' (*Times of India*, 21 November 1924).

It must be noted that this was not the universal view. Conversely, in 1928 the industrialist W.M. Alexander told a Queensland audience that 'the greatest danger threatening the sovereign power of the people today is the annual avalanche of industrial and humanitarian legislation designed to correct the inequality of wealth'. His argument here was a mixture of economics and eugenics. Re-distribution would lower productive output, thereby lowering the standard of living. Longer term, it 'directly fostered the less capable and less worthy sections at the expense of the more capable and more worthy, thereby threatening racial fitness in the competition for survival'. Presaging Friedrich von Hayek's *Road to Serfdom*, he also argued the 'ever growing volume of interfering and taxing laws left citizens with less and less freedom … it enslaved them' (*The Queenslander*, 5 January 1928).

The argument here was generally between communism or democracy (or indeed the self-proclaimed third way of fascism). Was state intervention necessary, in what form, and was the democratic state the correct means with which to correct the economic failings of the 1920s? But this did not necessarily mean agreeing with either Karl Marx or Henry Ford wholesale – many theorists within the capitalist system were thinking innovatively in terms of rebooting it. As Tawney has argued, previously

> competition [was viewed as an] effective substitute for honesty. Today that subsidiary doctrine has fallen to pieces under criticism; few would now profess adherence to the compound of economic optimism and moral bankruptcy which led a nineteenth century economist to say: 'greed is held in check by greed, and the desire for gain sets limit to itself'.
>
> (Tawney 1920: 27)

The world of Adam Smith and unfettered capitalism had been cast asunder by the First World War and the debate now centred over what came next.

In 1920, the British engineer Clifford Hugh (C.H.) Douglas published his short book on *Economic Democracy*. This book impressed leading celebrity intellectuals from Charlie Chaplin to Ezra Pound, and fostered what became known as the Social Credit Movement. Douglas had arrived at his theory through organising the research of the Royal Aircraft Establishment in Great Britain during the Great War where, he observed, the wages paid to workers were not equal to the total cost of goods produced. The masses, in short, were not paid enough to purchase the goods they themselves had produced. Here he borrowed from another contemporary thinker, J.A. Hobson, whose thoughts on 'the mass of people with inadequate power to purchase and consume' he quoted at some length (Douglas 1920: 26). This produced what became known as his 'A + B theorem' which, crudely put, stated if a worker's wage of A was not enough to purchase the good they had produced, it would have to be topped up with an extra payment of B, a 'National Dividend' of credit distributed by governmental agency. A state-sponsored subsidy to make up for low wages, in other words.

This was clearly a critique of contemporary capitalism, but it was not a call to *end* capitalism entirely. Rather like Keynes' later *General Theory*, Douglas came to save the market, not do away with it. As Douglas noted, the big danger facing mankind was 'the Servile State; the erection of an irresistible and impersonal organization through which the ambition of able men, animated consciously or unconsciously by the lust of domination, may operate to the enslavement of their fellows' (Douglas 1920: 21). But just as a communistic or fascistic state could produce this end, he argued, so too could contemporary Anglo-American capitalism. It is perhaps not surprising Charlie Chaplin was a fan – Douglas' reference to there having grown up a spirit of revolt against a life spent in the performance of one mechanical operation devoid of interest, requiring little skill, and having few pro- spects of advancement' could have come from an early treatment of his 1936 film, *Modern Times* (Douglas 1920: 33).

In the 1930s Douglasite Parties were formed in Australia and, with some degree of success, in Canada. But it was in the 1920s that the under-consumptionist arguments of the Social Credit movement began to gain their global toehold. The state, after all, had intervened in innumerable ways in many countries to secure victory in the First World War and so too, it was claimed, could it do so to correct the great evil of inequality. The point in all this was that in the 1920s inequality was very much a moral question. There were of course economic consequences – under-consumption and the need for welfare transference payments – but the fundamental question was how much inequality was a good or at least tolerable thing. This was a question debated as much, or even more so, within nations as it was between them.

Race and religion

Economics was not the be all and end all, however. The 1920s fell almost exactly in the middle of what was known as the Jim Crow era of American lawmaking with regard to racial issues. This involved the legal codification of a 'separate but equal' relationship between Americans of African and European descent. All this was a legal fudge designed to get around the Reconstruction-era Fourteenth Amendment of the United States Constitution which enshrined the principle that 'no State shall make or enforce any law which shall abridge the privileges or immunities of citizens of the United States ... nor deny to any person within its jurisdiction the equal protection of the laws'. To circumvent this, 'separate but equal' mandated that access to public services and facilities could be separated along racial lines – but the quality of each group's facilities had to theoretically be 'equal'. In reality, this nominal equality was a raw deal for African-Americans. At a day-to-day level, white schools tended to receive the best facilities possible within the economic climate of the day while many African-American schools had to rely on inferior facilities, used equipment and old textbooks. The two groups were indeed separate, but hardly equal.

Many states also sought to extend the 'separate' nature of the relationship. In 1924, Virginia passed its Racial Integrity Act which required the mandatory distinction of race at birth, with divisions into just two categories: 'white' and 'non-white'. This legislation was predicated on the 'one-drop' principle: the presence of even one ancestor of non-white origin would render a person 'non-white' in the eyes of the law, and thereby forbidden to marry anyone of European heritage. Although certainly at the extreme end of the scale, the principle of forbidding sexual relations between white and black Americans was one pursued by the majority of states in the 1920s. Thirty American states forbade miscegenation, the number reduced over the 1940s and 1950s before final de facto repeal occurred in 1967. In a sense this extended the type of negative eugenic thinking – the prevention of undesired births through means that included even surgical sterilisation – that is discussed in the next chapter. These restrictions on interracial marriage would remain in place until the 1950s, when the US Supreme Court struck down Virginia's statute.

In such a climate, African-Americans understandably began to consider whether their plight would require drastic action and the attention of some turned to the opportunities offered by Brazil. This was a complex story. In 1890, Brazil had prohibited immigration of black or Asian people unless specifically authorised by Congress, a provision extended in 1921 to specifically exclude any black immigration whatsoever. This was a conscious act of public policy to move Brazil away from being perceived as a 'backward' slave state (slavery only being abolished in 1888) and towards a free, republican polity. Progress meant whiteness to many leading politicians in the major cities, and thus the wholesale encouragement of dispossessed and disillusioned black Americans was not top of their agenda. That said, Brazil was still viewed as a viable option by African-Americans for three main reasons. Firstly, because prejudice was not exactly unknown in North America either. Secondly, because the Brazilian policy of *branquismo* – whitening – of the racial make-up of the country was predicated on the races mixing (again, explicitly prohibited in most American states). And thirdly, because the Brazilian government kept its white-first policy somewhat under wraps to international audiences. Advertisements appeared in American newspapers promising cheap passage, housing and long-term loans to able-bodied American workers. And thus, by the early 1920s, Brazil looked a viable option for many (Meade and Pirio 1988: 85–8).

Cyril Briggs, a contemporary black journalist, wrote that the fact that 'the colored races are in the majority' made South America generally a good choice for exploration. Brazil in particular formed an economic 'El Dorado' where farmers could gain a fortune because agriculture had been so neglected and thus offered such a profitable market where African-Americans could draw on the skills acquired during their period of long enslavement. Brazil could thereby serve as an example for the African masses across the globe to throw off their colonial oppressors and serve liberty, not just the white man (Meade and Pirio 1988: 89). In reality, as the 1921 legislation illustrated, fears in Brazil and America of the Africanisation of the population perhaps rendered them more similar than Brazil's friendly image would have it.

Yet the notion of black empowerment, whether it involved immigration or not, was a key feature of the 1920s. As Gregory Holmes Singleton has observed, this

> found general expression in orthodox religion, esoteric sects, labour-based brotherhoods, and a host of organizations ranging from the National Association for the Advancement of Colored People (NAACP) to Marcus Garvey's Universal Negro Improvement Association.
>
> *(Singleton 1982: 29)*

Garvey had moved to the United States from Jamaica in 1916 and began advocating racial separation and the creation of an African homeland for black Americans to relocate themselves to. By 1920, two million Americans had joined his organisation. Ironically, his efforts met with some support from white racists like author Madison Grant who shared the goal of increasing separation between the races and sending the country's African-American population beyond the country's shores. In 1925, Garvey was convicted of mail fraud and imprisoned, leading to a power struggle in the Universal Negro Improvement Association. He was released in 1927 but deported back to Jamaica and spent the remainder of his life travelling the world and preaching the gospel of pan-Africanism (Spiro 2008: 258–63).

The NAACP was far more moderate in its goals and tactics. Founded by W.E.B. du Bois in 1909, the NAACP had backed African-American soldiers serving the allied cause in the First World War, but would go on to demand greater equality of rights and opportunity as a result. In a sense this replicated trends seen in non-white colonies of the British and French empires. In his book *The Crisis*, du Bois argued that

> this country of ours, for all its better souls have done and dreamed, is yet a shameful land ... It has never really tried to educate the Negro. A dominant minority does not want Negroes educated. It wants servants.
>
> *(cited in Foner, 2005: 699)*

Education and skills thus formed one of five key tranches of activity for the NAACP. The other four were increasing employment, ensuring due and equal process under the law, raising voter turnout and tackling the problem of lynching.

The latter owed much to the resurrection of the Ku Klux Klan. The Klan, driven underground in the Reconstruction era, re-emerged in the 1920s – partly inspired by *Birth of a Nation*. As many as five million Americans are estimated to have been members in the 1920s, and the Klan dominated many areas of local politics. Through a so-called 'decade strategy' each member of the Klan was responsible for recruiting ten voters for Klan-backed candidates in local elections. Through this strategy, mayoralties were won in areas outside the south, including both Portlands, in Maine and Oregon. Colorado and Indiana effectively experienced a Klan takeover of the entirety of state government. It was rumoured that President Warren G. Harding had been inducted into the Klan inside the White House itself. More than 1,000 people were assaulted by Klan members in Texas and Oklahoma alone over the course of the 1920s, and between 1918 and 1927 more than 450 people were lynched in the South, usually following an allegation of sexual assault (or attempted assault) against a white woman. In the 1920s, the Klan symbol of the burning cross joined the white hats and robes as emblematic of the fear the Klan was spreading across a wide swatch of the country. Attempts to curtail the Klan's power were almost universally defeated, and an anti-lynching law in 1919 was blocked in the US Senate when southern senators filibustered it. The Klan's power would remain largely unchecked until after the Second World War (Cashman 1998: 213–15).

Beyond America and the Klan, it was clear that ethnicity and race were becoming increasingly significant in the post-Versailles political discourse. The 1920s indeed started with a form of ethnic cleansing that had begun when the First World War was still in full swing. The Armenian, Assyrian and Greek genocides perpetrated by Ottoman forces may have been initiated with the extermination of intellectuals in Constantinople in 1915 and escalated into widespread bloodshed soon after, but they also continued in sporadic form up to 1925. All told, one and a half million Armenians, 300,000 Assyrians and up to 900,000 Greek Christians may have been killed in a systemic programme of extermination that was condemned as a crime against humanity. In Ireland, the use of so-called 'Black and Tan' paramilitary troops by the British across 1919–21 was neither so obviously racialised nor was the scale anywhere near that of the Turks, but perceptions that the Irish were of sub-English intelligence and had proved cowards in the trenches of the First World War were not uncommon. In part the use of such paramilitaries represented both a desire to protect Irish Protestants loyal to the union, but also reflected the fear of what the Black and Tan troops – often unemployed ex-servicemen – might do on the British mainland. Better to export the problem, in other words.

Just as the Black and Tans pitted Protestant against Catholic, it is clear that religion still played a significant role in the psyches of many in the 1920s, though this was also declining in some nations. In the United States, around 6 per cent of the population were Methodist at the beginning of the decade and 3 per cent Southern Baptist. The 1920s saw the start of a still unreserved trend of the former falling sharply and the latter rising incrementally (to eventually overtake Methodism by the 1960s). From a sharp increase pre-war as a result of Italian and Irish immigration to the United States, Catholicism more or less stagnated at around 16 per cent of the US population in the 1920s, before rising in the post-1945 period largely due to increased levels of Hispanic immigration. Overall, around four in ten Americans were members of religious organisations in the 1920s, though levels of actual belief are harder to quantify.

Regardless of the actual number of practising adherents, religions took on an increasingly public role in some parts of the country, particularly the South. More than 61 per cent of southerners identified themselves as church members in 1926, in contrast with 54 per cent of the overall country. Many were fundamentalist Christians who believed in the literal word of the Bible, leading to an inevitable culture clash with the rest of the country and the modern world itself. In 1925, Tennessee science teacher John Scopes was arrested and put on trial for teaching the theory of evolution, which had been banned by the state's Butler Act in an effort to protect schoolchildren from 'atheist' science that contradicted the Book of Genesis. The ensuing legal proceeding, which became known as the Scopes Monkey Trial, became a national spectacle. Scopes was convicted of violating the Butler Act but the state supreme court, undoubtedly worried about the reputation the state was gaining as the result of the case, reduced Scopes' sentence to a fine. The Butler Act itself remained in effect until 1967 (Cashman 1998: 218–19). The conflict between modernity and religious tradition would not end in the 1920s but gain new prominence as the result of the media coverage given the Scopes Monkey Trial. Indeed, the teaching of evolution remains controversial in many southern states to the present day.

Fundamentally, however, the Butler Act was the result of evangelical Christianity's increasingly wide appeal in the United States. Historically Christian countries with different traditions would naturally see different incarnations of the emerging conflict between modernity and tradition. In the UK, the number of 15-year-olds confirmed in the Church of England reached a then-peak of just over three in ten by 1930, the majority of whom were girls (as has proved the case largely since), and seven in ten Anglican children were baptised by 1930, all told. Religious worship gave people an identity, but it was often shifting into other forms: the Labour Party for Catholics, the Conservative Party for Anglicans, the British Legion for both. Then, as now, the most obvious forms of inter-religious conflict stemmed from the football field. As Andrew Davies notes,

> the Old Firm rivalry served to inflame sectarian hostilities in Glasgow throughout the inter-war decades. Matches between [the two big local clubs] Rangers and Celtic mobilised tens of thousands of football supporters into bitterly opposed camps, with expressions of national and religious allegiance inseparable from exchanges of sectarian abuse and violence. Like the annual 'Orange walks', held to commemorate the victory of William of Orange at the battle of the Boyne in 1690, [in the 1920s] Old Firm matches brought ethnic divisions to the forefront of civic life and turned religious affiliations into the source of intense antagonism.
> *(Davies 2006: 201)*

If, as chapter 4 illustrates, the Mitropa Cup could use football as a trans-European means of dialogue, so too could domestic rivalries stir up passions.

Beyond Europe and North America, the increasing Westernisation of 1920s global society – which often went hand in hand with secularisation – was not welcomed by all. In 1928 in the city of Ismailia, Egypt, Hassan al-Banna founded the Muslim Brotherhood. He did so alongside six fellow workers of that most overt instance of Western imperialism, the British-owned Suez Canal Company. In fact, partly to try and placate such concerns, the company actually assisted with the construction of a new mosque for Ismailia, which would serve as the Brotherhood's new headquarters. Al-Banna's critique was that contemporary 1920s Islam had been corrupted by the West, and the necessary remedy was the implementation of Sharia law over all parts of society – including those within the reach of government and beyond. This was in large part to act as a counterpoint to the reforms of Kemalism discussed elsewhere in this volume. As modern Turkey adopted a range of acts to modernise its politics, society and economy – including civil equality for women, secularisation, and expanded state support for the sciences – the Brotherhood set out to define a new, or rather old, form of life as constituting a truer form of Islam. Such debates are clearly not just the preserve of history.

Health

Whatever one's religion, however, the likelihood was that one would get more years to practise it during the 1920s. Life expectancies increased dramatically across the globe during the decade, albeit with regional variation. In Brazil and China, the average life expectancy remained stagnant at a very young 32. In Uganda it even dipped, from 25 in 1922 to 24 five years later. The normality of death at a young age – when one considers the mourning attached to the young dead of the First World War in the West, killed in such *exceptional* circumstance – marked a real global divergence of fortune. Nevertheless, for the most part there was improvement in both the West and the areas subjugated by the West. In the British Empire territories of Canada (1921 – 57 years, 1930 – 59 years), India (1921 – 25 years, 1931 – 31 years) and Jamaica (1920 – 35 years, 1931 – 43 years) there were increases in life expectancy. In social democratic Northern Europe, citizens were, by 1930, expecting to live beyond 60 in Iceland, Norway and Sweden. But this did not take place in just the democracies: Italian fascism saw life expectancy increase from 50 in 1922 to 55 by 1931. Soviet communism, from a less-developed economic state, delivered an improvement from 25 to 36 during the same period (Gapminder n.d.: passim).

The causes of death also tell us much. The rise of the motor vehicle brought the dramatically increased possibility of road-related death – rising from 10.3 deaths per 100,000 Americans in 1920 to 26.7 by 1930 (US Commerce Department official Julius Klein dryly noted in 1928 that there were so many cars in the country that pedestrians were nearing 'complete extinction', notably ignoring the actual danger that the increase in vehicles had created) (Klein n.d., 'America Motorizing Mankind', 3). By contrast, the increased use of vaccination halved the numbers killed through influenza (207.3 to 102.5 per 100,000) and made a significant dent in the numbers dying through tuberculosis (113.1 to 71.1 per 100,000). Cancer death rates continued to rise (83.4 to 97.4 per 100,000), which would not be curbed until the 1990s. Similarly, deaths from cardiovascular disease increased from 364.9 to

414.4 per 100,000, a trend that did not begin to be reversed until the 1960s. The latter two of these causes of death to some degree represented the increased longevity discussed above.

In the 1920s general health in the West could be helped by more active life-styles. Unlike in the United States, with its huge ratio of cars to people, almost one in three British people walked to (their often labour-intensive) work in the 1920s, and a further one in six rode a bicycle on such journeys (Pooley *et al.* 2005: passim). For the over four in ten Britons travelling to work by public transport, things were a little less healthy, however. In the 1920s, on the back of increased demand, the London Underground introduced additional coaches to cope with the desire most commuters had to smoke. For a London famous for its fog, the most smoky atmosphere could often be found several metres below street level, therefore.

We deal with scientific and technological changes elsewhere, but it should be noted that significant medical breakthroughs were made which aided general longevity. In 1920 the Toronto doctor Frederick Banting successfully tested insulin on diabetic dogs and the first human trial was (successfully) conducted in 1922. Several people close to death (diabetes was a slow but certain killer prior to this point) were saved as this drug came on stream. Likewise, the Dutch scientist William Einthoven created the electrocardiogram in the mid-1920s which allowed a far greater understanding of the degenerations of the human heart – and won him the Nobel Prize in the process. And lastly, although its effects would not be felt until the following decade, in 1928 – somewhat accidently – the Scottish researcher Alexander Fleming discovered Penicillin. This has been used against many types of infection in the decades that have followed. These three discoveries in different parts of the developed world illustrate both the global nature of the 1920s, and their continual impact since.

Conclusion

The 1920s were more complicated than the popular image of the 'Jazz Age' have suggested. While the American economy boomed despite initial hiccups after the First World War's end, its international rivals saw more modest growth for the most part. Regardless, the image of wealthy aristocrats and the *nouveau riche* overindulging in sex and booze (in the American case, the latter despite being illegal under Prohibition) was not completely inaccurate. Low tax rates under Republican administrations throughout the decade were partially to thank for the expansion of wealth that the rich enjoyed in the United States, while in Europe the share of wealth owned by the richest members of society actually fell over the course of the decade, with the exception of France. At the same time, the average income of the lower 90 per cent of society generally rose over the decade as well. The rising tide does seem to have lifted most boats, at least initially.

While the 1920s were a period of increasing prosperity for most people, race relations remained troubling. The United States was still dealing with the aftermath of the Civil War and Reconstruction and struggling to extend rights to African-Americans in the face of Southern intransigence. The Ku Klux Klan's revival decades after the end of Reconstruction reflects the predominance that these questions still held in many people's minds. Elsewhere, the ethnic cleansing of Armenians, Greeks and other groups in the aftermath of the Treaty of Versailles provided a horrifying preview of extermination campaigns against other minority groups later in the twentieth century. The breakup of Europe's nineteenth-century empires had opened the door to campaigns of mass slaughter that would result in the deaths of millions.

Amidst these dramatic changes, religion provided many with a way to make sense of the world's changing facets. The 1920s witnessed the beginning of the decline in religious membership in Europe that has continued to the present day. On the other hand, fundamentalist Christians in the United States launched a concerted campaign to outlaw the teaching of modernist ideas, including evolution, that they saw as an affront to their religious convictions. In Ireland, Catholics and Protestants continued their campaigns of violence against one another, the latter group aided by the British government's brutal Black and Tans. In the Middle East, the Muslim Brotherhood represented an early effort to mobilise Islam against the imperial powers that had divided the former Ottoman Empire amongst themselves. While both the Ottomans and European powers had attempted to mobilise Islam for their own purposes during the war, after its end it became increasingly clear that Islam could most effectively be mobilised as a key facet of a 'war of liberation' against non-Muslim powers (the British, for instance, now held a Mandate for Palestine and the sacred city of Jerusalem, ironically achieving the goal of medieval Crusaders who had sought that very goal nearly a millennium before). The abolition of the Caliphate by Kemal Atatürk's secular government in Turkey helped open the door to new interpretations of Islam that would take on a variety of political and social implications as the twentieth century continued.

As the 1920s drew to a close, the lives of most people had improved to at least some degree. The economic collapse of 1929 would reverse much, but not all, of this social and economic progress. More widely, however, the issues that began to emerge over the role of class, race and religion would persist far beyond their end. In many senses, the questions in these areas that the world continues to face in the early twenty-first century have their direct origins in the discussions of the 1920s.

Questions

- How did the perception of social class change in Western countries in the 1920s? How 'equal' was the decade?
- How accurate was F. Scott Fitzgerald's portrayal of 1920s America in *The Great Gatsby*? Would it have been an accurate representation of 1920s Britain or Brazil, for instance?
- How did race relations and perceptions of race change over the course of the 1920s?

- How did the lives of average citizens around the world change in the 1920s? How did the lives of the rich generally differ from those of the poor?
- Why did the 1920s see such a divergence in average life expectancy between countries? What factors impacted these numbers?

Recommended further reading

Douglas, C.H. (1920), *Economic Democracy*, London: Cecil Palmer.
Frieden, J.A. (2006), *Global Capitalism: Its Fall and Rise in the Twentieth Century*, New York: W.W. Norton.
Tawney, R.H. (1920), *The Acquisitive Society*, New York: Harcourt.

Works cited

Alvaredo, F., Atkinson, T., Piketty, T. and Saez, E. (n.d.), The World Top Incomes Database via http://topincomes.g-mond.parisschoolofeconomics.eu/
Banks, R. (1929), *The Conservative Outlook*, London: Chapman and Hall.
Cashman, S. (1998), *America Ascendant: From Theodore Roosevelt to FDR in the Century of American Power, 1901–1945*, New York: New York University Press.
Davies, A. (2006), 'Football and Sectarianism in Glasgow during the 1920s and 1930s', *Irish Historical Studies*, 35, 200–219.
Douglas, C.H. (1920), *Economic Democracy*, London: Cecil Palmer.
Foner, E. (2005), *Give Me Liberty! An American History*, New York: W.W. Norton.
Frieden, J.A. (2006), *Global Capitalism: Its Fall and Rise in the Twentieth Century*, New York: W.W. Norton.
Gapminder (n.d.), 'List of Indicators', www.gapminder.org/data/
Klein (n.d.) Box 1, Julius Klein Papers, Hoover Institution Library, Stanford University.
MacDonald, M. (n.d.), Constant Surprise: A Twentieth Century Life, within the Royal Commonwealth Society Archive, RCMS 41/1, Cambridge University Library, Cambridge, UK.
Meade, T. and Pirio, G.A. (1988), 'In Search of the Afro-American "Eldorado". Attempts by North American Blacks to Enter Brazil in the 1920s', *Luso-Brazilian Review*, 25/1, 85–110
Nightingale, R.T. (1930), *The Personnel of the British Foreign Office and Diplomatic Service, 1851–1929*, London: Fabian Society.
Pendergrast, M. (2010), *Uncommon Grounds: The History of Coffee and How It Transformed the World* (second edition), New York: Basic Books.
Piketty, T. (2014), *Capital in the Twenty-First Century*, Cambridge, MA: Harvard University Press.
Pooley, C.G., Turnbull, J. and Adams, M. (2005), *A Mobile Century? Changes in Everyday Mobility in Britain in the Twentieth Century*, Aldershot: Ashgate.
Shaw, G.B. (1930), *Socialism: Principles and Outlook and Fabianism*, London: Fabian Society.
Singleton, G.H. (1982), 'Birth, Rebirth, and the "New Negro" of the 1920s', *Phylon*, 43, 29–45.
Spiro, J.P. (2008), *Defending the Master Race: Conservation, Eugenics, and the Legacy of Madison Grant*, Burlington: University of Vermont Press.
Tawney, R.H. (1920), *The Acquisitive Society*, New York: Harcourt.
UNESCO (2006), *Literacy for Life: Education for All*, Paris: UNESCO Publishing.
World Economics (n.d.), 'Historical GDP data' via www.worldeconomics.com/Data/Madis onHistoricalGDP/Madison%20Historical%20GDP%20Data.efp

3

SCIENCE AND TECHNOLOGY
IN THE JAZZ AGE

In March 1925 Calvin Coolidge became the first American President to have his inaugural address broadcast nationwide using the new medium of radio. In it, he promised to cut taxes, and, keeping with the isolationist sentiments of his Republican Party, he told the American people that, 'we have never any wish to interfere in the political conditions of any other countries. Especially are we determined not to become implicated in the political controversies of the Old World'. The United States, he concluded:

> seeks no earthly empire built on blood and force. No ambition, no temptation, lures her to thought of foreign dominions. The legions which she sends forth are armed, not with the sword, but with the cross. The higher state to which she seeks the allegiance of all mankind is not of human, but of divine origin. She cherishes no purpose save to merit the favor of Almighty God.
>
> *(Miller Centre n.d.: passim)*

While the presidential election of 1920 had been covered on radio stations across the country, as had the party's nominating conventions, this was the first time millions of Americans had the chance to hear their President's inaugural address as it took place. It was estimated that 25 million Americans from coast to coast had the ability to listen to the broadcast if they chose to do so. Coolidge soon began to appear regularly in radio broadcasts, beginning a presidential tradition that continues to the present day (Ponder 1998: 123).

Just over two years later, newspapers and radio broadcasts around the world were filled with another feat of both technological and human daring. On 21 May 1927, a 25-year-old American pilot named Charles Lindbergh landed his plane, the *Spirit of St. Louis*, at an airfield outside of Paris, where he was greeted by the American ambassador and a jubilant crowd of more than 150,000 people. Lindbergh had become the first person to fly solo across the Atlantic Ocean from New York City, a perilous journey of more than 3,000 miles, propelling him to the status of one of the world's most famous people literally overnight. As the news spread across the United States, celebrations spontaneously broke out across the country. At least one man in Washington State dropped dead from the excitement of the moment as he reached for an issue of the newspaper carrying the story (Berg 1998: 112–31, 136–7). Lindbergh was feted across Paris, honoured in London, and then returned to the United States, where President Coolidge immediately awarded him the Distinguished Flying Cross. By the time he arrived in New York City for a victory parade, it was estimated that more than 7.4 million feet of newsreel had been shot of the young aviator and that he had become the most photographed man in the world (the previous record for newsreel had been held by the young and handsome Prince of Wales, later to become the ill-fated King Edward VIII) (Berg 1998: 157–8).

These moments in the late 1920s were two of the most iconic of the decade. Indeed, the radio and the airplane in many ways epitomised the progress of the decade in a wide variety of ways. While Coolidge was the first American President to fully utilise the power of radio to communicate with the public, Lindbergh was the first celebrity to cross between visual media (photographs and newsreels) and the informational potential of radio worldwide. Newsreels of Lindbergh's landing in Paris took weeks to reach the United States by ship but radio broadcasts were immediately available, as were wire stories filed by the European correspondents of newspapers around the world. As David E. Kyvig has observed,

> Americans had known national figures before – political leaders, military heroes, even athletes – but with Lindbergh national radio networks began to demonstrate their ability to turn persons of accomplishment into celebrities … Hundreds of thousands of people who would never come close to Lindbergh could feel that they knew him as well as they knew a neighbor.
>
> *(Kyvig 2004: 83–4)*

Radio was therefore an important, though clearly not the solitary, reason why Lindbergh rapidly became one of America – and the world's – most admired and beloved heroes.

The world seemed to become smaller for many people in the 1920s, thanks largely to these important improvements to transportation and communication. Yet there was a perceived dark side to these innovations as well. By 1932, long-standing worries about the military applications of aviation technology prompted British Prime Minister Stanley Baldwin to ominously warn that in a future war 'the bomber will always get through' and imperil civilian populations. Radio, too, was seen to have dangers. Fearing the content that radio station owners might broadcast, in 1927 the US government created the Federal Radio Commission (FRC) to regulate both the operating frequencies and content of radio stations. Stations were obligated to serve a vaguely defined 'public interest' and were banned from broadcasting obscene or widely objectionable content. The conflict between the FRC (and later the

Federal Communications Commission that replaced it) definition of these terms and the First Amendment rights of station owners and radio commentators extends to the present day as courts still deal with challenges to the constitutionality of penalising stations because of the words used on their airwaves (Boyer 2002: 336).

These were not the only dangers perceived by commentators in the 1920s, however. With modern science providing the most sophisticated account to date of not only the laws of physics that underpinned radio and flight but also human biology, a new set of fears began to emerge in the medical community. These surrounded the idea that the modern world's advanced medicine, relatively salubrious living conditions and welfare programmes had created a situation in which human beings were actually declining biologically, at least in the West. In Europe and the United States, these concerns were frequently expressed in racial terms and focused on whether the industrialised world could continue to compete in the face of competition from other groups. As the conservative British churchman William Ralph Inge put the question in 1926:

> Will supremacy ultimately fall to those nations which, like the Anglo-Saxons above all others, have established a high standard of living, with varied and abundant food, comparatively short hours of work, many amusements and comforts of every kind, or to the cheaper races, who are accustomed to a simpler manner of life, and make fewer demands upon their environment? ... All talk of disarmament seems to be futile so long as peaceful penetration [of the West by non-whites] would mean the submergence of the whites.
>
> *(Inge 1926: 278–9)*

These types of worries about degeneration at home coupled with 'submergence' by non-white races were articulated by a wide range of biologists, anthropologists and public affairs commentators. On the more academic end of the spectrum was the eugenics movement, an international movement of individuals who sought to stem the 'degeneracy' they perceived in the modern world (Inge himself was a long-time member of the British eugenics movement). In practice, the eugenicists achieved a range of policy victories ranging from immigration restriction in the United States to compulsory sexual sterilisation programmes for the 'unfit' in many US states and in a range of European countries. By the end of the 1920s, eugenics seemed to offer a scientific and technological solution to many of the world's problems that were being increasingly linked to biology in both policy and scientific circles. Science and technology were thus Janus-faced in the 1920s. The world was rapidly becoming 'smaller', but at the same time there were increasing fears about the consequences that might follow.

Travelling by air

The airplane was not a new technology in the 1920s: early models had, after all, been used for both reconnaissance purposes and in combat during the First World

War. The usefulness of aircraft for both combat and civilian purposes was thus well established by the beginning of the decade. The main question of the 1920s was therefore not whether aircraft would play a major role in the world, but how far they would go in doing so. Science fiction fantasies had already envisioned a world where flying was widespread: H.G. Wells' 1908 novel *The War in the Air* provided a prescient account of secret races between world powers to develop new aerial weapons, with the result being a war that would end with the collapse of the world economy and no discernible victors. Wells' earlier novel *The War of the Worlds* had gone even further, and described the possibility of flight through space and between planets. Flight was well established in the popular imagination and its advances were thus eagerly anticipated as the 1920s began.

Yet the question of practicality remained. How far and high could planes actually fly? How fast could they safely be flown? How much cargo, either civilian or military, could they be expected to carry in the future? There were no clear answers to these questions as the decade began, but there were many who were eager to find them. In 1909, French aviator Louis Blériot had flown non-stop across the English Channel in just over 30 minutes, claiming a monetary prize and worldwide fame in the process. In the aftermath of the First World War, British newspaper magnate Lord Northcliffe, owner of *The Times* and *The Daily Mail*, sponsored a series of races and prizes to push aviation to its limits. His publishing rival, Lord Beaverbrook, offered similar prizes for feats of aeronautical daring, including a prize for the first flight from Britain to India (*Aerial Age Weekly*, vol. 11, no. 9, p. 1; Berg 1998: 90).

All of these, however, paled in comparison to the feat of crossing the Atlantic Ocean non-stop. In 1919, wealthy hotelier Raymond Orteig offered a hefty $25,000 prize (about $300,000 in 2015) for the first aviator from an allied country to accomplish the feat by plane (Zeppelins, discussed shortly, were therefore excluded from the competition). In 1924, the conditions were revised to allow aviators from any country to claim it. That same year, Lowell H. Smith and five fellow US Army officers managed to circumnavigate the entire globe using planes. The limits of flight were rapidly being expanded (Berg 1998: 84, 91).

By Christmas 1926, Charles Lindbergh's plans for a transatlantic flight attempt were taking shape. Lindbergh was an airmail pilot with a penchant for daring aerial feats who had joined the Missouri National Guard to gain access to the most advanced aircraft and flying techniques of the day. His plane, the *Spirit of St. Louis*, was classed as an experimental aircraft and was almost entirely custom built for the Atlantic crossing attempt (Berg 1998: 99–104). Around 7:30 a.m. on 20 May Lindbergh took off from Roosevelt Field outside New York City with the plane's fuel tanks so heavy that he removed navigational equipment from the cockpit and tore the edges from his maps to reduce the plane's take-off weight. Twenty hours later, with his body beginning to flag from exhaustion, Lindbergh took the plane perilously close to the ocean to allow the spray to enter the cockpit and keep him awake. Thirty-three hours after take-off in New York, Lindbergh touched down in Paris, becoming the first person in history to set foot in Europe only one day after leaving North America (Berg 1998: 124–6).

A jubilant crowd welcomed 'Lucky Lindy', and he immediately became the most photographed – and almost certainly the most famous – man in the world. Among the honours he received was *The Daily Mail's* aviation cup, established by Northcliffe. Returning to St Louis in mid-June, he found that more than two million pieces of fan mail and telegrams had been sent to him (Fitzhugh Green, in Lindbergh's 1927 *We*: 316). Lindbergh spent the rest of the decade touring the country, trying in vain to avoid constant press attention and serving as a consultant and public relations figure for a company called Transcontinental Air Transport, soon nicknamed the 'Lindbergh Line', that planned to offer international flights from the United States to far-flung destinations. By 1930, a range of companies including American Airlines had established regular cross-country and international flights. The era of passenger air travel had begun in earnest (Berg 1998: 189, 207).

While airplanes would become the truly iconic mode of transportation for the 1920s, much as trains had been in the nineteenth century, they were in fact not the first – or the most luxurious – way to travel by air in that period. In 1863, Count Ferdinand von Zeppelin had travelled to the United States to observe Union military manoeuvres during the Civil War. While there, Zeppelin observed the army's use of balloons for reconnaissance purposes and began to hypothesise about the possibility of using larger balloons for travel over long distances. By 1900, Zeppelin had developed prototype airships that could carry their own propulsion engines along with a sizable cargo. In essence, Zeppelin's airships would be huge airframes carrying bags filled with lighter-than-air gas such as hydrogen or helium. With sufficient amounts of gas in the bags, the airships would rise and be able to carry engines and cargo loads that could include either passengers or military

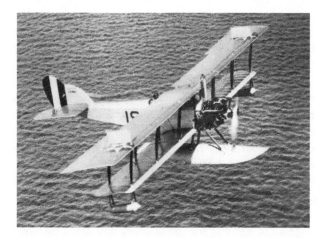

FIGURE 3.1 Air travel became increasingly popular after Charles Lindbergh's successful flight across the Atlantic, and aircraft technology began to advance rapidly toward the end of the decade, making the Curtiss N-9 seaplane, seen here, rapidly obsolete.

armaments. Through gradual improvements, by the 1920s Zeppelins were able to manage respectable speeds of around 80 mph in flight.

At the same time as Zeppelin was beginning to produce his airships, the French were also making advances with dirigibles along similar lines and in a period of rising tension between the two countries, both invested heavily in the aircraft. In 1908, one of Zeppelin's prototypes made a flight over the Swiss Alps, sparking the public imagination across Europe (de Syon 2007: 15, 36–7). Zeppelins soon became a source of Imperial German pride, and the British public began to fear that Zeppelins might become the vehicle to launch an invasion of the British Isles in the event of a war. Indeed, when war did come in 1914 the Zeppelin would play a role. The Germans managed to launch 57 Zeppelin raids against Britain, inflicting nearly 2,000 casualties and producing a backlash in the British press that was seen not only during the war but the subsequent General Election campaign. In November 1918 the electorate of Hull in the English north – heavily hit by the raids during the war – was greeted with local newspaper headlines such as 'What Hull Will Never Forget: The Murderous Work of the Zeppelins' and 'The Zeppelins' Foul Work: Striking Record of German Infamy' (Carr 2013: 58). Given the limitations of British planes at the time, little damage could actually be inflicted on the huge airships. The British public – stoked up by the vitriolic press – was outraged, and in 1920 the victorious allies demanded the dismantlement of the entire German airship fleet. German Zeppelin commanders had already destroyed most of the air fleet in 1919 to avoid handing their airships over to the Allies, further enraging the British (de Syon 2007: 72, 97).

By the 1920s, therefore, the Zeppelin's potential for both military and civilian purposes was well established. In 1922, the US Navy commissioned a cutting-edge new Zeppelin as a reparations payment, demonstrating that there was still strong military interest in the airships. In 1926, the allies agreed to lift the ban on German airship construction, in part because the Germans successfully argued that Zeppelins could be used for scientific purposes, including Arctic exploration (de Syon 2007: 126). In 1928, the *Graf Zeppelin*, a 236-metre dirigible with a luxurious passenger cabin replete with private rooms, was launched and flew across the Atlantic to the United States later in the year. The following year, the *Graf Zeppelin* flew around the world in just 12 days with heavy press coverage of the journey, making the airship an iconic source of German pride in the face of its post-war humiliation (the Zeppelin's appearance in the skies of Egypt led to a famous photo showing it flying over the Pyramids, combining the technological wonders of the ancient world with the modern in a single remarkable image) (de Syon 2007: 136–42). While the airplane and Charles Lindbergh epitomised American ingenuity and courage, the Zeppelin, both impressive and menacing at the same time, was Germany's answer.

All this being said, travel by air was still an impractical dream for most people in the 1920s. Despite the successes of the *Graf Zeppelin*, dirigibles were expensive to build, difficult to operate and fairly unsafe by even the standards of time. In 1925, the American-owned dirigible *Shenandoah* crashed in Ohio, killing its captain and other officers. The ensuing press frenzy did much to harm the reputation of airships in the

FIGURE 3.2 The *Graf Zeppelin* became a visible reminder of German industrial ingenuity and economic power in the late 1920s.

United States. Similarly, in 1928, the dirigible *Italia* crashed in the Arctic during a scientific mission, killing more than half a dozen crew and scientists on board. While impressive, Zeppelins and associated airships had clear flaws that would render them more or less obsolete by the mid-1930s (Duggan and Meyer 2001: 113, 135–6).

Following Charles Lindbergh's ground-breaking 1927 flight across the Atlantic, airplanes increasingly became the promising new technology in the American imagination. Airmail services expanded, as did passenger air services around the globe. However, given that planes lacked modern navigation and communication equipment, air travel remained treacherous, particularly in poor weather, and expensive. From a military perspective, most countries attempted to build up their air forces throughout the 1920s, with the British becoming the world's biggest exporter of aircraft engines and airframes. However, there were fewer than two dozen total models of plane being produced, and these were nowhere near enough to provide the diversity of air fleet that would ultimately be required in the next war (Edgerton 2005: 47). While both the Zeppelin and the airplane were symbols of the 1920s in their own rights, it would only be in later decades that both military and commercial flight would become widely available.

Radio

The exploits of Charles Lindbergh had been transmitted rapidly around the world thanks in part to a technology that was nearly the same age as flight itself. This was, of course, radio – the wireless transmission of audio using an antenna and receiver set. Early experiments with radio had been taking place since the nineteenth century and the transmission of wireless Morse code was in widespread use before the First World War, particularly by ships at sea (the ill-fated liner *RMS Titanic* had been able to wirelessly signal its distress calls in 1912, to the extent that they were received as far away as New York City).

Radio itself had been a truly international invention. In São Paolo, Brazil, the first wireless transmission of the human voice had taken place in 1900. Twelve years later the Italian Guglielmo Marconi had established his radio factory in Chelmsford, England, and on 31 August 1920 the first radio news programme was broadcast from Detroit, Michigan. The physical production of radios was an international endeavour, as Julius Klein, Director of the US Bureau of Foreign and Domestic Commerce, noted in a 1928 broadcast. Due to the wide array of components radio sets required, the 'truly magical scientific triumph' of producing radios was made possible only by 'a vast array of the innumerable circumstances and forces and movements that go to make up Foreign Trade' (Klein n.d., 'A Week of the World's Business': 2–3). Radio was intrinsically an international endeavour.

The 1920s thus saw the vast spread of the radio throughout the globe. This new technology did not advance without some panic, however. The *Argus* in Western Australia reported Marconi's comments on the psychosis surrounding this matter in 1922:

> Public fancy, he said, had taken pleasure in enlarging upon what had been called the wireless horrors that we might expect in the next war, if there was a next war. He believed, however, that if such developments did come about the means of combatting and counteracting them would quickly be found. One special form of delusion which seemed to be widely spread was that in some way certain persons were being used against their will as receivers for wireless waves, and that such waves injured them mentally and physically.
>
> (Western Argus, *24 January 1922*)

Such fears were eventually overcome, though the capacity for propagandistic damage by the wireless would become clear in the 1930s.

Still, this was not a victimless advance. In December 1924 *The Times* solemnly reported that

> in a written reply to Lieutenant-Commander Kenworthy [MP] who asked the Postmaster-General whether he would take steps to compel people with wireless sets to have corks attached to outdoor aerials, in view of the damage done to homing pigeons who come into contact with those aerials, Sir William Mitchell-Thomson states: 'as at present advised, I do not think it would be practicable'.
>
> (The Times, *20 December 1924*)

Similarly, the car radio was not invented without some difficulty: 'in the first attempts to receive broadcasting on running motor-cars the [Daimler-Marconi] experimenters found reception hopelessly distorted by the sparks from their own magneto and from those of passing cars'. Overcoming this matter was labelled by *The Times* as 'an engineering triumph of no small importance' (*The Times*, 10 August 1923).

By the mid-1920s, Anglophone radio listeners were plentiful. In 1925 there were an estimated 1.2 million wireless sets in Britain, and perhaps 20 million in the United States. Likewise in Belgium, France, Germany, Ireland and Spain 'telephony ha[d] met with considerable success' (*The Times*, 11 July 1925). And yet, in non-democratic Europe, there were still severe limits. *The Times* noted that

> it is not perhaps generally known that in Bulgaria the importation, sale or use of a wireless receiving instrument is prohibited by the Government. Wireless telephony has apparently created little or no interest in Greece, where broadcasting is not allowed. Broadcasting is also prohibited in Rumania, while in Yugoslavia the use of wireless receiving sets is only permitted to members of the Diplomatic Corps and to Consular Agents.
>
> *(The Times, 11 July 1925)*

Beyond Europe *The Times* saw

> no prospect of listening attaining popularity in the homes of ordinary folk [in India] such as it has won in this country. The great mass of the people gain a scanty livelihood from the cultivation of the soil, and have few interests outside their village life and the constant problem of making two ends meet.
>
> *(The Times, 21 July 1925)*

As late as 1937 there were only 50,000 radio sets for an Indian population of some 350 million.

It was in the United States, however, that radio most rapidly grew into a mature commercial industry. This was in sharp contrast to Britain, where the government established a monopoly on radio transmission by forming the British Broadcasting Corporation (BBC) in 1927 to replace the earlier and less well-established British Broadcasting Company. From 1927 onward, the BBC enjoyed a complete monopoly on the country's airwaves, and as a public corporation it was answerable to Parliament and, ultimately, the public. The British radio industry would thus begin its life as a non-commercial enterprise, funded by de facto indirect taxation, and not expected to make profits (and in fact forbidden from seeking to do so) (Coase 1950: 49–65). The Corporation's first Director-General was Sir John Reith (later First Baron Reith), who built the BBC into a broadcasting powerhouse by the late 1920s. Unlike commercial radio elsewhere, the BBC would be funded by a wireless licence that was a compulsory annual purchase for every radio set owner. In 1923 there were around half a million payers of the 10 shilling (half a pound) annual fee, with probably around 200,000 houses listening illegally for free. To give an indication as to some of the content, in the week of 28 October 1929 – when events spiralled out of control on the New York stock market – regional listeners in London were greeted with programmes on biscuit recipes, 'the forest peoples of Equatorial Guinea', and 'Hockey: tactics in attack and defence' (BBC Genome n.d.).

The business of America in the 1920s was business, however, not the provision of high-quality programming for a small annual fee. Unlike Britain, American radio broadcasting would therefore remain the preserve of corporations. In 1919, the US government intervened to prevent the sale of American radio stations to the British-based Marconi Company out of fears that foreign-controlled radio monopolies might have undesirable effects on the American people. As a result, General Electric negotiated a deal to purchase Marconi's extensive radio holdings in the United States and acquired a majority share in the Radio Corporation of America (RCA) that was subsequently formed. Its main rival would be formed by the American Telephone & Telegraph Company (AT&T), which controlled the phone lines across the country that would be essential for transmitting audio over long distances for broadcasting.

By 1921, more than 500 radio stations were operating around the country and in 1924 a nationwide network of stations was temporarily created to cover the presidential election that year. In 1927, AT&T and its partners formally created a network of stations that it called the National Broadcasting Company (NBC) while RCA created the Columbia Broadcasting System (CBS) as its rival. The creation of the radio networks – essentially, large numbers of stations that were linked together and carried the same programming for much of the day – allowed for higher quality programmes to be developed and distributed across a wide section of the country, hence generating huge advertising profits. By the end of the 1920s, both NBC and CBS were filling their airwaves with dramas, comedies, and musical programmes, with their networks soon spanning from the East to West coast of the country. Many of these were performed and broadcast live (Benjamin 2009: 5–7). By 1930, it was estimated that more than 40 per cent of American families owned a radio set, and in urban areas the number was estimated to be above 50 per cent. Profits for the networks and the station owners soared (Fortner 2006: 75–7).

As elsewhere, however, the American radio industry's rapid success raised important questions. Social commentators worried, not without justification, that the commercial focus of American radio would lead to dominance of lowbrow programming aimed at generating profits rather than bettering the audience. NBC justified its own focus on entertainment rather than educational programming by observing that educational radio stations generally failed and ceased broadcasting within only a few years, demonstrating that commercial viability was the key to success (Fortner 2006: 81). From the government's perspective, however, the push for constant profit would not necessarily generate desirable outcomes. In addition, radio's powerful reach might make politically or morally undesirable programming available to a wide audience.

In 1927, the government directly stepped into the fray by creating the FRC. The FRC had the power to ban programmes from broadcast (astrological readings and fortune telling were early targets) and ensure impartial political commentary. With the creation of the FRC, the government also created a system for issuing broadcasting licences for specific frequencies and the power to prevent stations from blasting one another off the air. Stations that did not comply with the FRC's regulations on what they could broadcast could have their licenses revoked, and indeed some stations that were deemed to be broadcasting questionable material were shut down in the final years of the decade (Benjamin 2009: 9). While the American radio broadcasting model gave corporations much of the power that was held by the government in Britain, there was clearly still a need for regulation.

At the end of the day, however, American radio was still about making money. In the heady days of the 1920s, radio company stocks soared in a manner startlingly reminiscent of Silicon Valley technology stocks in the twenty-first century. From the middle years of the decade to 1929, RCA's stock price went up more than 900 per cent despite never paying a dividend to its investors. Much as with American tech stocks in the early 2000s, the eventual crash was vicious, eventually wiping out 97 per cent of RCA's stock price (Business Insider 2012: passim). A prescient investor who sold their shares in the summer of 1929 would have reaped huge profits; the unfortunate soul who bought those shares lost almost everything. As discussed in the final sections of this book, these price fluctuations were not entirely coincidental, but in fact the result of serious market manipulation.

In contrast to the rapid success of radio in the United States, the development of radio in the non-European world occurred in fits and starts. In 1928, the Chinese government signed an agreement with RCA to develop a central radio station in Shanghai and five feeder stations across the country. In December 1930, President Herbert Hoover and Chiang Kai-Shek communicated over this network for the first time. This was a transnational feat – with the Shanghai to California cables being laid by Danish and British firms. A year prior to the Chinese agreement, wireless telegrams were beamed for the first time between London and Cape Town. Penetration to the heart of the African continent would have to wait however. Whilst it is true that South Africa's first radio broadcast (Mendelssohn's *Auf Fluegeln des Gesanges*) took place in 1923 and Kenya had its own radio station by 1927, this was mostly media to be enjoyed by British and European expatriates. Francophone and Lusophone Africa more or less followed suit in the 1930s with Mozambique (1933) and Senegal (1939) also seeing European-focused stations being set up. By the end of the 1920s, radio was becoming a truly global phenomenon. In 1932, King George V made the British monarchy's first-ever radio Christmas Broadcast across the Empire, beginning a tradition that continues to the present day. Radio had now become an indispensable tool of not only business but also governments.

The automobile

The automobile was not invented in the 1920s: indeed, like the airplane, it had played a major role in the latter stages of the First World War. Yet it was only after the war's end that the automobile reached its maturity and, in the United States at least, became a physical representation of modernity that, unlike the aircraft, was increasingly accessible to the middle class by the end of the decade. Elsewhere, the automobile would become almost synonymous with America and the Jazz Age.

The moving force behind the automobile's increasing ubiquity was Henry Ford, a Detroit industrialist who had begun his career as an inventor and machinist. In 1893, Ford had invented a prototype gasoline engine and built a version that was large enough to power a small vehicle for a short period. Three years later he produced a 'Quadricycle' – a carriage powered by a small engine – and in 1907 supervised the development of the Model T, a functional and durable automobile that was inexpensive enough to produce that it would be affordable by more than just wealthy motoring enthusiasts (Watts 2006: 38–9, 115–17). The Model T went into production in 1908 and in 1910 Ford transferred production to a new plant in Highland Park outside Detroit, and it was here that Ford again proved to be an innovator. Realising that the production process could be dramatically sped up by using an assembly line system in which workers would repetitively perform a single task on a moving line rather than doing several things while the automobile sat without moving, Ford implemented this system for every aspect of the production process. Following the introduction of the assembly line, the number of cars produced doubled in a single year (1913–14) while the number of workers declined nearly 10 per cent. The falling cost of production allowed Ford to lower the price of the car even further, making it affordable for more consumers. By the early years of the 1920s, Ford was producing more than two million Model Ts a year and had built more than half the automobiles on the road. Profits soared, and Ford's remarkable efficiency achievements became the inspiration for industrialists and governments around the globe (Grandin 2009: 35–7).

In the Soviet Union, Ford's assembly line became the model for the mass production of goods on a massive scale, often at the expense of quality. Ford's autobiography was even translated into Russian and became a best seller. Russian communism itself soon became a veritable cult of technological progress, revering both increases in production numbers and the creation of new innovations themselves. By the late 1920s, the Soviets were hiring foreign technical experts – including Americans – to help them improve industrial efficiency further, particularly in the tractor industry that was critical for agricultural production (Josephson 2009: 22–30).

Ford was not yet done innovating, however. In 1914 he announced that he was raising the wages of his workers to a startling $5 a day, almost double the wage of the average industrial worker. In return for the higher pay, Ford created a sociological department to manage the lives of his workers. The department's employees encouraged their fellow Ford employees to save money, abstain from decadent purchases (except for Model Ts) and lead moral and sober lives. Schools were established to teach immigrant workers English and to inculcate them with 'American' virtues (Watts 2006: 203–5). Ford also established and purchased a number of newspapers in the Detroit area to reach both his workers and the wider community. One of these – the *Dearborn Independent* – would soon become the source of controversy.

Ford's model of paying his workers substantially more than the prevailing wage in exchange for their loyalty, sobriety and diligence was a new model for industrialists who had traditionally relied on producing profits by paying their workers as little as possible and replacing them on an almost constant basis when they were too inefficient. Ford was thus seen as the visionary who had created a new form of capitalism, and his profits continued to soar. Despite a brief financial hiccup in the post-war recession of 1920 in which he nearly went bankrupt, by the following year Ford was pulling in record profits. In 1921, the Ford Motor Company was amassing profits of $8 *per second* when the factory was producing automobiles. That same year, the price of the Model T dropped from $575 to $348 (Benson 1923: 161–92). Former socialist presidential candidate Allan L. Benson remarked in 1923 there was no real separation between Ford's business activities and politics because, 'Whatever concerns the welfare of others concerns him. He believes we have only just started to make this world a fit place in which to live and wants to do everything he can to help the work along' (Benson 1923: 307).

By the mid-1920s, however, Ford's dominance had begun to erode in the face of new competition. His biggest rival, General Motors, began producing a range of automobiles that were technically superior to the now-dated Model T, and in addition began introducing new models on an annual basis. Ford was still producing only one model in one colour (black). Additionally, in 1925 the Chrysler company was formed, creating a third competitor to diminish Ford's market share. Both GM and Chrysler saw their market shares explode as they began to produce new models in the face of Ford's traditionalism. Ford eventually produced a reply to the challenge in the form of the improved and much larger Model A in 1927. By the end of the decade, nearly two million Model As had been sold, an impressive number but nowhere near the dominance of the Model T (Cashman 1998: 187–8).

FIGURE 3.3 The automobile epitomised the apparent triumph of modern industrial society in the 1920s and by the end of the decade was in widespread use across the globe, including in rural Finland, seen here.

At precisely the same moment that the competitive landscape of the American automotive market was changing, the British government attempted to restrict the export of rubber to the United States in an effort to raise the price and help the Empire's farmers. The result was a political firestorm in the United States, described in chapter 1, and a significant pushback against Britain by the US government. Never one for conventional solutions, however, Ford decided to build a massive rubber plantation of his own in the Amazon basin. The bizarre factory town in the Brazilian rainforest that resulted – naturally called Fordlândia – was a catastrophic failure and was eventually abandoned in 1945 (Grandin 2009: 24–8). While Ford's obvious passion for dramatic solutions to both practical and political problems was part of his appeal to the American public in the modernity-obsessed 1920s, it also led him in impractical and sometimes dangerous directions.

The latter of these were illustrated by a very public series of incidents that thrust Ford into the political arena in an unappealing way. During the First World War, Ford opposed US military intervention and actively campaigned against it. In 1915, he dramatically announced that he was going to take direct action to end the war by sailing a ship across the Atlantic with a number of prominent peace activists to convene a peace conference between the combatant nations. To put pressure on world leaders, he planned to broadcast wireless telegraph messages directly to soldiers in the trenches encouraging them to lay down their arms. This eccentric scheme met with initial difficulties when many of the invited activists and politicians declined to join the voyage and the American press made it the object of ridicule. The ship eventually sailed with Ford and dozens of activists on board but the voyage became a complete fiasco when a bout of influenza hit the passengers. Ford himself arrived in Norway to find almost no interest in his peace mission and, still recovering from illness, he returned home empty-handed (Watts 2006: 231–4).

This episode would have ultimately meant nothing, except for the fact that Ford had derived an outlandish conclusion from the experience. On board the ship, he claimed, the true group responsible for the war had been revealed to him: Jewish bankers. How he came to this specific conclusion is not entirely clear, but by the end of journey he was openly telling his fellow passengers that 'the German-Jewish bankers' had started the war to make profits and he later referred to 'the International Jew, the International Jewish banker' as a threat to world peace. On his return to the United States, his negative remarks about Wall Street financiers began to include references to 'New York Jews' and 'Kikes'. This was not the extent of his bizarre anti-Semitism: Ford banned the use of brass on the Model T because he believed it to be a 'Jew metal' and vocally denounced jazz as a form of Jewish-controlled music that was destructive to public morals (Watts 2006: 382).

In 1920, Ford took these conclusions to the public in a periodical entitled the *Dearborn Independent*. Ford had purchased the previously reputable local newspaper in 1918 and now intended to make it a mouthpiece for his views about the Jews. For two years, the paper published weekly articles denouncing the Jews as 'the world's problem' and reprinting libels from the notoriously anti-Semitic (and forged) *Protocols of the Learned Elders of Zion*. Ford's anti-Semitism was so widely known and insidious that Allan L. Benson reported that in the course of his interviews with Ford for an otherwise cloying biography, Ford abruptly refused to speak with him further until he had read a selection of anti-Semitic literature. At the same time, he reported, Ford insisted on drawing a distinction between 'Jewish international bankers' and individual Jews, many of whom he employed in his factories. 'I do not want any harm to come to them', he reportedly told Benson in the early 1920s (Benson 1923: 356–60).

Regardless of his intentions, by this point the anti-Semitic campaign had done serious harm to Ford's reputation. In 1925, Ford was sued for libel by agrarian activist Aaron Sapiro as the result of his claims about a Jewish world financial conspiracy. Specifically, the *Dearborn Independent* had claimed in 1924 that Sapiro was personally behind a Jewish conspiracy to control American agriculture for financial gain. Ill-advisedly fighting the case in court, Ford bizarrely claimed to have had no knowledge of the newspaper's articles and no influence on its content. The first case resulted in a mistrial when scurrilous allegations emerged from the Ford camp that a juror had been bribed by a Jew, and rather than face a second trial Ford agreed to settle the case. The *Independent* was duly shut down, Sapiro received a cash settlement and Ford formally apologised for the assertions of the newspaper, though he refrained from taking any responsibility for them and went so far as to again deny any knowledge of the contents of the paper (Watts 2006: 390–6; Baldwin 2001: 218–54). Few took his denials of responsibility seriously, and Ford would never escape the label of anti-Semite. In 1938, Adolf Hitler's government would award him a medal for his contributions to industrial production, his acceptance of which has contributed to the view that his anti-Semitic ideas never substantially changed from the mid-1920s. In these ideas, in fact, he would find an ally in Charles Lindbergh, who himself expressed the view that Jews could be a destructive force in society and received similar honours from Nazi Germany himself (Baldwin 2001: 281–92). The prophets of American modernity would thus find themselves tempted by the anti-democratic modernist visions that began sweeping Europe in the 1920s.

Regardless of his personal and political views, Ford had become an icon of American industry by the end of the decade. The rapid increase in the number of automobiles on the road quickly changed American society, with those able to afford personal vehicles soon beginning to move out of cities and toward the suburbs. In 1922 the first traffic signals appeared in New York City and were quickly adopted by other cities around the East Coast. In this changing social climate, cities began to change their physical appearances to attract attention. Tall skyscrapers, most iconically the Empire State Building in New York City, began to spring up in major cities in an effort to attract prestige for both their owners and the city itself. For young people, the automobile offered unprecedented freedom with the ability to drive literally anywhere and evade the supervision of both parents and society more widely (Cashman 1998: 187–9). Sex and cars quickly became linked in the American psyche, and the parents of young women began to fear the arrival of a young man with an automobile at their front door who might lead their daughter into sin. Henry Ford's affordable automobile had changed both the physical and the social landscape of America by the end of the 1920s.

Importantly, beyond the Fordlândia experiment, a global impact of the expanding automobile industry could also be felt. Between 1924 and 1928 car production skyrocketed: in France (44 per cent increase), Britain (54 per cent increase), Germany (500 per cent increase) and Italy (43 per cent increase). All told, the production of these Europe nations was less than a seventh of total American production (and about a quarter of the 500,000 units America was exporting in the mid-1920s), but they were upping their game in this sphere. In 1921 Ford was the leading car producer in the UK – with a fifth of the UK market compared to the tenth enjoyed by the Englishman William Morris (most famous for manufacturing the Morris Minor). As the decade progressed, however, Morris' share grew and Ford's fell to a situation where, by 1929, Morris had over a third of the British market and Ford just 6 per cent. This was of course still a reasonable share of a growing market, but the domestication of the automobile industry would be something Ford would have to cope with in the 1930s – particularly as nations began erecting tariff barriers to encourage domestic industry.

It was thus somewhat accurate to argue, as US Department of Commerce official Julius Klein would in 1928, that the rapid advance of the automobile worldwide was the result of how 'we [Americans] leaped at once into the forefront [of the automobile industry] and have maintained that leading position ever since'. Indeed, as he continued, California by then had two cars for every five of its residents while Germany could boast only one car per 157 inhabitants and Japan just one per 1,500 residents. On average, the rest of the world had one car per 277 people. China had only 20,000 vehicles in the entire country. This, he claimed, showed that 'some American Aladdin, we might almost think, has rubbed a magic lamp, and a host of incredible genii have conjured up a swift and splendid world of transportation in fulfillment of his wish'. As a result, more than 90 per cent of the vehicles on the road worldwide had been produced by American-owned plants in North America (Klein n.d., 'America Motorizing Mankind': 3; 'China in Transition: Conflict and Commerce': 5).

Yet even the optimistic Klein had to concede that the automobile industry had never been completely American. Foreign competitors, including Citroën in France and Rolls-Royce in Britain, developed their own domestic markets for specialised – and often luxury – vehicles. On the other hand, as Citroën himself admitted, the French automotive industry was far less efficient than American plants (and, indeed, many of his employees were trained in the United States to learn American production methods). American vehicles traversed not only the streets of major cities around the globe, but American trucks carried goods through rural areas worldwide. Klein predicted that foreign markets would soon absorb 'at least a million American cars a year' (Klein n.d., 'Foreign Triumphs of the American Automobile': 5–6). The Great Depression would intervene against this vision of unassailable US economic supremacy, but in the 1920s American companies undeniably dominated the international automobile industry.

Fears of degeneration

The development of the aircraft and the automobile were the engineering marvels of the early twentieth century, but, as with any practical innovation, they had naturally been underpinned by advances in theoretical science. Understanding how to make planes fly relied on understanding the laws of physics while Henry Ford's Model T had only been possible because of advances in combustion engines and metallurgy, among others.

Yet it was not just the physical sciences that advanced in the early twentieth century. As we noted in chapter 2 on class, the biological sciences and medicine both saw major advances during the decade that would begin to push life expectancies upward around the globe. The discovery of insulin in 1920 provided a means for diabetics to survive longer than ever before, changing the illness from a certain death sentence to a condition that could potentially be managed under the right circumstances. Two men shared the 1923 Nobel Prize in Physiology or Medicine for the discovery. In 1929, the same prize was awarded to two researchers for the discovery of vitamins and their importance for human growth and development. In 1928, Scottish bacteriologist Alexander Fleming noted that a particular fungus growing near bacteria cultures in his laboratory appeared to kill the bacteria. Studying the fungus more closely, Fleming derived a substance he called Penicillin from the fungus and determined that it could kill a wide range of bacteria that were known to cause human illness. His initial findings about whether Penicillin could actually cure these illnesses were inconclusive and generally ignored, but by the outbreak of the Second World War other experts would take up Flemings' findings and carry them further. Penicillin would become the world's first antibiotic to be produced on a mass scale and go on to save millions of lives that otherwise would have been lost to infection.

While these advances would prove effective in fighting some types of disease, physicians and biologists had long realised that other illnesses appeared to not be caught from other sick patients but instead seemed to run in families. This observation had been buttressed by a series of scientific findings about the inheritance of traits that had begun to emerge in the late nineteenth century. In 1865, Austrian monk Gregor Mendel presented a set of research findings he had derived from breeding pea plants in his monastery's experimental garden. Mendel had realised that by combining pea plants with certain traits (tall versus short, for instance) he could control the traits of the next generation of plants. His conclusion was that the physical traits of the pea plants were being carried on to their 'children' plants by an unknown force or substance. Even more striking was the fact that some traits ('tallness', for instance) seemed to overwhelm other traits when they were combined and did not blend together (so breeding a tall plant with a short one would create a tall plant rather than a medium one, for example), suggesting that some traits were 'dominant' and others 'recessive'. Not only were traits inheritable, Mendel had shown, but with sufficient knowledge it would actually be possible to make a probabilistic prediction about the traits of the next generation by examining the 'parents' (Kevles 1995: 41–2).

Mendel's startling conclusions were ignored until 1900 when they were redis-
covered by a number of researchers studying plant breeding and hybridisation. His
conclusions did not necessarily apply only to plants, however. In 1859, British
naturalist Charles Darwin had published *The Origin of Species*, a remarkable work in
which he argued that animal species had evolved into their present forms by the
process of natural selection, in which the most fit outbreed the least fit and thus
pass on their traits to the next generation. Over a suitably long period, natural
selection could lead to the emergence of new species entirely. While Darwin had
published this theory prior to Mendel's work with pea plants, it became obvious
after 1900 that Darwin's process of evolution might well be driven by the hereditary
forces that Mendel had discovered, thus providing a more complete account of
how evolution and natural selection could function. In addition, it quickly became
clear that evolution did not just apply to plants and animals, but also to humans.
Indeed, Darwin's half-cousin, Francis Galton, came to the conclusion that the
principle of natural selection had all but been abandoned in the modern world
thanks to modern medicine and welfare measures, leading to a situation in which
the least fit members of human society were actually breeding more than their
superiors. Thus, Galton would argue, human society had to take steps to prevent
the biological deterioration of society. Conversely, by ensuring the reproduction of
the most fit, society might be able to expect an actual improvement in its overall
quality. Galton called the field he founded 'eugenics', a Greek term roughly
equivalent to 'well-born' (Kevles 1995: 8–20).

By the 1920s, eugenics would be sweeping the globe. In 1904, a centre for
experimental hereditary research was established at Cold Spring Harbor, New
York, by biologist Charles Davenport. The laboratory soon became a collecting
centre for human pedigrees (family trees) showing the inheritance of both positive
(such as intelligence or physical prowess) and negative (including alcoholism,
tuberculosis or so-called 'feeble-mindedness') traits through the generations of
American families. By collecting vast amounts of such data, Davenport and his
associates hoped, it might become possible to fully understand the patterns along
which all such traits were inherited and, eventually, encourage the positive ones
while discouraging the negative ones (Kevles 1995: 45–6). The most certain way to
prevent the reproduction of the 'unfit' was through sterilisation – removing the
physical ability to reproduce through surgery. By 1911 six US states had legalised
eugenic sterilisation for residents considered to be carrying a hereditary illness that
it was deemed in the state's interest to prevent being transmitted. California soon
became the country's leading steriliser and would end up subjecting tens of thousands
of its residents, often non-white women, to the procedure before the Second
World War (Hart 2011: 127–9).

In Britain, the Eugenics Education Society (later renamed the Eugenics Society)
pushed for eugenic reforms including the exchange of hereditary health certificates
before marriage and, later, began to advocate voluntary sterilisation for the mentally
unfit. Unlike the United States, Britain did not embrace compulsory sterilisation for
its citizens, but other countries did: Denmark passed a national law allowing the

sterilisation of the 'feebleminded', as did Norway and Sweden, while the Canadian province of Alberta passed a sterilisation law of its own in 1928. By the early 1930s a majority of American states had passed sterilisation laws of some description, and in the landmark case of *Buck v. Bell* in 1927, the US Supreme Court upheld the right of states to forcibly sterilise their citizens. Throughout the 1920s, the US experience with sterilisation was the model on which other countries based their own eugenic sterilisation campaigns. In 1933, Adolf Hitler's German government would pass a far-reaching sterilisation law of its own, directly and explicitly based on the American model (the Weimar Republic had its own burgeoning eugenics movement, which often referred to itself as the 'race hygiene' movement). Most American eugenicists were flattered by the compliment, though some feared that the Germans would soon exceed their own accomplishments in the field (Hart 2011: 106, 161, 179–82).

The arguments presented by the eugenicists were not just applied to the 'feebleminded' and those believed to be carrying inheritable illness however. The logic of controlling the state's biological make-up was also used to justify the large-scale exclusion of 'undesirable' immigrants from the United States throughout the 1920s. In 1916, wealthy New York conservationist and socialite Madison Grant published *The Passing of the Great Race*, a book arguing on 'scientific' grounds that all of human history was determined by race. In keeping with the standard racist views of the day, Grant argued that the 'Nordic race' was the most advanced and responsible for virtually all positive developments of human society throughout history, while the lesser 'Mediterraneans' and 'Alpines' were mere followers at best and destructive barbarians at worst (Spiro 2008: 147–9).

Further, Grant claimed, the United States had originally been founded by Nordics but now faced mass immigration from other races that were threatening to overrun the country and, in his mind even worse, interbreed with the Nordics. According to Grant, the country had to protect its hereditary quality by shutting the door on undesirable immigrants and adopting eugenic policies to encourage the Nordics to breed in higher numbers. *The Passing of the Great Race* became an immediate sensation, selling only a modest number of copies but being widely cited by anti-immigration advocates throughout the 1920s (Spiro 2008: 147–66). In 1923, one of Grant's followers, Lothrop Stoddard, published *The Rising Tide of Color against White World-Supremacy* declaring that the 'white world' was under existential threat from non-white races that threatened to supersede it because of the loss of European life in the First World War (Stoddard 1920: passim). For both Grant and Stoddard, the world stood on the brink of destruction if radical change to ensure white supremacy were not enacted.

Although they placed emphasis on different elements of eugenics, the overarching issue was not just the preserve of racial obsessives, however. John Maynard Keynes, the noted British economist we discuss in depth from chapter 10 onwards, had been active in the eugenics movement since before the First World War. As David Singerman notes,

> his involvement spanned his entire professional career, from service as treasurer
> of the Cambridge University Eugenics Society in 1911 to membership of the

council of its parent national society in the nineteen-forties. Infamously, he assured the latter that eugenics was 'the most important, significant, and, I would add, genuine branch of sociology which exists'.

(Singerman n.d.: passim)

Nor was Keynes unique amongst economic scholars. Ruminating on the issue of the 'population question and world peace', the Swedish economist Knut Wicksell concluded in the early 1920s that 'the best way to prevent future wars was to lower the birthrate' (Jonung 1992: 364). Since there was a surplus of Swedish women and not enough men, the former might have to be persuaded to emigrate overseas.

Influenced by such population-based arguments, coupled with traditional racial prejudice and lobbying by the eugenicists themselves, the US government dramatically restricted immigration to the country over the course of the 1920s. In 1921, the Emergency Quota Act was passed after Grant directly lobbied key lawmakers. Under the law, a set number of immigrants would be allowed in from each country, with larger quotas set for Northern European ('Nordic') countries, and smaller quotas being given to Southern European countries. Ironically, this had the effect of allowing in a large number of German immigrants, despite the United States having just fought a war against the country, and excluding a large number of immigrants from countries with which the United States had been allied during the First World War (Spiro 2008: 209–10). Three years later, the Immigration Restriction Act lowered those numbers even further, allowing in a total of just 165,000 immigrants from all countries. All immigration from Asia was banned outright. Grant praised the legislation as 'an amazing triumph' while Stoddard proclaimed that 'America is saved!' (Spiro 2008: 232–3).

Between the passage of eugenic sterilisation laws around the globe and the draconian restriction of immigrants seeking better lives in the United States, the eugenics movement was riding high at the end of the 1920s. By the mid-1930s, it would be tarred by its associations with Nazism and, after the Second World War, would nearly cease to exist in an organised and public way. In 1930 that was all in the future however, and the eugenicists seemed to have offered governments an important scientific tool to manage the quality of their population and head off demographic disaster in the aftermath of the First World War. Just as the Model T and the *Spirit of St. Louis* were the outcomes of scientific advancement and breakthrough technologies, so too was eugenic sterilisation and immigration restriction, both of which were advocated by men and women who claimed to be basing their views on cutting-edge science.

Conclusion

In 1928, the economic optimist Julius Klein publicly summarised the United States' economic relationship to the world thus:

This export trade of ours means American cash-registers ringing their merry tune in the shops of Johannesburg or Harbin. It means, empty American kerosene-oil tins serving as cooking utensils over peasants' fires in the rice country of South China. It means safety-razor blades scraping the chins of blonde Swedes in Stockholm and of swarthy Africans in the Sudan. It means gay, enthralled audiences in the mining towns of Peru or the teeming native quarters of Tientsin watching the movies from America, with their flashing pageants of great events, their handsome heroes hanging from cliffs, their grotesque antics of the baggy-trousered 'comic' It means massive American machinery hewing and erecting public works needed by other peoples. It means American cosmetics in Cuban boudoirs – American electric refrigerators in sweltering tropical cities – American airplanes showing (in a manner to win the admiration of the world) the dauntless 'way of the eagle'.

(Klein n.d., 'A Week of the World's Business': 5)

This was the triumphalist rhetoric of a United States committed to the business of doing business, as its Republican administrations happily proclaimed throughout the decade. Certainly, the United States was not the only producer of goods consumed in far-flung places. Yet to an extent, Klein had a point. American industry was at the centre of the technological and manufacturing innovations that characterised the decade and while it was not alone in innovating, it was increasingly associated with the innovations themselves.

The 1920s opened the metaphorical door to the world of modern technology and conveniences that exists nearly a century later. Many of these innovations made the world 'smaller' by bringing far-flung people together. The obvious example is the radio, which rapidly became the 'must-have' appliance of the decade in every industrialised country and in many places that still lacked other basic conveniences. Even in remote areas of California's Sierra Nevada Mountains, a local resident reported to naturalist Gustav Eisen that both the physical and the social landscape had changed dramatically from only a few decades before:

Great changes have taken place since you were familiar with the pioneer aspects of the sierras: Numerous roads, great dams, electrical power, railroads, homes, reservoirs, mountain towns, villages, mark the forests and canyons! Where then were thousands of sheep and a few men tending them, and communication was by individual contact, now the aeroplanes fly daily (in summer) over the mountains, electric power lines, telephone lines thread their way to distant stock ranges, radio instruments in the humble homes of mountain dwellers. Even the Indian today rides with his squaw and papooses in an automobile, and many of them have phonographs in their cabins!

(Winchell 1930: passim)

Similarly, an American traveller to Central Africa in the middle years of the decade remarked that the spread of technology there had been both swift and seemingly unstoppable:

> What amazes one most in Africa is the astonishing rapidity with which civilization is spreading. Within our memory Central Africa was an impenetrable mystery, – a complete blank on the map. Now one can traverse it from end to end in motor cars and steamboats and trains equipped with every modern appliance for comfort … We even met people planning motor trips from the Cape to the Nile just as they do from New York to Los Angeles. With transportation come law and order, peace and safety, hospitals and schools … In place of the old ceaseless feuds, slave raids and expeditions for plunder, peace reigns.
>
> *(Denison, J.H. n.d.: 340)*

Certainly the progress of technology was positive from the European and American perspective, but often less so from the perspective of those being forced to adapt to a changing world. Noting that their travel group had often seen instances of physical abuse of Africans by whites, one of the previous writer's fellow travellers observed that, 'Every black man is, ipso facto, in the position of servant to every white man' (Denison, C. n.d.: 325). Technological advances were making the world a metaphorically smaller place, but only for those privileged enough to be able to partake in them.

Transportation improvements were at the heart of these changes. The airplane was far more than just a way to explore remote areas of mountain ranges but a new way of both travelling and conveying goods over vast distances that had previously taken weeks or even months to traverse. When 'Lucky Lindy' became the first person in history to arrive in Europe the morning after departing North America, he not only made himself the most famous man in the world but also heralded a degree of physical mobility never before experienced. While Charles Lindbergh and the airplane was the classically 'American' form of air travel, Germany's answer came in the form of the impressive but ultimately impractical Zeppelin, illustrating that the desire to produce the physical symbols of modernity were shared by more than just the victors of the Great War.

Similarly, Henry Ford became an icon of the 1920s not only because of his Model T but also the efficiency innovations his assembly line factories were able to demonstrate, and the immense profits that followed. In addition, the high salaries he paid his workers, often in exchange for their acquiescence to a set of rigid social rules, became the model for a new form of capitalism. Even outside the capitalist West, the USSR looked at Ford's innovations and attempted to put them to work on behalf of the workers rather than factory owners. For both capitalists and communists, increasing efficiency with modern tools and tactics was a symbol of the modern world.

Ford's rampant anti-Semitism was a clear black mark on his reputation, both at the time and since. As the example of the eugenics movement demonstrates however, scientific progress itself was not without its own dark side, and the increasing knowledge of human heredity that had its origins in the mid to late nineteenth century led to the emergence of a movement that committed itself to 'scientifically' managing human breeding. While many of the eugenics movement's efforts were directed at convincing the 'fit' to breed more, it also led to the surgical sterilisation of thousands around the world, and would be the intellectual inspiration for more human rights abuses over the decades to come. Increasingly convinced by both the scientific evidence being presented by the eugenicists and the lobbying efforts of wealthy patrons like Madison Grant, the US government all but slammed the door on immigration in the middle years of the decade. It would not be until the 1960s that the United States would once again become a land of opportunity for immigrants.

Science and technology were therefore multifarious endeavours in the 1920s, as they are in any era. The radio, the airplane and the automobile would increasingly make people's lives better around the world in the decades to come. At the same time, the rise of political extremism and the mass bloodshed of the Second World War would also be the legacy of these new technologies. At the end of the 1920s, however, the illusion of indefinite technological progress was still very much alive. It would take the experience of the Great Depression and the destruction of another world war, this time including nuclear weapons, to begin to open questions about the potential human consequences of such progress.

Questions

- What were the relative benefits of travel by plane versus Zeppelin in the 1920s? Why did planes overtake dirigibles as the primary form of air transportation in the years after?
- Beyond the physical daring of his flight across the Atlantic, what other factors and trends made Charles Lindbergh such a major celebrity in the late 1920s?
- Why did it prove impossible for the US government to have no role at all in the radio industry, despite rejecting the British model of public-service broadcasting?
- Why did the automobile become such an icon of modernity in the 1920s? What factors led to its widespread popularity in the US and elsewhere?
- Why was the American eugenics movement so successful in the 1920s? What wider cultural and social concerns was its success based upon?

Recommended further reading

Baldwin, N. (2001), *Henry Ford and the Jews: The Mass Production of Hate*, New York: PublicAffairs.

Berg, A.S. (1998), *Lindbergh*, New York: G.P. Putnam's Sons.

Briggs, A. (1995), *The History of Broadcasting in the United Kingdom, Volume I: The Birth of Broadcasting*, Oxford: Oxford University Press.

Spiro, J.P. (2008), *Defending the Master Race: Conservation, Eugenics, and the Legacy of Madison Grant*, Burlington: University of Vermont Press.

Stoddard, L. (1920), *The Rising Tide of Color against White World-Supremacy*, London: Chapman and Hall.

Watts, S. (2006), *The People's Tycoon: Henry Ford and the American Century*, New York: Alfred P. Knopf.

Works cited

Baldwin, N. (2001), *Henry Ford and the Jews: The Mass Production of Hate*, New York: PublicAffairs.

BBC Genome (n.d.), via http://genome.ch.bbc.co.uk

Benjamin, L.M. (2009), *The NBC Advisory Council and Radio Programming, 1926–1945*, Carbondale: Southern Illinois University Press.

Benson, A.L. (1923), *The New Henry Ford*, Funk & Wagnalls Company.

Berg, A.S. (1998), *Lindbergh*, New York: G.P. Putnam's Sons.

Boyer, P.S. (2002), *Purity in Print: Book Censorship in America from the Gilded Age to the Computer Age*, Madison: University of Wisconsin Press.

Business Insider (2012), 'Apple Walking in RCA's Footsteps', via www.businessinsider.com/chart-apple-walking-in-rcas-footsteps-2012-11

Carr, R. (2013), *Veteran MPs and Conservative Politics in the Aftermath of the Great War*, Farnham: Ashgate.

Cashman, S.D. (1998), *America Ascendant: From Theodore Roosevelt to FDR in the Century of American Power, 1901–1945*, New York: New York University Press.

Coase, R.H. (1950), *British Broadcasting: A Study in Monopoly*, London: Longmans, Green and Co.

de Syon, G. (2007), *Zeppelin! Germany and the Airship, 1900–1939*, Baltimore: Johns Hopkins University Press.

Denison, C. (n.d.), 'The Racial Problem in Africa', in *An African Log*, vol. 2, Appendix I, 325–331, Box 1, Marshall Bond Papers, Hoover Institution Archive, Stanford University.

Denison, J.H. (n.d.), 'The Progress of Civilization in Africa', in *An African Log*, vol. 2, Appendix I, 339–347, Box 1, Marshall Bond Papers, Hoover Institution Archive, Stanford University.

Duggan, J. and Meyer, H.C. (2001), *Airships in International Affairs, 1890–1940*, Basingstoke: Palgrave.

Edgerton, D. (2005), *Warfare State: Britain, 1920–1970*, Cambridge: Cambridge University Press.

Fortner, R.S. (2006), *Radio, Morality and Culture: Britain, Canada, and the United States, 1919–1945*, Carbondale: Southern Illinois University Press.

Grandin, G. (2009), *Fordlandia*, New York: Henry Holt and Company.

Hart, B.W. (2011), 'British, German, and American Eugenicists in Transnational Context, c. 1900–1939', Unpublished PhD thesis: Cambridge University.

Inge, W.R. (1926), *England*, New York: Charles Scribner's Sons.

Jonung, L. (1992), 'Knut Wicksell's Unpublished Manuscripts: A First Glance', in Blaug, M. (ed.) *Knut Wicksell*, London: Edward Elgar Ltd, pp. 358–366.

Josephson, P.R. (2009), *Would Trotsky Wear a Bluetooth? Technological Utopianism under Socialism, 1917–1989*, Baltimore: The Johns Hopkins University Press.

Kevles, D.J. (1995), *In the Name of Eugenics: Genetics and the Uses of Human Heredity*, Cambridge, MA: Harvard University Press.

Klein, J. (n.d.), Box 1, Julius Klein Papers, Hoover Institution Library, Stanford University.

Kyvig, D.E. (2004), *Daily Life in the United States, 1920–1940: How Americans Lived Through the Roaring Twenties and the Great Depression*, Chicago: Ivan R. Dee.

Lindbergh, C. (1927), *We*, New York: Buccaneer Books.

Miller Centre (n.d.), 'Inaugural Address' via http://millercenter.org/president/coolidge/speeches/speech-3569

Ponder, S. (1998), *Managing the Press: Origins of the Media Presidency, 1897–1933*, New York: St Martin's Press.

Singerman, D. (n.d.), 'Keynesian Eugenics and the Goodness of the World', unpublished manuscript.

Spiro, J.P. (2008), *Defending the Master Race: Conservation, Eugenics, and the Legacy of Madison Grant*, Burlington: University of Vermont Press.

Stoddard, L. (1920), *The Rising Tide of Color against White World-Supremacy*, London: Chapman and Hall.

Watts, S. (2006), *The People's Tycoon: Henry Ford and the American Century*, New York: Alfred P. Knopf.

Winchell, L.A. (1930), Letter from L.A. Winchell to Professor Gustav Eisen [c.1930], Outgoing Correspondence, Box 1, L.A. Winchell Papers, Fresno City and County Historical Society.

PART II

PART II

4

FILM, MUSIC AND OTHER PASTIMES

The 1920s were an age of celebrity, and in that glittering time there was no more wondrous a medium than film. Whilst Hollywood had been little more than a sleepy town on the edge of Los Angeles in 1914, five years later it had become the epicentre for a new form of entertainment that rapidly swept the world. As with most technologies in the post-Industrial-Revolution age, everyone soon wanted a piece of the action. Whilst nineteenth-century American industrialists would sometimes look enviously towards the capitalism of the old world (and seek in some ways to ape it), the 1920s would see these roles dramatically reversed when it came to film. In 1922 *The Times* of London confidently asserted that 'what the English producer needs, if he wishes to make a place for himself in the American [film] market, is courage' (*The Times*, 21 February 1922). Courage aside, it noted that 'he must select new faces, pretty faces – even if they are insipid ... He must not be afraid of indulging in a great deal of sentiment excluding always patriotism, an emotion that the American indulges in no country but his own.' But, worst of all, 'he must play deliberately for tears, repugnant though such an exhibition of emotion may be to a cultured English taste'. This was no easy ask – 'above all, he must spend money, lots of money' – but, with 20,000 American theatres outside of New York, the potential markets were big and the rewards (and profits) just as obvious. Perhaps this could be expected – though the volume of talent drain (Charlie Chaplin, Alfred Hitchcock and Cary Grant, to name but three) Britain experienced over the first half of the twentieth century arguably could not have been. But film, as we will see, took off beyond nations with such obvious linguistic and cultural ties to the United States. In a sense cinema served as a metaphor for the general global picture in the 1920s – Europe was in decline and the United States moving into the ascendency.

There were other global trends taking off in a big way this decade however – foremost amongst them sport and music. These too had significant relevance beyond their own individual expansion (lucrative for some though they indeed were). Sport allowed a peaceful means for citizens from former enemy states to achieve something closer to brotherhood. The great exception again was the world's newest superpower as American isolationism and exceptionalism somewhat extended into this sphere and the imperial British games of cricket and rugby achieved next to no penetration on the North American continent, nor did that more universal game of association: football (soccer, to Americans, as American football is and remains a wholly other entity). With the exception of track- and field-based Olympic sports, Americans then, as in later years, retained a penchant for games they had themselves invented, while showing a relatively small amount of interest in more international games. For American sport fans, the 1920s would be dominated by the 'national pastime' of baseball and the stars that were increasingly becoming national heroes. The biggest of these was George Herman 'Babe' Ruth, a remarkably talented all-round player and one of the greatest hitters of all time.

On the other hand music – particularly jazz – would rival film as a successful American export throughout the 1920s. The combination of African-American migration from the American South to a more tolerant North, together with improving technologies surrounding radio broadcast and general sound equipment, led to an explosion of interest in jazz. But jazz was merely part of a wider youth-based rebellion against pre-war norms of staid domesticity. New fashion statements, smoking, increased confidence when discussing pre-marital sex and actually carrying it out were all symptomatic of a new cultural age. Together with the 1960s, the 1920s was perhaps the decade in which global culture – best expressed through what people did with their spare time – changed the most in the whole gamut of the twentieth century.

Hollywood and beyond

During the 1920s 'Hollywood' as an industry took off. The small, anarchic and low-budget cinema of the First World War era was replaced by the age of movie moguls. As film historian Steven J. Ross notes, 'the 1920s signaled the rise of a new type of film industry, an oligarchic studio system centered in Los Angeles and financed by some of the largest industrial and financial institutions in the nation' (Ross 2011: 6). Foremost amongst these was Louis B. Mayer – a global citizen in more ways than one. Born in Minsk in Tsarist Russia in 1884 the former Lazlo Meir only arrived in the United States 20 years later and initially set out with the modest ambition of renovating a clapped-out movie theatre in Haverhill, Massa-chusetts. Yet he was quick to see an opportunity when one arose. Gaining the exclusive New England rights for D.W. Griffith's polemic *Birth of a Nation* in 1915, Mayer started his own production company which in 1924 merged with two others to form Metro-Goldwyn-Mayer, or MGM. Whilst other movie chiefs – certainly Charlie Chaplin – began to strive for high art, Mayer's logic was simple: after the horrors of the First World War and with bouts of economic uncertainty, people wanted simplistic escapism. And he was right – even in the Great Depression of the 1930s MGM would never fail to turn a profit.

The 1920s saw the unstoppable advance of Hollywood. In 1920 almost half the American population visited the movies on a weekly basis and by 1930 the cinema industry was approaching full coverage. This had significant consequences for American society and politics. As Ross notes, the 1920s saw the dawn of a 'Washington–Hollywood' alliance that was entrenched for several decades (if indeed it has fully dissipated to this day), and 'studios hesitated producing any film during the 1920s that was overtly favorable to labor or radical causes' (Ross 2011: 27). In part this emanated from the spirit of the Palmer Raids of 1920 – when 4,000 alleged communists were arrested in more than 30 American cities. The atmosphere of anti-Bolshevism in the United States was a portent of later McCarthyite sentiment in the 1940s and 1950s. Charlie Chaplin managed to span both – falling under FBI surveillance from 1922 – but then he always maintained creative independence due to his personal wealth and leadership of United Artists. This independence pushed him down some eclectic political avenues – he became friends with leftists such as Max Eastman and later Upton Sinclair – as well as leading to some questionable artistic choices (though duds like *A King in New York* and *A Countess of Hong Kong* were decades away). In the 1920s, however, it also produced classics like *The Gold Rush* and *The Circus*.

In 1922, the year after his successful film *The Kid* (which drew heavily on his impoverished London youth), Chaplin was worth a reported $5 million – equivalent to more than $60 million in modern money. Chaplin's comedy (and his bank balance) were thus safe enough, but his politics were beginning to come more and more to the fore. In 1921 he ranted against the workings of contemporary capitalism in a controversial interview:

> 'Many people have called me a socialist,' said Chaplin as he paced up and down the room, 'my radical views have been much misunderstood. I am not a Socialist, nor am I looking for a new order of things. But I believe that conditions can be much improved and that the lives of the working classes can be made far more pleasant than they are. For a long time capital has held sway and declared that the present order is the only one, but Henry Ford's methods rather disprove that don't they? He is getting all the business of the country because he is fair. He gives value received for his merchandise, and on the other hand he considers his workers, pays them a fair wage, and has made profit sharing absolutely practicable. You can't feed labor a lot of words anymore.'
>
> *(Carr 2017: passim)*

His views on Ford were perhaps slightly generous. Certainly, as chapter 7 notes, Chaplin's positive inclination towards Jews would not have chimed with Ford. But the crucial point was that Chaplin was not the only filmmaker with a 'message': for conservative-leaning Hollywood moguls like Mayer, cinema's expansion was a tool to spread the good right-wing gospel. For all the liberal voices like Chaplin, the key powerbrokers in 1920s cinema were usually Republicans. In 1921 the Motion Picture Producers and Distribution Association (MPPDA) appointed its first head,

Will Hays – formerly Postmaster General under Republican President Warren G. Harding. The MPPDA's initial function was to keep the costs of film production low by encouraging studios to make films which would limit the number of cuts made by state censorship boards (states then charged studios for each foot of film cut from a film and for any edits of title cards). In the late 1920s the MPPDA morphed into a self-regulatory body of its own and, after a Catholic Priest Daniel A. Lord authored a set of guidelines on what he considered 'desirable' behaviour in the movies, the MPPDA under Hays soon made it – from 1930 – its role to police the motion picture industry itself. This would usually be in a more small 'c' conservative direction. But it was not just Hays. Al Jolson – whose *Jazz Singer* launched the use of sound that would hit Chaplin in other ways – organised Broadway stars to work for Harding in 1920 and Calvin Coolidge in 1924 (Ross 2011: 61). Although he would later support Roosevelt in the 1930s, in 1928 William Randolph Hearst leant his weight to Herbert Hoover's successful bid for the Presidency. This was largely the work of Mayer, of whom it was said people would send scripts to the White House knowing they would find their way into Mayer's hands one way or the other. The ties ran deep.

FIGURE 4.1 British actor Charlie Chaplin's iconic 'tramp' character made him one of the richest actors in Hollywood history during the 1920s.

At least for Chaplin, the reviews remained good into the mid-1920s. As *The Times* murmured approvingly of his next venture: 'all those who enjoy a hearty laugh should go to see *The Gold Rush*, of which one of the especial recommendations is that even when the humour is at its height it is never in the least vulgar' (*The Times*, 15 September 1925). Unfortunately for the little tramp an enemy was waiting around the corner, and that enemy was *The Jazz Singer* (1927). *The Jazz Singer*, starring Al Jolson, was America's first full-length film which including a brief section of audio, in this case Jolson singing on screen. It was the first time that audiences had actually seen an actor speak on screen. Earlier filmmakers – including Chaplin's business partner D.W. Griffith – had incorporated short sound vignettes before a main silent feature, but the two minutes or so of spoken dialogue (no voice was heard until 17 minutes into the film, keeping the audience in suspense) in *The Jazz Singer* revolutionised the industry in proving a solid business case for moving away from silent cinema. Outside of academia, the actual content of *The Jazz Singer* – a Jewish man exiled from his community and appropriating an African-American art-form (whilst 'blacking up' in make-up) – has been rather lost in the sands of time amidst the film's commercial success. It would go on to be the most lucrative film in Warner Brothers' history, though was hampered by the fact it slightly outstripped the technology of the time: many movie theatres did not yet have the technology to cater for sound, and thus it ran as a silent film in several key markets. Still, for an investment of around $425,000, Warner Brothers eventually recouped just shy of four million.

For all Chaplin's talk of 'art' and the base nature of the new 'talkies' the reality was that Hollywood was big business. The big studios sold stock to Wall Street investors which provided nearly $1 billion in capital by 1922 (Ross 2011: 57). These investors naturally wanted a return on their capital, and thus the price of the average movie ticket increased from 25 cents in 1924 to 35 cents by the time of the crash in 1929. It would subsequently dip back down to around the 1924 level during the depression of the 1930s. But the fact was that Hollywood, like Wall Street, was something of a bubble in which demand had to be maintained. And this mattered for Chaplin's friend the worker too. By 1929, around 150,000 Americans were employed in some manner connected to the motion picture industry. At this time the industry was around $170 million in profit and paying around $10 million annually in corporate taxes. Chaplin's independence meant he could postpone dealing with the talkies until 1940 – his *City Lights* (1931) and *Modern Times* (1936) remained essentially silent films even if he experimented with various forms of sporadic sound. However, for his great contemporary Buster Keaton things were a good deal more difficult. Having signed with Mayer's MGM in 1928 – a decision he later regarded as the worst of his life – Keaton became a victim of the new studio system. Renowned for his daredevil escapades – most famously in *Steamboat Bill, Jr.* standing still whilst a house collapsed on top of him (Keaton standing in a small portion where an open window meant he would not be crushed) – he discovered that MGM did not want to put their investment at risk. Stuntmen were soon employed but, as

Keaton remarked, 'stuntmen don't get laughs'. An industry built on one form of art suddenly had to change to another.

In any event, 1920s cinema was not just comedic, and the most glamorous swashbuckler of this era was Douglas Fairbanks. Together with Chaplin, D.W. Griffith and Mary Pickford, he founded United Artists in 1919. Whilst Chaplin worked out his previous contracts the fledgling independent company was largely funded by the successes of Fairbanks' popular costume pieces – *The Three Musketeers* (1921), *Robin Hood* (1922) and *The Gaucho* (1927) formed an impressive run of films that, in essence, freed up the room for Chaplin to experiment artistically with more dramatic works. Like Chaplin, Fairbanks would struggle with the transition to the 'talkies' and initially dithered – he opened 1929's *The Iron Mask* with an introductory monologue, but performed the actual film as a silent work.

His lover, and from 1920 wife, Mary Pickford was just as famous. Dubbed 'America's Sweetheart', Pickford had actually been born and grew up in Toronto (she later made a point of re-acquiring her original citizenship in later life, stating 'I want to die a Canadian'). With Fairbanks and Chaplin, Pickford promoted Liberty Bonds during the First World War, and sold one of her famous curls for $15,000. In 1929's *Coquette* – for which she won the Academy Award for Best Actress – Pickford styled her trademark ringlets into a bob. In proof that the 1920s were not immune to gossipy news, *The New York Times* carried the story of her new haircut on its front page. She, like her husband, would not prosper in the talkie era of the 1930s, however. Still, the two became the stuff of legend within their own lifetimes. Together Pickford and Fairbanks owned a famous 18-acre estate labelled Pickfair by the media. Located in Beverly Hills, the list of guests was rivalled only by Cliveden, the Astors' property in England, as the must-visit abode of choice. Throughout the 1920s Albert Einstein, Charles Lindbergh, the Roosevelts and H.G. Wells all visited Pickfair, and the Mountbattens used part of the estate as their honeymoon suite. One of the most celebrated homes in the world during the 1920s, it was later demolished in 1990 by its then-owner, actress Pia Zadora.

The international flocking to Pickfair was quite symbolic. If Hollywood had been established as the empire of film in the 1910s, the 1920s were the decade that made film a global success story which reached from European metropolises to the developing world. For instance, by 1928 there were around 300 cinemas in British India, though only 60 in the Indian states. These were mostly urban, and cinematic penetration beyond the big cities was rare indeed. But this new market meant a new type of film, and there was also a concerted attempt to make a distinctly Indian film. As *The Times of India* noted, 'Indian cinema audiences naturally prefer films that interpret Indian life, and the Indian cinematograph industry should therefore be ready to cater for the coming demand'. This, however, was easier said than done. As the newspaper noted, 'most of the studios in India are hopelessly inadequate. Few are equipped with the all necessary light, and few employ directors and camera-men who have had instruction in successful Western technical methods of production'. However, there was some hope:

within the borders of India lies some of the loveliest and most varied scenery in the world. Thus there should be an immediate demand for good Indian films not only in India and [areas of Indian settlement such as] South and East Africa, but also in Europe and America.

(Times of India, *12 December 1929*)

The notion of making a non-American type of film was one that united many a territory. Readers in Adelaide, Australia, were told that

it may be fairly said that the average American taste determines for the most part the character of the fare provided in their picture halls for the Australian people, and if, as many think, the state of culture is not so far advanced in America as in British communities, it is not perhaps surprising that the inferior standard should be reflected in the films.

(Adelaide Advertiser, *11 March 1927*)

Weimar Germany perhaps produced the most famous response to Hollywood's domination: Fritz Lang. Lang had served in the Austrian army during the First World War in Romania and Russia, and had been wounded three times. He suffered shell shock in 1916 and, partially to heal such psychological wounds, began scribbling down notes for future film treatments. Together with his wife Thea von Harbou, Lang wrote several classic films throughout the 1920s from the Dr Marbuse Trilogy to, most famously, 1927's *Metropolis* and what became 1931's *M. Metropolis* told a story of class difference set in a future dystopia (albeit one bearing several hallmarks of the contemporary fad for Art Deco). It was a huge commercial risk – costing a record-breaking five million Reichsmarks – and involved the input of three studios all told, Paramount, MGM and the German company UFA. The latter took a decidedly political turn when, in April 1927, the industrialist Alfred Hugenberg took over the running of UFA. Since all participating studios had retained the contractual right to cut anything they deemed inappropriate, Hugenberg cut Lang's film by around a quarter of its original length – removing much of Lang's Catholic iconography and supposedly 'communistic' subtext. In 1933 the DNVP (Deutschnationale Volkspartei) led by the same Alfred Hugenberg would go on to be coalition partners in Adolf Hitler's first administration, albeit with Hugenberg himself swiftly removed from any effective influence.

Two countries divided by a common language

For all that film was emblematic of global convergence, it is worth offering something of a brief corrective here. Perhaps the two most 'global' nations in the 1920s were Britain – with its vast geographic empire – and the United States, the coming economic powerhouse. In a sense, this book marks the point at which the latter replaced the former as a truly dominant global player. But given their common heritage, the advances in airplane and radio technology discussed in chapter 3, and the artistic and cultural ties outlined in this chapter, it is perhaps surprising to discover that they were – to borrow a phrase alternatively attributed to Oscar Wilde and

George Bernard Shaw – two countries divided by a common language throughout the 1920s. Two examples, trivial enough in their own right, demonstrate this.

The first concerns the simple Hot Dog, a staple of American culture to the present day, and a man named Waldorf Astor. Waldorf Astor was a cultured man. He had been born in New York before settling in the UK at the age of ten in 1889. He later married an American, Nancy, and both became Members of Parliament. In 1926 he set out on a world tour where he became acquainted with a snack devoured by many. By way of context, it is important to set out that references to the Frankfurter sausage as a Hot Dog had appeared in the American press since the early 1890s. Yet in his diary in July 1926, whilst passing through California, he recorded that

> all through the U.S.A. one notices that Hot Dogs may be obtained. A Hot Dog is apparently a sausage and dates from an old joke that the contents of the sausage was dog! Now 'Hot Dog' is the recognised description for sausage.
>
> *(Astor 1926)*

Astor's ignorance may seem minor, but it is remains interesting. Was it a class issue? Was the Eton-educated Astor simply not *au fait* with a food largely the staple of the American working class? Was it a national issue? Or was it a technological one? Had the gospel of fast food homogenisation not spread by the 1920s? In reality, all are in large part true. There were limits to the global 1920s, therefore.

A second example concerns another English expatriate, the romantic author Elinor Glyn. By the 1920s Glyn was based in Hollywood and mixing with the stars. Yet evidently she had some difficulty understanding them – or at least liked informing English correspondents of their strange manner of talking – for she kept a list of 'Americanisms'. Some of this was rather *sui generis* – 'He's batty about some night club girl. He's gone plumb nuts about this little wren!' or 'thehellyasay!' (helpfully bracketed 'surprise'). But other terms seem almost modern valley girl – 'he's kind of falling for you' or 'don't you never quit (drop the subject)' (Glyn n.d.). In part, of course, this was a relic of the pre-talkie era. American voices could be heard on radio but not on the big screen. The homogenisation of a universal, predominantly Americanised English language would take a few decades to reach fruition.

Music and nightlife

Debates over homogenisation were also true of music and nightlife, though here the American cultural influences made clear earlier inroads. Certainly there can be few more enduring symbols of the 1920s than jazz. This was famously a black art form in a white-dominated world, initially basing itself in the New York borough of Harlem, and its dissemination also touched upon issues of both race and class. As the Marxist historian Eric Hobsbawm – writing under the pseudonym Francis Newton – noted, the crucial factor in the development of jazz, as of all American popular music, the factor which more than any other accounts for the unique American phenomenon of a vigorous and resistant folk-music in a rapidly expanding capitalist society, is that it was never swamped by the cultural standards of the upper classes. (Newton 1960: 43)

Emerging out of New Orleans and the Deep South, black migration to northern American cities in the 1910s produced a jazz diaspora that resulted in several different sounds. The sheer proliferation of jazz as an industry created work for many – by the early 1930s there were around 60,000 jazz bands and almost 200,000 professional musicians in the United States (Newton 1960: 64). Ironically, this number included white musicians seeking to restore the 'true' New Orleans sound from a supposedly bastardised form of music Louis Armstrong in Chicago or Duke Ellington in Harlem (both African-American) had moved towards. Such cultural appropriation was always a possibility – indeed the various 'schools' such as bebop or swing – were often terms created by white music critics often more hazy on the details than such intellectual grandstanding suggested. But the art form as a whole (evidenced by the success of Ellington's 'Creole Love Call' and the show tunes of George and Ira Gershwin) was a worldwide sensation. Not everyone was pleased. One Australian told the *Sydney Evening News* that

when [jazz] grows older it may become civilized … Or some inventor may discover a silencer the wearer of which will be able to sleep and smile in the presence of a whole orgy of saxophones and other super noises of our modern civilisation.
(Sydney Evening News, 30 December 1927)

But the fact that this debate was even taking place at all was testament to the fact that this person had lost that particular argument.

Jazz was closely associated with sex from its inception. The term itself originated in the early twentieth century as a slang word for sex, and the rhythms, instrumentations and lyrics of popular songs were risible to traditionalists (song titles were themselves often suggestive: 'Squeeze Me', 'I've Found a New Baby', along with 'Creole Love Call', were among the decade's hits). Moral panic over both sex and the racial aspects of jazz soon resulted. Henry Ford's *Dearborn Independent* published an article in 1921 headlined 'Jewish jazz becomes our national music' that described the musical form as being 'of Jewish origin' and controlled by Jewish companies trying to destroy American values:

Monkey talk, jungle squeals, grunts and squeaks and gasps suggestive of cave love are camouflaged by a few feverish notes and admitted to homes where the thing itself, unaided by the piano, would be stamped out in horror … In decent parlors the fluttering music sheets disclosed expressions taken directly from the cesspools of modern capitals, to be made the daily slang, the thoughtlessly hummed remarks of high school boys and girls … It is rather surprising, is it not, that whichever way you turn to trace the harmful streams of influence that flow through society, you come upon a group of Jews?

(Various Authors n.d.: 178)

Anti-Semitic slurs and moral panic aside, jazz rapidly became popular among American young people who were able to play the music at home thanks to the phonograph. While many radio stations in the 1920s remained reluctant to play music associated with the African-American community, the phonograph made it possible to play music of any sort in the privacy of the home. In 1927, a survey of African-American homes in a destitute section of Georgia found that none had a radio, but almost 20 per cent had a phonograph (Kyvig 2004: 202). In a community suffering from deep poverty, this clearly showed the priorities of those with any amount of disposable income. Jazz itself become more 'respectable' for white audiences after George Gershwin composed 'Rhapsody in Blue' in 1924, demonstrating that the more respectable and traditional instruments of the piano and orchestra could be fused with jazz to produce exciting results (Kyvig 2004: 70–80). Jazz became the hallmark American music of the 1920s to the extent that author F. Scott Fitzgerald branded the decade as 'the Jazz Age'. The fact that the music was always associated with youth, sex and illegal alcohol throughout the decade made Fitzgerald's nomenclature even more imbued with significance.

There were certainly other ways to enjoy an evening if one were not interested in jazz, however. Travelling through the French capital to promote his film *The Kid* in 1921, Charlie Chaplin took in several of the evening hotspots. At the Palais Royale in Montmartre he remarked that the Parisian scene was 'a novelty. Different. Seems several steps ahead of America. And it has atmosphere, something entirely its own, that you feel so much more than the tangible things around you'. Amused by a woman wearing a monocle and entranced by 'simple, exotic, neurotic music', he people-watched for several minutes. A couple were

> dancing a tango. It is entertainment just to watch them. The pauses in the music, its dreamy cadences, its insinuation, its suggestiveness, its whining, almost monotonous swing. It is tropical yet, this Paris. And I realize that Paris is at a high pitch. Paris has not yet had relief from the cloddy numbness brought on with the war. I wonder will relief come easily or will there be a conflagration?
>
> (Chaplin 1922: 109)

Crossing the border later in the tour he conversely noted that 'Germany is beautiful. Germany belies the war ... Men, women and children are all at work. They are facing their problem and rebuilding. A great people, perverted for and by a few' (Chaplin 1922: 114). At Berlin's Scala café he was disappointed at the lack of 'pretty girls' but was impressed with the 'modernist style of architecture'. This included

> mottled sea green walls, shading into light verdigris and emerald, leaning outward at an angle, thereby producing an effect of collapse and forward

motion … The whole effect is weird, almost ominous. The shape of the room in its ground plan is itself irregular – the impression is that of a frozen catastrophe. Yet this feeling seems to be in accord with the mood of the revelers in Germany today.

(Chaplin 1922: 116)

As for Chaplin's homeland, as Richard Bennett noted, in the 1920s 'London provided a gay and illegal night life … [where] it was always possible to buy drinks at exorbitant prices out of hours' (Bennett 1961: 115). Foremost amongst this revelry was the Irishwoman Kate Meyrick. Meyrick ran the famous 43 Club in London's Gerrard Street, Soho. She was often in and out of prison – five times in total – as she flouted drinking laws brought in during the First World War. Her interests lay beyond Soho however: Regent Street's Silver Slipper saw its polished glass floor experience a police raid over Christmas 1927. For all the risk, the rewards for such dicing with the law were obvious though, with Meyrick – a woman who had come to London with barely a few pounds to her name in 1919 – amassing over half a million pounds by the late 1920s. Despite the then Conservative Home Secretary William Joynson-Hicks often being regarded as to the right of Mussolini, Meyrick remained remarkably trouble-free given the open and financially lucrative ways in which she was flouting the law. Partly, one suspects, this was because so many influential types – politicians, journalists, legal big-wigs and general opinion formers – were making use of such facilities. At a profit of around £100,000 per jail term she served, this was probably an arrangement many contemporaries would have taken.

The situation was ostensibly quite different in the United States, where the Eighteenth Amendment to the US Constitution had banned the production and sale (though technically not the consumption) of alcohol beginning in January 1920. The Volstead Act, as Prohibition was frequently known, was somewhat farcical from the start: the ban applied to beverages with more than 0.5 per cent alcohol, covering both beer and hard liquor, but did not apply to beverages that had not been proven to be intoxicating. As a result, California grape growers were legally able to ship 'grape juice' that included a label 'warning' that if the juice were allowed to sit and ferment for 60 days it would develop 12 per cent alcohol content. The California grape industry quadrupled over the decade as a result, helping give birth to one of the state's biggest industries today (Kyvig 2004: 20–1). Home cider makers and 'moonshiners' – illegal alcohol makers, usually in the rural American South, producing hard liquor at night in the woods, hence the nickname – continued to skirt the law throughout the decade. Dedicated home moonshiners around the country found they could make (often dangerous) hard liquor in their bathtubs, with the result being colloquially referred to as 'bathtub gin'. More respectably, beer and even whisky could be legally obtained from a pharmacy with a doctor's prescription (Kyvig 2004: 22). A national Prohibition Unit was established to enforce Prohibition against violations of the law, but funding and salaries were low, making the agents easy prey for bribery and corruption. Members of Congress themselves flouted the law, consuming alcohol in Washington restaurants, and, as will be seen, President Harding himself was known to drink heavily with Washington journalists, among others (Cashman 1998: 213).

At the same time, outside America's big cities, the available evidence indicates that Prohibition was reasonably effective. Average liquor consumption per person was estimated to have dropped by nearly half from the pre-First-World-War period to 1921 (Cashman 1998: 210; Kyvig 2004: 24). A nationwide study in 1926 indicated that in most medium-sized American cities, alcohol consumption had disappeared almost entirely. By the late 1920s, the cost of illegal alcohol on the black market had been driven up so high that most middle-class families could no longer afford to partake on a regular basis. At the same time, consumption of Coca-Cola skyrocketed, as did that of coffee (Kyvig 2004: 21).

The major American cities were a very different story, however. Illegal 'speakeasies' – secret bars, often behind an unmarked door, a basement or a back room – flourished in the big cities. The New York City police commissioner claimed in the middle years of the decade that there were around 32,000 speakeasies in the city at the height of Prohibition (Cashman 1998: 212). By definition, speakeasies were beyond the scope of the law, meaning that there was not only no police protection for patrons but that they were also run by criminal enterprises rather than reputable business owners. Every form of vice could generally be found, and violence was common. Even the highbrow press could hardly print enough stories highlighting the scandals that took place in them. 'Patrolman is shot in barroom hold up' read the front page of *The New York Times* in 1929, covering the story of a police officer who had stopped at an 'alleged speakeasy' (with the exact address given, presumably in case readers wanted to inspect the premises themselves) and was critically wounded when the establishment was robbed by gun-toting robbers (*New York Times*, 23 December 1929). Throughout the year, *The New York Times* used the term 'speakeasy' more than 500 times in its pages, mostly in stories related to homicide and other violent crimes (ProQuest n.d.).

Violence and illegal alcohol were integrally related beyond speakeasies as well. Canada's vast and mostly rural border with the United States became the centre of massive alcohol smuggling operations by 'bootleggers' who took great risks to bring their products to American cities (and claim huge profits). In addition to the obvious danger of capture and imprisonment, bootleggers often fell out with one another with violent results. Al Capone became the most famous gangster in the country's bootlegging racket, taking control of wide swathes of Chicago and netting an astonishing $105 million in profits in 1927. With the mayor of Chicago and other politicians in his pocket, Capone operated a vast criminal enterprise and was only brought down by federal officials when it emerged that he had not reported his (illegal) earnings on his federal tax returns (Cashman 1998: 212).

While Capone presented himself as a businessman, violence was part-and-parcel of his techniques. On 14 February 1929, six of Capone's mob rivals and another man were brutally executed by mobsters wearing police uniforms and armed with Thompson submachine guns in a Chicago garage in what became known as the St Valentine's Day Massacre. The story became front-page news across the country, and *The New York Times* was among the papers casting clear blame on Capone and Prohibition itself for the violence. 'The killings have stunned the citizenry of Chicago as well as the Police Department, and while tonight there was no solution, the one outstanding cause was illicit liquor traffic', the paper reported (*New York Times*, 15 February 1929).

These constant stories of lawlessness, violence and moral decline began to wear on the American public. Alcohol brought many undeniable social ills, but the rise of organised crime and the level of violence that seemed to be permeating society were becoming increasingly worrying to many. Americans were constantly inundated with press coverage and stories about how readily the law was being flouted in the country's big cities, creating a distinctive allure for young people around the country who wanted their own taste of the excitement and flocked to the urban areas. F. Scott Fitzgerald's *The Great Gatsby* was only one of the novels of the era that were rife with tales of booze-soaked parties and the outlaws who had become obscenely rich selling alcohol at inflated prices. Prohibition would not formally be brought to an end until the ratification of the Twenty-First Amendment in 1933 (because the Volstead Act had become national law through a Constitutional amendment, it took another amendment to repeal it). By then, support for Prohibition had declined precipitously. A nationwide survey in late 1936 reported that 65 per cent of Americans would not support the reinstatement of national prohibition if given the option (Gallup 1936). Significantly, however, the end of the Eighteenth Amendment did not mean that alcohol became legal immediately everywhere. States, counties and cities were allowed to ban alcohol at the local level, and, at the time of writing, hundreds of US counties, mostly in the South, remain officially 'dry'.

Outside the United States, Prohibition had distinct effects as well. In 1921, the US Congress passed a bill allowing the Coast Guard to search all foreign vessels before they entered American waters and confiscate those found to be unloading illegal alcohol. This legislation was particularly directed at British captains, who were known to smuggle in alcohol from the Bahamas, and the law clearly flew in the face of international law since the vessels were to be boarded while they were still in international waters. (The British Foreign Office chuckled bitterly over the fact that the War of 1812, along with numerous other Anglo-American diplomatic incidents, had been partially precipitated by the Royal Navy boarding American vessels on the high seas to search and seize them, and now the shoe had ended up on the other foot.) In the end, a compromise was reached in which the British were allowed to serve and carry alcohol on passenger liners docking at US ports as long as the booze was safely stowed, giving British liners a huge commercial advantage over American companies, which were strictly forbidden from serving alcohol even when they were at sea (Moser 1999: 33–4). While resulting in a victory for both sides, the episode illustrated the strange contortions that Prohibition had created in the international sphere. At the same time, European alcohol consumption was changing as well. French wine production rose from around 59 hectolitres in 1920 to 65 by 1929. Conversely, German production fell by around

16 per cent. As transport links re-emerged after the war, many international wine connoisseurs began to buy French and turn their noses up at the produce of their former enemy.

Fashion and sexuality

Another hallmark of the new era emerging during the 1920s was the clothing worn by young women. By the mid-1920s, skirts rose to just below the knee from a near full-length pre-war look, and the amount of material needed for a complete woman's outfit shrank from around 20 yards before the war to less than ten by the flapper age of the 1920s. This did not happen overnight. Developments in fashion were relatively slow and piecemeal until the mid-1920s with a more adventurous (or, for more conservative contemporary commentators, debauched) style coming more or less into being alongside the economic pick-up experienced by nations from Germany to America at this time. With increased disposable incomes, both men and women wanted to have fun. For women, out were long, flowing locks of hair and the shorter 'bob' became the haircut of choice for the 1920s would-be fashionista. The debate whether all this sexualised or de-sexualised women is certainly contentious. On the one hand, the pre-war hourglass figure with emphasis on the bust was out. On the other, shorter skirts meant an increased focus for men's eyes on women's legs. In any case, some changes were partly just technological. Prior to the 1920s many garments had been fastened with laces or buttons. But the 1920s saw the development of the zipper, and this opened the way to new styles (and, for women, increased wearing of trousers).

As described elsewhere in this volume, as sexual mores changed there were significant societal and demographic consequences. In the Netherlands, where the General League of Roman Catholic Caucuses remained the largest political party throughout the 1920s, illegitimate births as a percentage of the total fell from just over 2 percent of all births to around 1.7 per cent between 1920 and 1930. In more left-leaning Germany, the 1920s saw 150,000 illegitimate births, a figure which halved in the early 1930s before bouncing back up under the Nazis (and their desire for the master race to replicate itself regardless of marital constraints). The English legal system also began to adapt to the new terrain. Under English law a bastard was unable to become an heir to property, a situation which it was difficult to rectify even with the subsequent marriage of their parents. The Legitimacy Act of 1926 changed this by legitimising the birth of a child if both parents subsequently married one another (providing neither party had been married to someone else in the interim). Conversely, as soldiers returned from the war marriage rates increased drastically too – in 1913 the German marriage rate had been 7.7 per 1,000 people, by 1920 it was 14.8. People clung to different forms of living.

The changing sexual mores of the 1920s also affected groups that had previously been confined to the margins of society, and while widespread toleration of non-heterosexual relationships was still decades away, important changes were already taking place. In the 1890s, British sexologist Havelock Ellis had already scandalised society by publishing on 'sexual inversion' (homosexuality) and pederasty. Flying in the face of Victorian social views, Ellis argued that there was nothing intrinsically unnatural about same-sex relations. In 1928, Radclyffe Hall published the novel *The Well of Loneliness* describing a lesbian relationship, sparking the trial of the author on obscenity charges and the confiscation and destruction of the book by British authorities. It was only after the Second World War that the novel would become widely available. While both Oxford and Cambridge Universities, not to mention London, had thriving homosexual sub-cultures in the 1920s, they were still kept in the shadows by both the law and social conventions (Kennedy 2008: 27–9). Economist John Maynard Keynes was among the men who actively pursued illegal sex with other men in the under-ground gay culture of London and Cambridge, actively recording the details of his hundreds of encounters in a series of remarkable lists (Davenport-Hines 2015: passim).

Ironically, given what would come under the Nazis, in the 1920s it was Berlin that briefly became the centre of this new sexual openness, as bars and nightclubs catering to homosexuals and cross-dressers sprang up across the capital (the musical and 1972 film *Cabaret* has popularly illustrated these aspects of 1920s Berlin). Inspired to scientifically analyse the phenomena he was witnessing, Berlin sexologist Magnus Hirschfeld, himself gay, established the Institute for Sexual Science to conduct large-scale examinations of human sexuality in 1919. In the early 1920s, Hirschfeld coined the term 'transsexual' and amassed a large collection of erotica and other artefacts in the course of his research. In 1921 he was instrumental in creating the World League for Sexual Reform, an organisation dedicated to openly studying and discussing issues related to sexuality and reproduction. In addition to its research aspects, Hirschfeld's institute offered treatment to those suffering from sexual issues ranging from physical impotence to 'deviant' desires including pederasty. A number of his patients were Nazi Party members, the vast majority of whom, a colleague later claimed, were 'not … sexually normal' (Kennedy 2008: 31). Hirsch-feld's Institute would be shut down and physically destroyed by the Nazis in 1933, and he would narrowly escape by fleeing to Switzerland, where he died in 1935. The razing of the Institute was an illustration of the repression that rapidly descended on Germany's gay community after Hitler's rise to power, and homosexuality soon became punishable by confinement in a concentration camp or worse.

Sport

American sports expanded greatly throughout the 1920s. On 20 August 1920, the owners of four Ohio-based teams – the Akron Pros, Canton Bulldogs, Cleveland Indians and Dayton Triangles – gathered to form a new professional league. Initially called the American Professional Football Association (APFA), the new body began life with two 'shutouts' (the first of which was a 48–0 victory by the Rock Island Independents over the St Paul Ideals). In 1922 the APFA changed its name to the instantly recognisable National Football League (NFL) and expanded to new territories including New York (the Giants joining in 1925) and Detroit (the then Panthers joining the same year).

Baseball too increased its reach. Following the 1919 Black Sox scandal – when eight Chicago White Sox players were accused of intentionally losing games after being bribed by professional gamblers – the sport got back on its feet remarkably quickly and made efforts to rebuild its reputation with the appointment of a new hard-nosed commissioner and the lifetime banning of eight White Sox players involved in the case. Losing the heart of their team, the White Sox were devastated for decades and would not make it back to the World Series until 1959 (Reisler 2006: 237). Scandal aside, the first two decades of the twentieth century had generally been known as the dead-ball era – low-scoring matches exacerbated by both the poor condition of the match balls used by many league teams (the ball was rarely if ever replaced during the game, making it difficult for the batter to see as it became darkened over the innings, and it was often deemed permissible for the pitcher to deliberately damage or misshape the ball to gain an advantage over the batter), and the sheer size of many fields preventing large numbers of the much-desired home runs. Improvements to both made the game more exciting for 1920s fans.

The year 1919 also saw another historic moment when the New York Yankees purchased Babe Ruth from the Boston Red Sox, with the latter not winning another World Series until the early 2000s as a result of the 'Curse of the Bambino' that had supposedly befallen it. Two years later the New York Yankees would make their first World Series final (lost 5–3 to the New York Giants). But in 1923 their first World Series title would arrive, with further triumphs in 1927 and 1928. Ruth was rewarded for his efforts and in 1922 signed a contract worth an astounding $52,000 a year (the number so chosen because Ruth claimed he had always wanted to make 'a grand a week') (Creamer 2011: 254). This was approaching the then presidential salary of some $75,000, and would soon surpass it. However, the wealth was in no way universal for players of the era: in 1927, when Ruth made $70,000, the next highest paid player made just $17,500, and most made far less (Creamer 2011: 351). Ruth was evidently worth more to the Yankees than many of their remaining players combined.

Part of the reason for these dramatic amounts of money becoming attainable was the fact that Ruth was far more than just a professional athlete; he was a cultural phenomenon. The rapid growth of radio taking place at precisely the moment he entered national prominence immediately made him a celebrity across the country, and his penchant for hitting home runs endeared him to fans who were willing to flock to the ball park – and pay for tickets – to see him slug the ball rather than tactically hit singles and doubles to advance runners, as traditional baseball strategy and managers had advocated. There was certainly no shortage of homers to drive the fans and the radio audiences wild: Ruth hit 59 in 1921, and ended the season with a batting average of .378 (meaning he hit the ball more than one third of his times at bat, which is very high and difficult for a player to do) (Reisler 2006: 239). In the 1927 season he broke his own record by hitting 60 home runs while still batting a remarkable .356 (Reisler 2006: 266–7).

Off the field, Ruth was larger than life and a hero to millions of young Americans. He was a notorious womaniser despite being married, and had a renowned appetite for illegal booze, cigars and food. His hard-luck story of having grown up in a Baltimore orphanage, only to be redeemed from the vagaries of this existence by his baseball prowess, was perhaps the most quintessentially American story one could conceive. His ego was undeniably huge, he often had a crude tongue, and he showed little to no respect for any form of authority. Meeting President Warren G. Harding on a hot Washington day, he reportedly remarked to the country's chief executive, 'Hot as hell, ain't it, Prez?' The press, and the public, could hardly get enough of him (Creamer 2011: 20–5, 319).

The 1927 season was the peak for the Yankees, with Ruth now joined in the starting line-up by a young Lou Gehrig, who matched Ruth in home runs for most of the season. Ruth knocked his record-breaking sixtieth home run in the second to last game of the season but it was Gehrig who won the Most Valuable Player award. The Yankees won a record number of games that season and swept the

FIGURE 4.2 George Herman 'Babe' Ruth was not only the greatest hitter of his generation, but also became a hero to millions of Americans and an international celebrity.

Pirates in the World Series (Creamer 2011: 308–10). In 1930, Ruth signed a two-year contract with the Yankees for $80,000 a year, giving him a larger salary than President Herbert Hoover. The Yankees would once again sweep the World Series in 1928, but not win again until 1932. Ruth played his last full season in 1934 and died of cancer in 1948 at the age of just 53. His Yankee teammate and rival, Gehrig, tragically died in 1941 at the age of 37 after being diagnosed with the degenerative disease amyotrophic lateral sclerosis (ALS), often now referred to as Lou Gehrig's disease.

American football and baseball were fundamentally US sports. While figures like Ruth and Gehrig were household names in the United States, in most other countries they were known primarily as celebrities rather than as athletes. Ruth, for instance, was appalled when he visited Paris in the mid-1930s and found that he was virtually unknown there (though he had received a hero's welcome when he visited Japan and took part in several games against Japanese teams there). In London he found more receptive audiences and even took a brief cricket lesson, demonstrating the obvious similarities between the two sports (Creamer 2011: 381–2).

For most of the world, however, it was not baseball or cricket that was the sport of primary interest, but football (soccer, to Americans). Association football was burgeoning in popularity at the same time as baseball was expanding in popularity in the United States. In the three summer Olympics of Antwerp 1920, Paris 1924 and Amsterdam 1928 football was played by male competitors (women would have to wait until 1996). In 1929 Uruguay was chosen to host the first FIFA World Cup of 1930 over bids from Italy, Sweden, the Netherlands and Spain. But it was in club football where perhaps the greatest breakthroughs occurred. In 1923 Bolton Wanderers defeated West Ham United in an English FA Cup Final attended by over 125,000 people, the largest attendance for a football match in the world to that point.

But the interest in football went beyond such one-off occasions, and indeed beyond international borders. In the early 1920s several states that had been part of the old Austro-Hungarian Empire – including Austria (1924), Hungary (1925) and Czechoslovakia (1926) started professional football leagues. The central European café of the 1920s – particularly in Jewish areas of major cities – was often full of conversation over the tactics, personalities and results of such entities. Crucially however, the Austrian association believed this was high time for a transnational network of football clubs and so, in 1927, the Mitropa Cup was formed. Initially involving two teams each from Austria, Hungary, Czechoslovakia and Yugoslavia, Italian clubs entered the competition from 1929 with other central European nations following in the 1930s. Two of the early winners – Sparta Prague and Ferencvaros – would go on to become big names in European football in later decades. The Mitropa Cup itself is regarded as a forerunner to the present UEFA Champions League.

The economics of soccer remained much more modest. In the year Babe Ruth signed his $52,000 a year contract, the maximum wage for a British footballer was capped at £8 a week (£6 over the summer), with the potential for a loyalty bonus of £650 over five years. To have earned £400 a year through soccer would have been a positive extravagance and this maximum wage legislation remained in place until the early 1960s. Transfer fees remained limited too. In 1928 Arsenal signed the first £10,000 player, David Jack from Bolton Wanderers. The lack of professionalism that then marked the game can be gleaned from the fact that in order to negotiate the fee downwards from Bolton's request for £13,000, the long-serving Arsenal manager Herbert Chapman took his counterpart negotiators out to get drunk. Meeting in a hotel with Bolton officials, Chapman tipped a waiter £2 to have himself served 'gin' and tonic with the gin removed, and his own club administrator 'whisky' and dry ginger with no whisky. The Bolton representatives were given no such remission and as they became ever more intoxicated the price gradually dropped.

Whilst football was an English export largely at this stage to Europe (and European communities in Latin America), cricket was an almost exclusively imperial affair. In the 1920s the de facto test-playing nations – the highest, five-day form of international competition – were England, Australia, South Africa, New Zealand (not formally a test-playing nation but often included in Antipodean tours) and the West Indies (whose first test was played in 1928). Australia would win the famous 'Ashes' series against the mother country in 1920/21 and 1924/25 with England achieving victory in 1926. This was still a relatively convivial affair played by gentlemen, though many of the same competitors were involved in the infamous 1932/3 'Bodyline' Ashes – when England elected to bowl hard and fast at the batsman's body in order to induce him to prod his bat at the ball in self-defence and provide an easy catch. At the time this was considered extremely controversial, though sporting norms would surely change as the decades moved on.

Conclusion

The 1920s were certainly not all roaring or upbeat, but in significant ways people did indeed begin to enjoy life again after the horrors of war. Hollywood movies started as a fad that would never last, but by the beginning of our period (and certainly by mid-way through it) they had become the primary form of escapism that would dominate Western life until the take-off of television in the 1940s and 1950s. Similarly, in 1920s Germany the Nazis complained about the 'negroid wailings' of jazz but politically they were nowhere and the sound of jazz was everywhere. By the 1940s jazz had become so mainstream that the Nazis created a swing band of their own ('Charlie and his Orchestra') to combine hit American tunes with pro-German propaganda lyrics ('Let's Go Bombing' was the title of one such bizarre song) for broadcast to Britain and the United States. Fitzgerald's declaration that the 1920s were the 'Jazz Age' was a reflection of not only the music's popularity but also its social associations with sex and alcohol.

Both of these were also controversial throughout the decade. Sexual mores changed rapidly, with women's skirts getting shorter and, as the chapter on gender notes, the expansion of women's opportunities in a number of areas. However, progress would only go so far: 'respectable' women were still expected to marry and return to more traditional roles afterward, while homosexuality was still not a discussed topic in most places, with a few notable exceptions. In the United States, alcohol became one of the decade's key social touchstones, with Prohibition creating a widespread reduction in drinking habits but at the same time being flouted in the country's big cities and capital. The rise of organised crime, and the violence that came with it, scandalised many and led to the question of whether Prohibition was desirable even if it had reduced alcohol consumption. By the mid-1930s, a strong majority of Americans were not in favour of returning to the 'dry' days of the 1920s.

Beyond film and music, the popular entertainment of the 1920s revolved around sport. In the United States, baseball was the national pastime, with Babe Ruth captivating the national imagination and becoming a hero to millions. He was joined by a roster of superstars who became at least locally famous and often had national name recognition as well. The World Series would annually captivate the country, thanks to the emergent technology of radio that could narrate its games on a real-time basis to listeners around the country. The newsreel of course also had an impact, making Babe Ruth recognisable to fans as far away as Japan and Britain.

Outside the United States, where other sports remained dominant, sport became a truly global affair with increased transport links making it possible to operate transnational football competitions (and plan for a 1930 World Cup in South America), and allow the British Lions Rugby team to visit South Africa in 1924 (losing all but one of the four matches) and Argentina (winning all nine games) in 1927. By 1928 46 nations (including, for the first time after the war, Germany) were competing at the Olympic Games in Amsterdam with almost 3,000 athletes being selected for competition. India's first gold medal in field hockey and Uruguay's victory in the football tournament were evidence of the increasing global nature of the 1920s – as was Coca-Cola's first Olympic sponsorship that year.

All told, the 1920s are often associated in the popular imagination with glamour, decadent parties, flappers and illegal booze (the latter in the United States, at least). As our (second) chapter on class shows, this was not a universal experience, nor was it the experience of most. Yet the images of the decade created by Fitzgerald and the literary scene of the era were clearly rooted in some elements of truth. There was fun to be had in this turbulent decade and whether experienced second-hand through movies or the more direct route of the speakeasy, many were determined to have it. With the impending economic crash that would end the decade (and all the problems this brought global citizenry), this was probably no bad thing.

Questions

- What factors led to Hollywood films becoming so internationally popular in the 1920s?
- Did Prohibition fail in the United States? Why or why not?

- Why was jazz viewed with such suspicion in the United States? What factors led to its eventual success?
- Why was Babe Ruth able to gain a level of international fame that no other athlete had ever been able to achieve?

Recommended further reading

Kennedy, P. (2008), *The First Man-Made Man*, London: Bloomsbury.

Kyvig, D.E. (2004), *Daily Life in the United States, 1920–1940: How Americans Lived Through the Roaring Twenties and the Great Depression*, Chicago: Ivan R. Dee.

Newton, F. (1960), *The Jazz Scene*, London: Monthly Review Press.

Works cited

Astor, W. (1926), Journals held at the University of Reading, MS 1066/1/36, 26 July.

Bennett, R. (1961), *A Picture of the Twenties*, London: Vista.

Carr, R. (2017), forthcoming political biography of Charlie Chaplin, London: Routledge.

Cashman, S.D. (1998), *America Ascendant: From Theodore Roosevelt to FDR in the Century of American Power, 1901–1945*, New York: New York University Press.

Chaplin, C. (1922), *My Trip Abroad*, New York: Harper and Brothers.

Creamer, R.W. (2011), *Babe: The Legend Comes to Life*, New York: Simon and Schuster.

Davenport-Hines, R. (2015), *Universal Man: The Seven Lives of John Maynard Keynes*, London: William Collins.

Gallup (1936), via The Roper Center for Public Opinion Research, www.ropercenter.uconn.edu

Glyn, E. (n.d.), Journals held at the University of Reading, MS 4059, Box 24.

Kennedy, P. (2008), *The First Man-Made Man*, London: Bloomsbury.

Kyvig, D.E. (2004), *Daily Life in the United States, 1920–1940: How Americans Lived Through the Roaring Twenties and the Great Depression*, Chicago: Ivan R. Dee.

Moser, J.E. (1999), *Twisting the Lion's Tail: American Anglophobia between the World Wars*, New York: New York University Press.

Newton, F. (1960), *The Jazz Scene*, London: Monthly Review Press.

ProQuest Historical Newspapers (n.d.), *The New York Times* with Index.

Reisler, J. (2006), *Babe Ruth: Launching the Legend*, New York: McGraw-Hill.

Ross, S.J. (2011), *Hollywood Left and Right: How Movie Stars Shaped American Politics*, Oxford: Oxford University Press.

Various Authors (n.d.), *The Jewish Question: A Selection of the Articles (1920–22) Published by Mr. Henry Ford's Paper The Dearborn Independent and Reprinted Later Under the General Title of The International Jew*, London: M.C.P. Publications.

5

ART, LITERATURE AND THE CONVERGENCE OF CULTURE AND POLITICS

If Hollywood constituted the home of the burgeoning cinematic empire, it was in Paris where literature's leading names gathered during the 1920s. During the decade referred to in French as *les années folles* – the crazy years – many gathered in the Francophone world to artistically chronicle them. Indeed, T.S. Elliot, F. Scott Fitzgerald, Ezra Pound and Wyndham Lewis were but some of the names who passed through the city of lights in that period. There they wrote, discussed and debated literary ideals, had affairs, and tried to make sense of a changing world. The safe age of 1914 had been torn apart by the horrors of war, and the sense of transience about the new world – with its jazz, its cocktail parties, and its changing (and loosening) morals – marked the work of all such figures.

And then there was Ernest Hemingway, who moved with his then-wife Hadley Richardson to Paris in 1921. His five years in the French capital were chronicled in his posthumously published work *A Moveable Feast* (1964). The inspiration behind this work tells much about the way the Hemingways lived in the 1920s. In 1956 the Ritz Hotel in Paris tried, eventually successfully, to convince Hemingway to reclaim two small steamer trunks he had stored there since his March 1928 move to Florida (second wife now in tow). These held numbered pages of fiction, general notes, books, and even old clothes. Not much from these scribblings made it into the final manuscript, though they seem to have provided the impetus for Hemingway to set pen to page.

It is a good thing he did. Together with *The Sun Also Rises*, Hemingway's 1926 novel that included depictions of Anglo-Americans enjoying the seedy café life of contemporary Paris, *A Moveable Feast* forms a vital historical record of an important period in literary history. By the first chapter, the sheer relentless alcohol consumption of such authors – outside, for many, their home of Prohibition-era America – becomes obvious. Pitching up at a café on Paris' Place St Michel one rainy afternoon, Hemingway begins writing with just a café au lait for company.

This was quickly followed by a half-carafe of dry white wine. Then a Rum St James. Then the customary drink of kirsch 'when I would get towards the end of a story or toward the end of the day's work' (Hemingway 1964: 16, 21). And this was a relatively light afternoon.

For all the *post facto* glamour afforded to such figures, their existence was often less than secure. Hemingway kept the wolf from his Parisian door by regular journalism and was forever chasing the big cheque. For most of these authors, that cheque eventually came, but it was not always the luxury of *The Great Gatsby* for them afterwards. Hemingway and Richardson raised their son Jack (known as 'Bumby') in a two-room flat with no hot water and no inside toilet. Whittling away his afternoons at the Musée du Luxembourg, Hemingway's predilection for Cezannes, Manets and Monets was certainly nowhere close to being met with actually owning one. Only with the publication of his fictionalised memoir *A Farewell to Arms* in 1929 did Hemingway achieve financial independence.

He, like many an author, did have a (usually) friendly patron in the form of Gertrude Stein, however. The Stein salon at 27 Rue de Fleurus became something of a legend. A cadre of artists, authors and thinkers arrived, dropped off a manuscript, partook of a drink, and awaited Stein's verdict. This was all intentionally set apart from the world around them – as Hemingway recorded, Stein

> did not like to hear really bad nor tragic things, but no one does, and having seen them I did not care to talk about them unless she wanted to know how the world was going. She wanted to know the gay part of how the world was going; never the real, never the bad.
>
> *(Hemingway 1964: 57)*

She held forth on a variety of topics, and advised the young writers before her that they

> can either buy clothes or buy pictures. It's that simple. No one who is not very rich can do both. Pay no attention to your clothes and no attention at all to the *mode*, and buy your clothes for comfort and durability, and you will have the clothes and money to buy pictures … Buy the people of your own age – of your own military service group. You'll know them. You'll meet them around the quarter. There are always good new serious painters.
>
> *(Hemingway 1964: 25)*

And yet there was always one fault line between those of Stein's age (born in 1874) and those born in the 1880s and 1890s. This was given famous voice in the most mundane of locations, a trip Stein took to get her faulty Model T Ford car fixed. When the garage's *patron* had become upset at his mechanic's lethargy in addressing Stein's problem, he told his younger protégé that 'you are a *generation perdue*'. 'That's what you all are', Stein told Hemingway. 'All of you young people who served in the war. You are a lost generation' (Hemingway 1964: 61). When asked to clarify this, Stein remarked that 'you have no respect for anything [and] you drink yourselves to death'. Hemingway, ironically, queried her assertion regarding alcohol. But the wider claim regarding the impact of the war on this generation was astute. Hemingway himself denied it. Staring at a statue of Marshall Ney, a general during the Napoleonic Wars, with a cold beer in hand he declared 'the hell with her lost-generation talk and all the dirty, easy labels' (Hemingway 1964: 62). And yet sitting at the Closerie des Lilas, Hemingway noticed those who wore

> Croix de Guerre ribbons in their lapels and others … [with] the yellow and green of the Medaille Militaire, and I watched to notice how well they were overcoming the handicap of the loss of limbs, or the quality of their artificial eyes and the degree of skill with which their faces had been reconstructed.

'In those days', he remarked sharply, 'we did not trust anyone who had not been in the war, but we did not completely trust anyone' (Hemingway 1964: 74).

To this 'lost generation', the war had also imbued a sixth sense – the ability to both weave tales, and detect when others were doing similar. As Hemingway noted, 'in Italy when I was at the war …, for one thing that I had seen or that had happened to me, I knew many hundreds of things that had happened to other people who had been in the war in all of its phases'. This 'gave me a touchstone by which I could tell whether stories were false or true' (Hemingway 1964: 181). This was a point that extended beyond the written word in the 1920s. As discussed elsewhere in this work, several political ideologies attempted to lend meaning to the experience of the First World War. This was most obviously true in the case of German and Italian Fascism – explicitly predicated on the lessons of the ex-servicemen – but the democracies were not above doing similar: mainstream British politicians such as Clement Attlee, Anthony Eden and Harold Macmillan all wore their military titles into Parliament, and all sold a narrative of the war experience for electoral gain (Carr 2013: passim).

Most importantly in terms of culture, Hemingway's oeuvres of this period gave light to what became known in literary circles as the 'Iceberg Theory'. This was the assertion of a minimalist style of prose that described what characters were doing rather than their motivations behind such actions. Arguably – particularly when describing the events of conflict – this provided a means whereby authors could maintain a degree of cognitive dissonance from their creations. But it lent a particular style to the work of Hemingway – a matter of fact, descriptive voice that concealed a barely contained rage behind the mundane. Hemingway's sentences were long and windy rather than analytic.

He was not the only author sheltering beneath the iceberg, however. Ford Madox Ford, whom Hemingway encountered in Paris, would write his famous *Parade's End* tetralogy between 1924 and 1928. The protagonist of these novels is Christopher Tietjens, a bright statistician at the British Treasury who later serves during the First World War. His wife Sylvia is brash, raucous and prone to affairs, his lover Valentine an outgoing suffragette taking on the establishment. Tietjens, for all his ability, remains passive. Events – the war, his marriage – seem to pass him by. He is portrayed as an anachronism, the last relic of stoic, Tory England. The world had left him and his kind behind.

The poignancy of the conflict would also be chronicled by Robert Graves (who wished the British nation *Goodbye to All That* before promptly fleeing the symptoms of post-traumatic stress disorder to Mallorca) from one side, and Erich Maria Remarque's *All Quiet on the Western Front* from the other. In *The Nation*, the author Robert Herrick compared Hemingway and Remarque:

> both 1929 novels deal with the filth of war, but the American's outsider status guarantees its 'amateurish taint.' Hemingway's dirt is the squalor of the 'boudoir, the brothel and the bar' – the milieu of the Ambulance driver – not the 'clean human dirt' of the soldier: 'We were amateurs in the great struggle, never rightly understanding what it was all about, often generous and gallant and efficient amateurs, but never quite grown up; so that our literature drawn from that source must have the unsubstantiality and superficiality of the amateur'.
>
> *(Hutner 2009: 112)*

Arguably this was a little harsh: Hemingway had after all been wounded by a battlefield mortar and won the Italian Silver Medal of Bravery. But it was clear that tragedy sold.

On the other hand, so too could politics. Theodore Dreiser was another to reflect on 1920s mores. Dreiser was a committed socialist who visited the Soviet Union in the late 1920s. He was also fiercely opposed to the racism inherent in parts of the Southern United States, with his early work touching on the Jim Crow laws, lynching, and the general second-class status afforded to African-Americans. His big breakthrough came, however, with his 1925 novel *An American Tragedy* (later remade as the 1951 film *A Place in the Sun* and, later still, forming much of the inspiration for Woody Allen's 2005 *Match Point*).

An American Tragedy remains a classic telling of the rise and fall of a man of initially modest means in 1920s America. It takes its protagonist, Clyde Griffiths, from humble circumstance through to mixing with the high and mighty. Offered the chance to take a further step up the social ladder through acquiring a wealthy spouse, Griffiths hatches a plot to murder the one encumbrance to this – his pregnant girlfriend. In the end he protests his innocence at her eventual demise, and the murder scene is played ambiguously. But – guilty or not – the novel presents her murder as in some ways a logical end to his social climbing, and he concedes the guilt of at least wishing her dead. Interestingly, throughout the story the media is presented as both Griffiths' inspiration and his undoing. He acquires the idea to kill his girlfriend from a newspaper article but, later, it is the newspapers that frame him as a ruthless murderer before soon, after he appeals his conviction, moving on to fresher stories. This uncaring, individualistic form of capitalism was Dreiser's perpetual enemy and inspired him to join the Communist Party in 1945. The 1920s were wrought with such existential dilemmas.

The novel itself was changing throughout the 1920s. As Gordon Hutner has noted, 'when William Dean Howells died in 1920, his passing symbolised the transition between the end of one era, American Victorianism, and the beginning of another, American modernism' (Hutner 2009: 37). In a sense this was a more pessimistic form of literature, but it also involved retaining much of the previous social commentary. For Hutner, 'throughout the 1920s, one can observe efforts that decry modernism and wail over the emergence of a monstrous mass culture at one and the same time' (Hutner 2009: 44). We touch on Charlie Chaplin elsewhere in this volume, but his friendship with authors like Dreiser certainly coloured his own left-leaning art. The worry about a fast-changing world, ripped asunder by the horrors of war and potentially inclined to regress even further united both politicians and literary figures alike.

One of these new, modern writers was Upton Sinclair, whose campaign for the governorship of California in 1934 was the culmination of the sustained use of literature to make political points. His 1906 novel *The Jungle* had made his name through a tale of the poor conditions faced by Chicago immigrant labourers, but had largely captured the public attention due to its depiction of unsanitary conditions in the meat packing industry. The 1920s saw several instances of this type of radicalism. In the 1925 tract *Mammonart* Sinclair applied the socialist sense to a variety of historical painters, composers and authors. This was one of six works in his so-called 'Dead Hand' series of books which criticised the view of Adam Smith that an 'invisible hand' would guide people's self-interest in a manner that would deliver wide benefits for society as a whole.

Along similar lines, American author Sinclair Lewis spent the decade writing novels pillorying the small town life that had been idealised in Horatio-Alger-type stories for decades in the United States. *Main Street*, published in 1920, painted unflattering portraits of the provincial attitudes and ill-founded beliefs that were still common among the American population (Lewis was himself from small-town Minnesota, and drew upon this background throughout his works). Two years later, *Babbitt* parodied the superficial pretentions of a small-town businessman, and, in 1927, *Elmer Gantry* focused on the story of a preacher who had fewer genuine religious commitments than an interest in making money and attracting women. In addition to becoming one of the best-known (and wealthy) authors of the period, Lewis would be awarded the Nobel Prize in Literature.

F. Scott Fitzgerald, discussed elsewhere in this work, became the author who perhaps most closely represented the spirit of the decade. A severe alcoholic who struggled with his wife Zelda's mental health problems, Fitzgerald's 1925 *The Great Gatsby* is likely the best-known novel representing life for the rich and famous in 1920s America. Ironically, the book did not initially sell well and Fitzgerald considered it to be a failure at the time of his premature death in 1940. In addition to his most famous work, however, Fitzgerald also penned *Tales of the Jazz Age*, a compilation of short stories that included 'The Curious Case of Benjamin Button'. *The Beautiful and the Damned* (1922) and *Tender is the Night* (1934) both explored the decadence of jazz-age life in the United States and abroad (along with the struggles of shell shock, mental health problems and alcoholism).

Beyond the fictional realm, the post-1918 period saw a flurry of critiques focusing on the very notion of modernity. Most famous was Oswald Spengler's *Decline of the West* which suggested that every civilisation had a shelf-life of around a thousand years, and the West was approaching its own decline: democracy leading to concentration of wealth and a media that claims to be free and critical of the status but in reality is anything but was a natural trend in his eyes. In this fatalistic view of the world, the West stood at the abyss of its own destruction. Spengler had begun to write his magnum opus in 1911 and made several revisions throughout the First World War before its two-volume publication in 1918 and 1922.

In terms of historiography and humanity's understanding of its recent past, the 1920s saw the publication of *The Rise of American Civilisation* (1926) by Charles and Mary Beard which was a largely male-centric account of American history which also minimised the slave experience. In Britain, economic studies by R.H. Tawney highlighted the importance of religion in the rise of capitalism, whilst Lewis Namier began his long career of prosopographical studies with a 1929 account of George III. Outside of Europe, studies began to turn away from the high political and towards the everyday – particularly in Japan through the work of historians like Tsuda Sokichi. But, overall, it is fair to say the grand narrative of big figures making or breaking history still dominated the canon.

Indeed, it was perhaps with two Marxists, Georg Lukács and Antonio Gramsci, that literary and cultural criticism found its most perceptive critics. For both, history was clearly a living, breathing thing. For Lukács, the experience of the failed Hungarian revolution of 1919 had only strengthened his belief that all history was the history of class conflict. His book *History and Class Consciousness* (1923) – which posited that Marx had been misunderstood as being obsessed with commodities and not his true interest, people – was swiftly condemned by Moscow and withdrawn from publication (to be republished in the 1960s).

For Gramsci, the consequences of being a Western Marxist in the 1920s were even worse – the fascist dictatorship in Italy locked him up for 11 years of imprisonment. But there, something of a small comfort admittedly, he could write and think. In his *Prison Notebooks* Gramsci put forward the notion of hegemony – the winning of the hearts and minds of the working class. He believed that purely economic explanations of the rise of Mussolini involving a conspiratorial elite advancing the figure who would most bend to their will was no longer enough. Western Marxism, embodied through these two figures who would come to prominence in the post-1945 epoch, had been born.

Art and design

With the dislocation of war came the dislocation of art across the globe. From 1922 onwards the Mexican painter Diego Rivera painted murals across several cities – eventually spanning from Mexico City to San Francisco and Detroit.

Schooled in pre-war Paris, Rivera had witnessed the birth of the cubist tradition under Picasso and Braque, and taken much on board. Cezanne was also an inspiration. In 1922 Rivera joined the Mexican Communist Party and his pictures often had a distinctly political bent. His mural at the National Palace in Mexico City took six years, involved over 100 frescoes, and remains to this day. In 1927 he visited Moscow where he was commissioned to paint a mural for the Red Army club, but he would be expelled due to perceived anti-Soviet leanings – which in turn contributed to his expulsion from the Mexican Communist Party. As Gerry Souter notes, to

> succeed in Mexico [Rivera] had to embrace art for the common people, art that taught through recognisable images, art that became part of the architecture symbolising the merger of government, its history, the natural abundance of the land and the will of the people. He embraced an art form that was the product of a collective of talents. All this came together at a point in history where Diego Rivera stood commanding the tools and the imagination to bring this proletariat form of storytelling into fruition.
>
> *(Souter 2012: 109)*

Thousands of miles away in Paris, two equally famous names were getting acquainted. In 1926 Salvador Dali moved to the French capital where he encountered his great idol, Pablo Picasso. Dali was already an eccentric – he had cultivated sideburns, a coat and knee-breeches – but this association unleashed his surrealist experimentation to a degree which helped him paint perhaps his most famous work, *The Persistence of Memory* (with its melting pocket watches). In some senses however he was going against the grain. Picasso and others such as André Derain were undergoing what became known as the 'return to order'. This took artists away from avant garde experiments with cubism and back to realistic, often classical imagery.

In tandem with this shift, Art Deco – although the term would only normally be applied in retrospect – exploded as an architectural and artistic phenomenon in the 1920s. Although a slightly open-ended art form, it usually comprised a neo-classical element, often including geometric shapes and sharp, contrasting colours. Art Deco was ostentatiously grandiose and could be seen in booming cities across the globe. From the various buildings seen along Wilshire Boulevard in Los Angeles to (although only constructed from 1932) the plans for the new Senate House in London, Art Deco was an attempt to meld past and present. Nowhere was this more obvious than in the 30 metre tall statue of Christ the Redeemer in Rio de Janeiro. Not only was the style itself Art Deco, but the use of a radio-operated floodlight system (installed by Marconi) to aid the opening ceremony was testament to a future-looking focus too.

At the same time, the post-war era saw an expansion of artistic endeavours consciously attempting to question the status quo that had dominated before the First World War. In Germany, the Expressionists drew upon the mental trauma of war and its lingering effects to produce films, music, literature and painted images.

The Expressionists largely saw themselves as a response to the intellectual optimism of the nineteenth century and the view that scientific progress would inevitably improve the human condition. In contrast, the Expressionists highlighted the emotional experience of life, particularly in its darkest and most passionate moments. First World War veteran Otto Dix's *Sex Murder* depicted the grisly murder of a naked woman with a well-dressed man in a bowler hat, possibly the perpetrator, gazing on the bloodshed with what appears to be a smirk. Meanwhile, his 1924 etching *Stormtroopers Advancing Under Gas* depicted soldiers in dehumanising gasmasks launching an attack against an unseen enemy. In both cases, the combination of extreme violence coupled with the ambiguities of the image created a sense of pronounced disquiet for the viewer. Similarly, artist George Grosz lampooned both the government and the military in his works, earning him the ire of conservatives. For the Expressionists, the war had changed everything and their art was the vehicle they would use to explain their experiences (Crockett 1999: 57, 72–4).

As Eric Weitz has also noted, 'Weimar-era photographers also broke new aesthetic and theoretical ground. Convinced that photography was *the* artistic medium of modernity, they used camera and the pen to define its relationship to other art forms and our way of experiencing the world' (Weitz 2007: 214). Perhaps the most prominent exponent of this art form was the Hungarian émigré Lazlo Moholy-Nagy. Moholy-Nagy had fled Hungary when the communist revolution after the First World War had given way to authoritarian counter-revolution. Establishing a reputation in Berlin, his most famous photographs captured peaceful shots of the bustling metropolis often taken from above. He would eventually coin the dogma of 'the New Vision' that expressed his contention that photographs could reveal a new way of perceiving objects which the human eye would often miss. After the Nazis came to power his work – like many foreigners' – dried up and he eventually sought refuge in moving to London in 1935. Whilst Art Deco spoke to the successful melding of traditional and futuristic elements, there were limits here.

Colonialism and politics outside the West

As Toshiko Ellis has argued (Ellis 1999: passim), culture – including poetry and prose – was both reflective of changes in the world around it, and seeking to influence the contemporary agenda. This was particularly true of Japan. The 1920s began in Japan with an emperor, Yoshihito, plagued by neurological problems. This era – known as the Taishō period – lasted until the Emperor's death in 1926 (when he was succeeded by his son, the more militarist Hirohito) and was marked by the hoarding of power by a series of elder statesmen surrounding the emperor and increased autonomy for the Japanese Parliament. In 1920 the conservative-leaning Seiyūkai ('friends of constitutional government') were the dominant force in Japanese politics and continued to hold key positions in the cabinet throughout the 1920s. This administration faced many forms of criticism however. Prime Minister Hara – who sought to control inflation, re-draw the electoral map to ensure Seiyūkai dominance for time immemorial, and re-adjust the Japanese economy to the post-war world – was assassinated in 1921. Non-political technocratic prime ministers were appointed to steer Japan into the mid-1920s and, in order to forestall communistic agitation, a Public Security Preservation Act was passed in 1925. This new law was sold as a non-partisan means of maintaining the *kokutai* (parliamentary sovereignty) or system of private property, but was highly ambiguous. *Kokutai* as a concept was extendable to ideas of national character or identity as much as the parliamentary chamber, and thus the government had virtually dictatorial means to stamp out any form of dissent – political, artistic, or both. The Tokkō – secret police – were given a vast range of new powers, including a 'Thought Section of the Criminal Affairs Bureau'.

Japanese art and culture had to operate in this milieu. For conservative-leaning Japan, the country was being caught in a pincer movement of Western decadence and Russian communism. As Ellis notes, the way Japan 'looked' was changing:

> one of the most striking features of the cultural scene of Japan in the 1920s was the emergence of an urban mass culture of an unprecedented scale centering around the rapidly growing city of Tokyo. Various elements of everyday life newly introduced from the West, including Western fashions, customs, and ideas, were quickly absorbed and integrated into the lives of the urban populace.
>
> *(Ellis 1999: 723)*

This imbued within the Japanese intelligentsia a feeling that they were living in a moment that represented a fundamental juncture in human history.

On the one hand, as elsewhere, this produced an explosion in left-wing thought. As Ellis states, in the 1920s,

> the social position of poets and writers had also changed: they were no longer tied to the privileged class of the well-educated and had lost their status as cultural elites. 'Literature' had gradually developed into a self-generating and a self-regulating system.
>
> *(Ellis 1999: 725)*

Perhaps most provocatively, this included a new Japan Proletarian Literary Association with its own journal, *Senki (the Fighting Flag)*, in 1928. Eighteen issues of the journal were banned in all, but it still managed to maintain a peak circulation of 26,000. For such writers and thinkers, progress could mean Moscow more than it meant Manchester or Michigan. Equally, there was a slight anti-Western turn amongst other intellectuals. Many felt that the Westernisation of Japanese public life from the films discussed in chapter 4 to the café culture we will see in chapter 6 was fundamentally a negative development. Old Meiji Japan may not have had everything right, but it had been right to resist such developments, or so they argued. In the 1930s this cadre of poets and thinkers – in publications such as *Cogito* and *Jihon Romanha* – began to re-assert what they saw as the true Japan. A self-proclaimed cultural renaissance soon followed which provided something of an intellectual backdrop to the new, aggressive foreign policy pursued under Hirohito.

The global order against which Hirohito would protest attempted to execute a form of cultural and educative resistance too, however. Importantly, the 1920s saw the establishment of several new universities across the British Empire. The University of Dhaka in modern-day Bangladesh, Makarere University in Uganda, the Imperial College of Tropical Agriculture in Trinidad, Mandalay College in Rangoon, and Raffles College in Singapore were all founded in this decade. From early in the 1920s, university leaders in the Anglophone world were predicting two trends, that science would grow in importance and that the United States would soon eclipse Britain as the leading global educative power. Both were to varying degrees true, and the British concession of adopting the 'American' PhD as a method of post-graduate assessment from 1917 was seen as symptomatic of this. But if the tide was turning in many ways the university system still formed an adjunct of empire. Between 1900 and 1918 no professors from continental Europe had been recruited to the teaching staff of the University of Manchester. Some European appointments began to appear in the 1920s, but these were still heavily outnumbered by imperial-born candidates – the British preferred to draw on the sons of their colonies (Pietsch 2013: 154). Similarly, the University of Oxford's affiliation scheme – permitting students from within the Empire and beyond to use their previous university experience to shorten any Oxford degree by a year – continued into our decade, with the University of Hong Kong gaining this status in March 1920. Academic ties could often be as diplomatic as they were learned.

Of a different order altogether was the *satyagraha* philosophy preached by Mohandas (frequently known by his title of Mahatma) Gandhi. Although Gandhi's famous 400 kilometre Salt March – a protest against the levies on that good the ruling British then charged – would not take place until 1930 his leadership of the anti-colonial Indian National Congress from 1921 saw *satyagraha* writ large. The phenomenon of *satyagraha* – literally 'the insistence upon truth' – took many forms of which non-violent resistance was the most famous. As D.C. Grover observes, 'the *satyagrahi*'s selfless action persuades the public and his adversary of truth. As truth is the goal, non-violence is the means. Non-violence seems to mean the complete avoidance of any evil in thought and in action' (Grover 1977: 13). For Grover, the Gandhian dialectic contended that 'the crisis the world is experiencing is not essentially a political or economic one, but a moral and spiritual one' (Grover 1968: 227). In a world which arguably relied on these first two phenomena there were limitations here – 'Gandhi [does not] suggest how intercultural, political institutions can guide the non-West from a series of villages to one accommodating modern influences' (Grover 1968: 234) – but *satyagraha*'s lack of a concrete 'political' programme was also arguably one of its greatest selling points. In binding up means and ends Gandhi was able to avoid the traditional 'terrorist or freedom fighter' dilemma associated with many a revolutionary movement. As discussed in our first chapter, this dovetailed effectively with a British empire which was beginning to doubt its own moral validity.

The literary (and indeed global) angle to all this was two-fold. Firstly, Gandhi's *satyagraha* was profoundly influenced by the work of a novelist, the nineteenth-century American Henry David Thoreau. Having read *Walden* – the account of Thoreau's period of immersing himself amidst nature in a Massachusetts log cabin – when a lawyer in pre-war Johannesburg, South Africa (Gandhi was thereby another truly 'global' revolutionary of this era), he repeatedly remarked how influenced he had been by its content. Thoreau's combination of self-reliance and simple living did indeed seem tailored to the movement that Gandhi would eventually lead (Hendrick 1956: passim). But *satyagraha* also produced an intellectualising of Gandhi and his ushering into such august circles – both in India and the wider world. Of the latter Gandhi humorously stated, 'I have been known as a crank, faddist, mad man. Evidently the reputation is well deserved. For wherever I go, I draw to myself cranks, faddists and mad men' (Lal 2009: 282).

Yet this had effects beyond the written word or intellectual debate. By 1923, with membership having 'increased enormously' in the two years of Gandhi's leadership, there were over 100,000 members of the Indian National Congress (Krishna 1966: 419). With *satyagraha* changing the debate and the manner in which the British could respond to the idea of India independence, as the 1920s moved forward some form of revision looked ever more likely. Symbolically, the very moment our decade ended, at midnight on 31 December 1929, the Indian National Congress raised the flag of India in Lahore (now in Pakistan). Borrowing from the spirit of the American Declaration of 1776, a few weeks later Gandhi – with Jawaharlal Nehru – issued their Declaration of Independence declaring the inalienable right of the Indian people to have their freedom. The Salt March may have been the immediate consequence, but independence remained the long-term goal. The 1935 Government of India Act conceded partial devolution of power from Westminster (building on the reforms of 1919 we discuss in chapter 7), and the Second World War would lead to the creation of a fully free India. Spirituality and matters of culture had played their role in shifting such discourse.

Such machinations did not merely affect the British, however. As Dirk Hoerder notes, 'in the mid-1920s the sisters Nardal from Martinique established a salon in Paris as a center of debate and literary development where Antillean, US, and West African intellectuals met' (Hoerder 2012: 576). But Francophone debates were often centred outside the Metropole itself. An important voice here was that of René Maran, born at sea off the coast of Martinique and the first black writer to win the prestigious Prix Goncourt in 1921. Having served the French Colonial authorities in Africa, he went on to pen his prize-winning *Batouala: A True Black Novel* after the First World War. Rather like Hemingway and the Great War, Maran was also accused of not knowing of which he wrote. Some felt (and continue to feel) that Batouala's Caribbean background left him not best placed to comment on Africa – in that sense, therefore, that the 'black' experience was not universal in our global 1920s – but many view the portrayal of anti-colonial sentiment inherent throughout the book as crucial in developing the counter-cultural narrative to the colonial regime. Hemingway remarked that through the book 'you

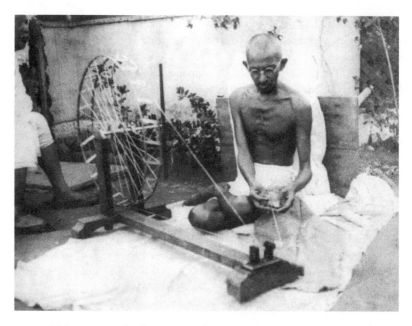

FIGURE 5.1 Mahatma Gandhi, here pictured at a spinning wheel, became an inspiration for millions in the decade in which this image was taken.

see the white man as the black man sees him … and that means it is a great novel'. If Chaplin in the West was *just* a clown, he would not have been so feared by those in high office – and the same rang true of culture in Africa and Asia. Literature, spirituality and poetry provided an avenue to shift public opinion on injustice, and that in itself was important.

Conclusion

Art and literature worldwide underwent significant changes in the 1920s. From the American expatriates drinking heavily in Paris cafés to the German Expressionists and poets in Japan, the overarching theme of the decade was the questioning of authority and the rejection of progressive optimism. The most popular literary characters of the period were men and women that audiences could directly relate to, particularly those who had seen the death and destruction of the First World War. In contrast, F. Scott Fitzgerald's work illustrated the glamorous and decadent, but ultimately superficial (and occasionally criminal), lifestyle enjoyed by the wealthy in the United States, while Sinclair Lewis brutally parodied the small town lifestyle that had been venerated in American mythology in the previous century (and still is to the present day, to some extent). Upton Sinclair used his pen to draw public attention to pressing social justice issues, to great effect. In the nonfiction realm, concerns over cultural decline and collapse, also born out of the First World War, dominated the popular works of the era.

Outside the West, art and literature were less directly impacted by the experience of war but were increasingly oriented toward political agendas of their own. Gandhi sought to promote a particularly Indian form of philosophy – *satyagraha* – for the ends of the independence movement whilst the Japanese intelligentsia looked not only at Moscow but at their own past for inspiration for a new cultural turn. Both, in their way, rejected the Western lifestyle that the cinema and the written word were propagating. As the 1920s ended culture could be both international and profoundly nationalistic.

Questions

- How did artists and writers respond to the experience of the First World War?
- Why did so many expatriate artists flock to Paris in the 1920s?
- How did politics affect art and literature of the 1920s?
- What was the relationship between art and literature and power in the 1920s?
- What did Gertrude Stein mean when she described the young people around her as a 'lost generation'? Was her assessment accurate?
- What were the major differences between Western and non-Western culture in the 1920s?

Recommended further reading

Crockett, D. (1999), *German Post-Expressionism: The Art of the Great Disorder 1918–1924*, University Park: Penn State University Press.
Fitzgerald, F.S. (1925), *The Great Gatsby*, New York: Charles Scribner's Sons.
Hemingway, E. (1964), *A Moveable Feast*, London: Jonathan Cape.
Lewis, S. (1922), *Babbitt*, New York: Harcourt, Brace and Co.

Works cited

Carr, R. (2013), *Veteran MPs and Conservative Politics in the Aftermath of the Great War*, Farnham: Ashgate.
Crockett, D. (1999), *German Post-Expressionism: The Art of the Great Disorder 1918–1924*, University Park: Penn State University Press.
Ellis, T. (1999), 'The Japanese Avant-Garde of the 1920s: The Poetic Struggle with the Dilemma of the Modern', *Poetics Today*, 20/4, 723–741.
Fitzgerald, F.S. (1925), *The Great Gatsby*, New York: Charles Scribner's Sons.
Grover, D.C. (1968), 'Dimensions of Satyagraha in Contemporary World', *Indian Journal of Political Science*, 29/3, 227–234.
Grover, D.C. (1977), 'Satyagraha and Democratic Power Structure', *Indian Journal of Political Science*, 38/1, 10–29.
Hemingway, E. (1964), *A Moveable Feast*, London: Jonathan Cape.
Hendrick, G. (1956), 'The Influence of Thoreau's "Civil Disobedience" on Gandhi's Satyagraha', *New England Quarterly*, 29/4, 462–471.
Hoerder, D. (2012), 'Migrations and Belongings', in Rosenberg, E.S. (ed.), *A World Connecting: 1870–1945*, Cambridge, MA: Harvard University Press, p. 576.

Hutner, G. (2009), *What America Read: Taste, Class and the Novel, 1920–1960*, Chapel Hill: University of North Carolina Press.

Krishna, G. (1966), 'The Development of the Indian National Congress as a Mass Organisation', *Journal of Asian Studies*, 25/3, 413–430

Lal, V. (2009), 'Gandhi's West, the West's Gandhi', *New Literary History*, 40/2, 281–313.

Pietsch, T. (2013), *Empires of Scholars: Universities, Networks and the British Academic World, 1850–1939*, Manchester: Manchester University Press.

Souter, G. (2012), *Rivera*, New York: Parkstone International.

Weitz, E.D. (2007), *Weimar Germany*, Princeton: Princeton University Press.

6

WOMEN AND SOCIETY

The 1920s are redolent with symbolism for the advancement of women. The classic example of the 1920s woman was the notorious 'flapper' who could be seen smoking, drinking, driving and, horror of horrors, adopting a liberal attitude toward sex. We are also familiar with the oft-cited notion of a pioneering new woman who could vote, work and exercise greater autonomy over her life than her mother or grandmother could have dreamed. As historian Lucy Bland has noted, 'the modern woman-cum-flapper, a figure found across all classes, represented modernity, mobility, new opportunities, a brave new world, a break with pre-war world of chaperones, Victorian values and restrictive clothing' (Bland 2013: 3). These developments were all in significant part true; the stereotype was not without foundation. And yet there were also clear limitations in both social and economic freedoms here. In the West, as Maureen Honey has argued,

> in the 1920s women could envision autonomy, but they had only the vaguest of notions concerning a public sphere that would speak to their concerns and provide meaningful experience. Until they could link overtly male oppression to the nature of public activity as well as to the home, the dream of empowerment would remain a fantasy and the ability to transform what one claimed a hazy illusion.
>
> (Honey 1990: 39)

In other words, the formal rights women were gaining were not necessarily yet the indicator of genuine equality: they were now permitted to play a game determined by men, but not yet help set its laws (literally, in the case of many global legislatures, as we will note).

Such trends have received significant comment. As Jane Fenoulhet has observed, 'women's suffrage does not in itself represent a large step forward – at least not if democratization is defined as the increased participation in society of those previously excluded' (Fenoulhet 2007: 110). Angela Kershaw and Angela Kimyongür concur:

> [European] politics [in the 1920s] continued to be defined as a masculine sphere, even after the granting to women of the right to vote and to stand for election; in literature, women's writing was excluded from the canon and thereby from serious consideration; in professional life – journalism, public service or education, for example – women had to fight for recognition and resist discourses which often sought to relegate them to the private sphere.
>
> *(Kershaw and Kimyongür 2007: 1)*

But Europe remained something of a progressive vanguard. In areas of Asia, as we will note, having six children or more remained the norm in the 1920s – mitigating against even acquiring the limited new freedoms won in the West. There were also clearly different dynamics where gender intersected with race. As Kshama Sharma notes, African 'women began to organize in the 1920s, mainly in the laundry, clothing, mattress, furniture and banking industries' (Sharma 1989: 82). Yet this was tied into a wider struggle: 'the common exploitation and oppression of all Black people in South Africa led women to join forces with men against the system which chains them as human beings' (Sharma 1989: 83). Despite the demarcation of this chapter, women's movements were not always about policies geared just towards women. The oppressed then, as in later years, sometimes sought a broader movement for change.

Voting

For all the above caveats, the 1920s was an era of clear headline gains. Most obviously, the First World War proved a significant catalyst to the enfranchising of women. In 1914, precisely seven territories across the globe allowed women to vote at a national level – with Australia and New Zealand being joined by Norway, Finland (then a client state of the Tsarist regime in Russia), the Cook Islands, the Pitcairn Islands and the Isle of Man. Female voting at a national level was the practice of only a handful of nations, and in global terms was almost an eccentric activity. More men voted in the German elections of 1912 than the number of women enfranchised at that time throughout the globe. Famously however, the war and its vicissitudes greatly expanded female suffrage – the Provisional Government gave women in Russia and her territories the vote in July 1917, and a deluge of nations followed suit after the cessation of hostilities in November 1918. By 1920 victorious nations such as Britain and the United States had permitted women to vote in national elections, whilst new European nations (or old ones with new democratic constitutions) like Austria, Germany, Hungary and Poland also marked new eras with a new, wider electorate incorporating both the sexes. In the United States, women first voted in the presidential election of 1920 and played no small role in the election of Warren G. Harding, a candidate who was seen as physically attractive and generally appealing to female voters. The fact that he also supported Prohibition while his Democratic opponent argued that alcohol should once again be legal only further enhanced his standing with America's women. His wife, Florence, also directly courted the female vote on the campaign trail and in the White House (Ponder 1998: 113–14).

Where enfranchisement did occur in our period however, it was often conditional. Britain gave all men over the age of 21 the vote in 1918 for the first time, but maintained pre-1918 property requirements for women who wished to vote (as well as introducing a higher age threshold of 30). Puerto Rico's 1929 extension of voting rights gave only literate women the vote, whilst in 1930 South Africa opened up voting to women of European racial stock, but not the African majority. By the end of the 1920s several large states – including France and Italy in Europe, China, India and Japan in Asia, Liberia and Ethiopia in Africa and Argentina and Chile in South America – permitted no form of female voting at national elections. Despite the Western 'flappers', female voting was still in other words a minority pursuit. And yet the 1920s saw significant changes. Small new footholds were established for global female suffrage in Burma (1924), Mongolia (1924), Tajik and Turkmen Soviet Republics (both 1924), and Ecuador (1929). Where the vote had been given just after the war it was also often extended as male politicians, grudgingly, conceded that inequalities in age or property qualifications could no longer be justified. Moving Britain's 1928 bill to equalise voting qualifications between men and women, the Lord Chancellor – Lord Hailsham – stated that

> It is sometimes canvassed whether the vote should be regarded as a right or as a responsibility. If it be a right, a right by which the voter can protect himself and his class from injustice or oppression, then surely women have as much need of that protection as men. On the other hand, if it be a responsibility, a responsibility for the proper government and administration of our affairs, then women have shown themselves no longer to be unfit to share that responsibility. For my part I look forward to seeing men and women together sharing a common ideal of citizenship, sharing equally the burden of Empire which rests upon our people, equal partners and coheirs in a democracy which has been slowly built up through the centuries and to which it is our privilege tonight to set the coping-stone.
>
> *(House of Lords* Hansard, *21 May 1928, vol. 71, col. 167)*

So, to this British Conservative politician, women needed the vote under a Burkean rationale of defending oneself from tyranny, but they had also earned the right through their endeavours. This was quite a shift given such types would often have resorted to the Elizabethan concept of 'weak and feeble' women just two decades earlier.

The question, in such instances, was what came next. The 1920s afforded several post-suffrage vehicles for women to act *en bloc* however, and pacifism was one such instance. In the United States the National Committee on the Cause and Cure of War 'suggested that traditional notions of gender solidarity and women's special place in politics continued to exert a powerful, motivating influence on white, middle-class women's organization for more than a decade after the suffrage victory' (Zeiger 1990: 69). These associational nodes were to some degree a product of pre-war organisations, but they now had greater teeth. As women entered the world of work so too did they require and gain new organisations to cater for this. In Bristol, England schoolmistress Ethel Parr set up the first Venture Club – modelled on the Rotary Club – to offer woman-to-woman networking, collaborating and socialising (McCarthy 2008: 533). With new activities came new forms of co-operation – even if some experienced a slow birth. The Netherlands Society of Female Citizens, for example, fell from 5,000 members in 1924 to half that by the end of the decade (Fenoulhet 2007: 112).

For all the advances, politics was something of an exception (and particular nodes – parties – already of course existed). Though the first woman MP to sit in the British House of Commons – Nancy Astor – was elected in 1919, women's political representation remained extremely limited during the 1920s. The upper chamber, the House of Lords, was barred to women until 1958. But even in the Commons there were just 14 MPs at the peak point of the 1920s, the 1929 General Election. At that election Margaret Bondfield would become the first female Cabinet Minister in Ramsay MacDonald's new administration, but several female politicians of even the small sample that made it into the Commons were known more for having famous male relatives than their own credentials. Ruth (wife of Hugh) Dalton, Cynthia (wife of Sir Oswald) Mosley and Megan (daughter of David) Lloyd George were not the only ones to reach the benches of Westminster partly through association with prominent male patrons. In percentage terms the 1929 female representation in the three major parties was 2 per cent for the Liberals and Conservatives, and 3 per cent Labour. And this in a nation that, thanks to the war, was 52 per cent female. Votes for women had been granted in electoral terms, but barely in terms of various legislatures.

In the United States things were even more restricted. Although the first woman was elected to the House of Representatives in 1917 in the form of Jeanette Rankin, she served only one term (later to be re-elected in 1940) and progress in the 1920s was limited. The 67th Congress of 1921 saw four women in the House and the first woman Senator. But the circumstances of the latter were extremely odd. In 1922 the Senate race in Georgia was blown wide open when the incumbent Thomas E. Watson died prematurely. Since the state Governor Thomas W. Hardwick was a candidate for the Senate, he wanted to appoint a temporary successor who would be no threat to his candidacy. As a means of also attempting to secure the newly enfranchised female vote, he chose Rebecca Latimer Felton. Felton was married to a member of the House of Representatives and adopted a controversial political position in most areas. On the plus side, she campaigned for equal pay for equal work. On the other hand she was a vocal advocate of lynching and the last member of Congress to have been a slave owner. But she remains the United States' first female Senator – if only for a day.

When Governor Hardwick unexpectedly lost the election to Walter F. George the victorious Democratic candidate, who would serve until the 1950s. George was expected to take office immediately upon the reconvention of the Senate on 21 November. However, after lobbying from both Felton herself and local women's groups George conceded to allow Felton to be sworn in for a day and serve until George undertook his office from 22 November. This was an odd episode in more ways than one – nominal progress achieved through a profound reactionary. That progress was, however, limited. By 1929, the 71st Congress, there were still only nine women in the House of Representatives, 1.7 per cent of that chamber. The first elected Senator would not arrive until 1932.

The United States, for context, was not the only Western nation where representation remained modest. North of the 49th parallel Agnes McPhail was the only female Canadian MP from 1921 until 1935. In Australia there were no female parliamentarians at a federal level until the Second World War, and indigenous women were banned from voting in such elections until 1962. Europe fared only mildly better. The German Reichstag had 32 women in 1926 (6.7 per cent of the chamber), and the Dutch had elected eight female Members of Parliament by 1929. In the Netherlands in particular a veneration of the notions of 'motherhood and home' meant this small band had an important role in blocking regressive legislation. As late as 1937 a bill was put forward to ban all married women from paid employment. For all we may mythologise the 1920s as a decade of unbridled progress, history can always move backwards as well as forwards.

Sex

When it comes to social progress we have, as mentioned, the culturally ingrained image of the sexually liberated flapper. But it is important to note that these new social mores did, however, also produce a significantly conservative counterpunch. In Britain, fears about miscegenation between white women and 'aliens' – particularly those of Chinese or African descent – abounded. As Lucy Bland observes, in the early 1920s 'British women's marriages to Chinese men not only deemed them "aliens" legally and morally, but physically as well, their bodies were said to age prematurely, and their facial features gradually to acquire an Oriental look' (Bland 2013: 79). As discussed elsewhere in this volume, in many countries – and many American states – such congress between those of European and non-European stock was explicitly forbidden by law.

But the worry was not just about women and racial mixing, for in Catholic Ireland a general fear of 'sex and the single girl' was even more prevalent in the 1920s. Before the British withdrawal from Southern Ireland after the creation of the Irish Free State in December 1921, Irish elites had been able to blame any perceived immorality on the influence of Anglo-Saxon troops. But the problem, as Maria Luddy has noted, was that 'when the British garrison was gone ... levels of sexual immorality appeared to rise rather than decrease in the new State'. A 1926 sermon by the Reverend Dr Gilmartin referred to a state of dress amongst women 'bordering on the indecent', and it was nearly always women – and their bodies – who were blamed for the alleged said moral decline. In the new Ireland women were to be simultaneously worshipped as the vehicle to 'return the nation to purity', and pilloried when they were viewed as dipping below this exalted role (Luddy 2007: passim).

It is true that the English were still blamed by some. A Father Devane, addressing the 1924 Irish Inter-Departmental Committee of Inquiry Regarding Venereal Disease, remarked that 'it will be found, in many cases, the girls who acted as camp followers to [British] Black and Tans etc, were the same who pursued the [Irish] Free State troops, conveying in not a few cases infection'. Though not exclusively, this essentially put the blame on Irish prostitutes. Statistically however, this case did not stand up. The Committee's report, which was not published, concluded that venereal disease was 'disseminated largely by a class of girl who could not be regarded as a prostitute' – and that seven in ten cases could not be attributed to such sources (Luddy 2007: passim).

The conclusion many Catholic conservatives therefore drew was that *all* women were to blame. With a rise of over 7 per cent in the number of illegitimate births between 1926 and 1929, the advocates of this course had some support for their paranoia. For the first-time unmarried mothers – so-called 'hopeful cases' – there would be access to short-term institutional care (run by nuns) for them and their child. For those mothers on their second or third child, there was the prospect of detention in such an institution for up to three years. This stance was not intended to be penal, but it must have felt like prison to many. Like the various gradients afforded to differing levels of criminality, women were housed depending on their sexual experience. Perspectives on sex in the 1920s did not run just one way. To the unfortunate young woman in rural Kerry or Mayo, the glamour of Hollywood or Piccadilly must have seemed a world away – as it indeed was.

Perhaps the defining image of women in the 1920s: the sexually liberated woman with (perhaps illegally in the case of America) a drink in her hand cannot also be accepted without some qualification. In colonial Zimbabwe (then Rhodesia and under the rule of the British), elite male black Africans fought a lengthy rear-guard action against the right of young women to drink with their male counterparts. This desire to prohibit 'joint drinking' was largely, as with other discriminatory measures, motivated by fears over sexual relations. Class was not totally divorced from this picture (black African elites also generally rejected the beer hall lifestyle because of the working-class clientele and non-European liquor) but gender was a constant reference point in many Rhodesian communities.

Western attitudes toward African women continued to reflect the colonial and often Orientalist fascinations of the nineteenth century, particularly when women and sex were involved. An American woman travelling with friends from Cairo to the Cape in the middle years of the decade reported that women in Egypt ('the far famed mysterious women of the east') were generally covered from head to toe and 'their life must be far from a happy one'. While the country's men were 'lounging about engaged in idle conversation' the women 'would be carrying great jars of water from the river or bundles of wood for the fire on their heads, while balancing a baby on one hip and with perhaps a ragged child holding on to their skirts' (Davidson n.d.: 333).

Passing into the Belgian Congo, the travellers encountered the Mangbetu people, a group famed for binding the heads of infants to distinctively shape them, along with their artistic achievements. Unlike the Egyptians, the Mangbetu were reportedly 'extremely good looking' and since the arrival of colonialism the role of women had allegedly changed:

> As they may no longer, as a tribe, work off their surplus energy in war, they pass their time in beautifying themselves for the fascination of the opposite sex and in thinking up new forms of immorality, for, alas, these charming people are said to have no morals at all and to be past masters especially in the subject of sex. Birth control is universally understood and practiced although this, as well as their method of secret poisoning, is kept as a tribal secret, not to be imparted to the white man. Such extreme sophistication in combination with their primitive mode of living made them the most interesting people we visited.
>
> *(Davidson n.d.: 335)*

In the final reckoning, this traveller concluded, Africa's women had it rather good in comparison to their counterparts in the West:

> On the whole, the lot of African women seems to be a very happy one ... Since the advent of the whites, the native man has suffered in many ways without affecting the women – as in forced labor in the mines, and as Africa becomes more and more civilized women's position will undoubtedly deteriorate but it will be a very long time indeed before her life can approach in dullness and suffering that of the women in our slums.
>
> *(Davidson n.d.: 336)*

The most Westernised women on the continent were allegedly to be found in South Africa, where native women 'in dress and general appearance are very much like our own negroes – at least those we saw seemed to be' (Davidson n.d.: ibid.).

African colonial subjects themselves would have surely disagreed with these analyses in many ways. In 1925, a Rhodesian land commission heard complaints from African men that 'when they go to work their wives are subjected to temptations owing to the proximity of large numbers of unmarried men' (West 1997: 646). This patriarchal attitude merely built upon existing legal statute. In the eyes of the law, African women were not adults in their own right, and were under the legal tutelage of a male guardian – be he a father, husband or other elder. The Native Adultery Punishment Ordinance of 1916 had also criminalised the act of adultery by married women, but had not extended that judgement to their male counterparts. The law remained a one-way street.

Across the globe, sex and womanhood continued to be linked in a negative manner throughout the 1920s. For one, prostitution was a continued source of debate in 1920s Bombay. Pointing to the League of Nations and general global opinion 'decidedly in favour of abolition' with regards to prostitution, a correspondent to *The Times of India* noted the previous presumption in favour of regulated zones – Red Light Districts, in later parlance – should be replaced by an out and out ban. There was also a distinction between brothels run by male pimps and female madams. According to the contemporary legislation, male-owned brothels could be subject to government sanction, but female-run establishments fell outside the purview of the law. This produced 'a great danger to the physical and moral well-being of the people of the city and as such calls for urgent action' (*Times of India*, 25 August 1928). Again, if we are to view the 1920s globally then the picture of female advancement demands such correctives.

One reliable measure we have regarding women's empowerment was the age at which women married for the first time. Here again we can glean a great global divergence. Whilst the average Indian or Bangladeshi girl would not see 13 before they were married for the first time, the 1920s saw a marked increase in the age amongst Western women. Whilst women in the United States were scarcely above the age of majority (21) at the average time of their first marriage in 1920, by 1930 this had risen dramatically to 31. There was also an increase in Canada from 23 to 24 over the same timeframe. British, New Zealand and Swedish women were all married on average around their mid-20s – suggestive of a life before wedlock (Gapminder n.d.: passim).

The number of children per woman also tells us much. Whilst the pattern in many countries remained that marriage in effect saw women take a dramatic step back from the workplace, this was further entrenched by the number of children women would (largely) have to raise. In general the trend, as today, was an inverse relationship between economic development and children per woman. In many European nations such as Austria, Denmark, France, Germany and the UK women were having on average less than 2.5 children each in 1928. In North America the ratios were a little higher – 2.7 for the United States and 3.3 for Canada. But in Asia, Japan (5.1), Taiwan (6.3), the Philippines (6.1) and Sri Lanka (6.4), they were a good deal higher – a product of lower ages of marriage, and higher infant mortality (Gapminder n.d.: passim).

Further, information about reliable methods of birth control became increasingly available throughout the 1920s. In the United States, most information about birth control methods and devices remained illegal under anti-obscenity laws (prominent birth control advocate Margaret Sanger had already been arrested on such charges in 1916, bringing widespread attention to the issue). The vast majority of the birth control information that was available was explicitly directed at married women, and virtually no prominent advocates were willing to publicly support unmarried women using those techniques. Sanger's famous pamphlet *Family Limitation* identified the goals of the birth control movement thus:

We hold that children should be:

1   Conceived in love.
2   Born of the mother's conscious desire.
3   And only begotten under conditions which render possible the heritage of health.

(Sanger 1924: 10)

The fact that in Sanger's view the only reliable way to ensure that these goals could be met was the 'scientific' distribution of information gave her campaign an added urgency. British birth control advocate Marie Stopes put her views in similar terms, telling 'working mothers' in a 1925 pamphlet that,

No one told you how to give yourself a good long interval to pick up between the children; I am going to tell you how to do this so that you may bear *strong* children, and be happy bearing the children, because you have them when you are really *well*, and want them yourself.

(Stopes 1925: 3)

Even among its staunchest advocates, the discourse over birth control in the 1920s was almost exclusively focused on giving married women the right to choose when they would have children rather than giving unmarried women control over their fertility and sexual choices. Married women were now given the right to sexual pleasure without the worry of constant pregnancy in the context of their marriage; unmarried women were effectively told to wed before they would be extended the same right.

FIGURE 6.1 The 1920s birth control clinic, here operating out of a caravan, provided a new – if status limited – freedom for millions of women.

This was little comfort to the moralisers, however. Across the Western world, the spread of birth control led to a nearly hysterical moral panic in many circles. Catholics were the most vocal critics, viewing contraception as an attack on the traditional family and an affront to divine will. Protestants were potentially more receptive, though senior Church of England leaders were ambivalent in their responses to the movement. Some physicians and demographers had differing objections. Recognising that many European countries had birth rates already below the replacement rate of two children per couple, some objected that birth control was likely to reduce those numbers further. Demographers associated with the eugenics movement, discussed already, feared that birth control might lead to an increase in the numbers of the 'unfit' if contraceptive techniques were used primarily by the highly educated. The fact that Stopes and Sanger targeted much of their propaganda at working-class women was as much a reflection of this concern as it was a genuine interest in helping the poor (Soloway 1990: 264–6).

While much of Europe had already tipped toward declining birth rates by the 1920s, perhaps the most interesting trends in the period lie in Italy and Russia. In these countries the decade had two dictatorships operating completely different policies towards reproductive rights that produced similar outcomes. In 1920 the Soviet Union became the first European nation to legalise abortion in all circumstances. This was for the pragmatic purpose that since the dislocation of so many years of conflict, many women would be unable to protect and feed their child, and thus would likely seek abortion anyway. Better therefore to have the procedure carried out by a trained doctor than a rural amateur. The outcome here was a sharp decline in the number of births per Russian woman, from over 6 in 1920 to 4.5 by 1933.

Yet in a Catholic Italy whose fascist dictatorship was fetishising the cult of the mother and the importance of upping the national birth rate, a similar trend could be detected. Between 1923 and 1933 the ratio fell from 3.9 to 3. Here, in a sense, we have contraception beating dictatorship – something which naturally worried Benito Mussolini who often referred to the evils of industrial urbanism as a sterilising force, and ordered local newspapers to print lists of provincial birth rates as a nudge (or shove) towards further childbearing. A national population target of 60 million for 1950 was even set – though in the end the regime would fall before it became clear they had fallen over 13 million people short.

Education and the workplace

In the West then, both marriage and child rearing had been replaced, in varying degrees, by gainful employment. Teaching formed a significant proportion of female employment in most Western states in the 1920s. In the UK 76 per cent of teachers were female in the late 1920s, a figure lower than the 83 per cent of women teachers in the United States. For such women, the 1920s were challenging in two key regards. Firstly, it was official policy in many areas to encourage men to enter the teaching profession (particularly a problem in times of economic depression, when employment opportunities generally were fewer). In Western Australia, the wartime increase of male representation in the teaching profession from 30 to 36 per cent was met with the 'hope that increase will continue'.

From 1926 this was actually economically disadvantageous for the state. That year Western Australia passed a law setting the 'basic wage' at £4 5s per week for adult males and £2 7s for adult females. Thus, as Sally Kennedy shows, 'from a situation where the unclassified female teacher's salary ranged from 87–93 per cent of the unclassified male teacher's salary, the wage adjustments undertaken meant the new range was 66–81 per cent: from a position of near equal pay for equal work to a greater wage differential' (Kennedy 1983: 20). There were reasons to encourage greater male participation in teaching, and to re-integrate former soldiers back into the workforce, but this was something of a zero-sum game where women suffered as a result.

Female labour market participation remained limited in several nations. Although there was increased participation amongst every age group between 20 and 65 in 1920s Canada, across the age spectrum most Canadian women remained economically inactive by 1931. Between 1921 and 1931 the female percentage in work all increased: of 20- to 24-year-olds, from 35 per cent to 42 per cent; of 25- to 34-year-olds, from 17 per cent to 22 per cent; and of 35- to 64-year-olds, from 10.7 per cent to 12 per cent. But these statistics still indicated that marriage remained a bar to advancement. Once marriage (and children) came along, many women left the workforce. For Canadian employment guidance advisers however, the upward trend overall was cause for optimism. As Veronica Strong-Boag has pointed out, such individuals were generally

> subscribers to a Whig view of history, [and] congratulated themselves that there was in modern Canada a wide range of jobs suitable for girls. Among these they included stenography, nursing, bee-keeping, millinery, retailing, clerking and telegraph operating. According to them modern opportunities made it unnecessary for respectable young women to seek employment in 'masculine' fields such as carpentry, electrical work, automobiles, iron and steel and the like.
>
> *(Strong-Boag 1979: 134)*

In Britain the Sex Disqualification (Removal) Act 1919 made it illegal to not hire a woman because of her gender. It was, however, easier to get this on the statute book than it was to normalise it amongst contemporary businessmen, and there was an uneasy relationship between those men returning from active service and expecting to resume their former professions, and the women they would often displace. A Mr H. Key, secretary of the London Employers' Federation, remarked in 1920 that he had 'no sympathy with the girls who work for a hobby' who should be removed from their posts to accommodate 'the male employees who are now released from the army'. But he did concede that 'efforts must be made to find employment for the women who are obliged to work' (*Auckland Star*, 2 January 1920). To some degree this happened. As Martin Pugh has observed, a dramatic increase in secretarial and administrative employment in offices created a new and steady demand for female workers. As a proportion of the British labour force women continued at just under 30 per cent, in fact seeing a mild increase from 29.5 per cent in 1921 to 29.8 per cent ten years later (Pugh 2008: 183). A similar trend was seen in the United States. During the 1920s, the number of women in nineteenth-century-style domestic employment fell substantially, while more than two million entered office jobs. On the other hand, most of these women were excluded from joining labour unions, with the exception of garment workers (Cashman 1998: 190).

Offices were one boom area for women, but waitressing soon proved to be another. In many cities the growth of the café and café culture meant a concurrent demand for serving staff, usually women. In Tokyo the 1920s saw the mass expansion of the *jokyu* – female waitresses – as cafés grew and grew. The number of waitresses in Tokyo increased from around 7,000 in 1925 to over 15,000 by 1929. As cafés shifted from a space akin to a salon away from home to one which catered for a more middle-class clientele, the *jokyu* were in high demand. And yet we must be careful not to completely equate female advancement in the workplace with urbanisation. In 1920s Indonesia, for instance, women were performing over half and sometimes up to 80 per cent of the labour-intensive work of rice farming – planting, weeding, harvesting and other such activities (Benjamin 1996: 80).

As ever, what women could do depended on their skill-sets, and these could vary. Even within the Soviet Union female literacy rates varied drastically. West of the Ural Mountains over four in ten women were able to read and write. In the Uzbek and Turkmen Republics less than one in ten possessed similar skills. Elsewhere, areas still in large part agrarian such as Indonesia saw even lower rates of between 1 and 2 per cent. A lack of education, combined with still developing economies, kept women's employment options rather limited.

Leisure and culture

In a syndicated article, *The Times of India* reported the views of Gilbert Adrian, costume designer for MGM films, as to what the 'woman of the world ... should wear'. He noted that 'every garment she possesses must be stamped with the hall-mark of her vivid attraction'. Bright colours were to be used in the evening, if at all. The daytime called for 'severely tailored suits softened by no frilly touches'. The woman of the world apparently did 'not follow fashions, but creates her own' (*Times of India*, 18 July 1929). As noted already, in Britain there was a clear and discernible shift away from the Edwardian hourglass silhouette towards a thinner, tubular look. This involved ditching dresses with pronounced waistlines, discarding whalebone corsets and buying bras designed to flatten, rather than augment, women's breasts (Pugh 2008: 171). On the other hand, high-heeled shoes were generally frowned upon since it was assumed that the woman who used them would eventually displace her uterus and be unable to give birth (Pugh 2008: 172).

The new woman also augured a new women's press. In the United States in particular, women's magazines told of heroines throwing off the shackles of male oppression and leaving towns – often located in the Midwest – to move to the big city, often New York (Honey 1990: 32). Here the new woman cast off family demands with all the marginalisation that brought and became more of an individual in her own right. Interestingly, as Maureen Honey notes, this imagined city could be a mixed blessing: 'it frees her from the shackles of home, but it is full of false gods and is based on the principles of self-aggrandizement, competition and materialism, which are alien to her upbringing' (Honey 1990: 31).

One of the most shocking mores that was abandoned in 1920s America surrounded smoking. Traditionally seen as an exclusively male and decidedly unfeminine practice, public relations guru Edward Bernays realised early in the decade that women were a huge untapped market for tobacco companies and launched an advertising campaign to associate cigarettes with female liberation. Dubbed the 'torches of freedom' campaign, Bernays – who was the nephew of psychoanalyst Sigmund Freud and adapted many of his uncle's ideas to his campaigns – convinced millions of women that smoking was not only sexy but also a way to overcome male oppression. In 1928, he wrote in a short tract entitled *Propaganda* that conscious control of public opinion was the only way to maintain a democratic system, lest it collapse in the face of extremism and incompetence. Over the decades to come, Bernays would play an outsized role in influencing both the US population and the country's government (Bernays 1928: passim).

Martin Pugh has observed similar overall trends in the UK. Alongside previous publications such as *My Weekly* and *Home Chat* came, from 1922, *Good Housekeeping*. This originally American publication brought numerous equivalents – *Women and Home, My Home, Modern Woman* and *Wife and Home*. As Pugh notes,

> these magazines prospered on the basis of a standard formula comprising romantic fiction, marriage-and-husband tips, fashion, health and beauty, baby care, cookery, knitting patterns, dress-making, gardening and flower arrangement. In the aftermath of the war they increasingly emphasised household management especially for middle-class readers now struggling to find or to afford domestic servants.
>
> *(Pugh 2008: 174)*

Retailers soon jumped on the magazine bandwagon. The expansion of credit after the war, coupled with the general increase in incomes and available goods, led to a mass expansion of mail order firms catering to largely female audiences with glossy catalogues offering a wide range of goods. The push for convenience and labour saving was increasingly making it into the domestic sphere that most women still inhabited.

Beyond the magazine, longer-form novels also began to pick up on the theme of the newly liberated woman. *La Garçonne* was published in 1922 in France and translated as *The Bachelor Girl* a year later. The protagonist, a young woman, uses the infidelity of her fiancé as a springboard to live life on her own terms. This included promiscuity – shocking to many at the time – and would see its author, Alfred A. Knopf, lose his *Légion d'Honneur* as a result. The panic such publications helped foster is worth relating. In 1929 an article appeared in *The Times of India* which described 'the historical see-saw of the sexes'. It continued:

> when women today arrogantly flaunt a triumph which they claim at long last we have won from eons of subjection to man and man-made law, their self assertion, based upon complete ignorance of the facts, is as pitiful as it is grotesque.
>
> (Times of India, *25 June 1929*)

There was further to travel for half the globe's population.

Protest

Whilst the 1920s saw consumerism for some, it also witnessed protest by others. One crucial interaction between women and politics was through the Communist Party of South Africa. Through members like Mary Wolton and Josie Palmer, women helped forward a radical class- and race-based discourse which challenged the (pre-Apartheid) South African regime. However, it was not just in South African cities where women became active. In the agricultural Eastern Cape, many men left the region to seek work in urban areas. This left women isolated and at the mercy of local traders to whom they sold their produce – often wheat or maize – and from whom they purchased their daily necessities. These traders, sensing a captive market, would often charge extortionate rates for their basic foodstuffs whilst offering minimal prices for the goods they themselves purchased. The matter was made worse by traders stockpiling goods over years with poor harvests, thus meaning that in fallow – high-cost – periods they did not have to purchase from local women. Under leaders such as Anne Sidyiyo, women undertook to boycott these traders and forcibly removed the goods of those buying from them. This led to arrests and appearances in court, but it forced the traders into a climb-down and prices became regulated.

Another campaign centred around the drinking of beer in the Natal. Beer was popular amongst Zulu men and the brewing of the product allowed women to make a small profit and thereby gain the independence associated with running a small business. The government, however, was suspicious of these green shoots of independence and, in any case, wanted a piece of the profit that could be made. Passing the 1928 Liquor Act, the South African government began to raid local producers and restricted brewing to municipal concerns. This municipal brew was often sold at four or five times the previous price – making it unpopular all round. Across the small towns of the Natal women marched into the municipal canteens and assaulted male customers in protest. In July 1929 in Durban 2,000 whites clashed with 6,000 blacks, and 120 people were injured and eight died. The 1928 Liquor Act remained in place, but the movement was illustrative of the willingness of women to contest the oppressive use of state power to restrict their liberties.

This was replicated in several countries. The Indian National Congress – the independence movement dedicated to overthrowing British rule – had from the late 1880s included women in each of its meetings. As Gandhi's nationalist protests increased in prominence throughout the 1920s, so too were women increasingly drawn into the struggle. Bengali women joined picket lines against the regime, as did Sikh women across India. And, through Madeleine Slade, women's support for Indian independence truly went global. Dubbed Mirabehn, the English daughter of a British Rear-Admiral read the French essayist Romain Rolland's accounts of Gandhi and believed he constituted a twentieth-century Christ. Mirabehn moved to India in November 1925 where she lived for over 30 years and supported the struggle for independence which eventually bore fruit in 1947.

Further east in Japan, protest could also be seen. In February 1921 the Japanese Parliament passed a bill to allow women to attend political meetings. Defeated in the Upper House, this right was nonetheless secured a year later. Two months after the initial 1921 bill the Red Wave Society – a socialist organisation – was formed under the leadership of Yamakawa Kirkue. This was a profoundly anti-capitalist body, arguing that the inevitable consequence of capitalism was not only Marxist serfdom, but ultimately prostitution and enslavement. The end goal here was always suffrage (achieved after the Second World War), but following a 1923 earthquake in Tokyo (which killed more than 100,000 people) such organisations often provided relief for the destitute and dispossessed. As the decade progressed, the Tokyo Federation of Women's organisations was formed, which continued to push the case for the vote. Whilst first-wave feminism had delivered the vote in areas of the West, across the globe there were still battles to be won in this regard.

Conclusion

The 1920s were a period of immense change for many women, but it is easy to overstate the extent of these changes. In essence, the decade saw the emergence of a vanguard in several areas – including employment, sexual rights, social habits and literature. These movements ranged from the few parliamentarians in democratic legislatures to women holding off from marriage and experiencing something of an independent life for a little longer. But, inevitably, there was only so much that could be altered in a ten-year window of time. The rise of totalitarian regimes with their idea of male-centric political power, the need to re-accommodate brave former combatants of the First World War in various nations' labour markets, and limited educational opportunities (particularly surrounding literacy) meant equality across the board remained elusive.

While women entered the Western political scene *en masse* for the first time in the 1920s, there were very few female elected officials in any country. Women became a major demographic force for politicians courting votes as the result of female enfranchisement, particularly in the United States and in Europe, but many still felt strong social pressure to vote in accordance with the wishes of husbands or male relations. On the other hand, it was the 1920s that truly extended the process of bringing women into politics on a mass basis.

The two most critical limiting factors for women before the Second World War were lack of educational and professional opportunities, coupled with lack of control over their reproductive rights. Women's colleges dated back to the nineteenth century but there was still tremendous social prejudice against women entering the workforce on a large-scale basis. Virtually all female employees were unmarried women, with it being viewed as unseemly for a married woman to work rather than raise a family, which consequently limited the career prospects for the vast majority. Secretarial work offered perhaps the most promising career for most women, though it is certainly true that a number of pioneering women began pushing the social envelope and seeking careers beyond the traditional limits.

Reproductive control also remained elusive for many. Despite increasing scientific knowledge of reproduction, social anxieties and repressive laws prevented the majority of women from being given access to reliable birth control knowledge and methods. Quacks selling cure-alls, flawed devices and back-alley abortions harmed the lives and bodies of many, with often tragic results. It would not be until after the Second World War that birth control would be seen as an important health issue for women, and not until the 1960s would the US Supreme Court actually rule that the state had no right to ban the use of birth control in the privacy of the bedroom (in the case of *Griswold v. Connecticut).* Until birth control became legal and widely available, the lives of most women still revolved around pregnancy and childbearing. However, the 1920s saw the early signs that the tide was shifting in favour of access to contraception. Margaret Sanger and Marie Stopes saw their movements as extending a basic right to women, though both were careful to circumscribe their efforts to married rather than single women (and, as noted, their eugenic views led them to often focus their efforts on the poor and working class). The sexual revolution of the 1960s would eventually carry the discussion over female sexuality and reproduction to a more liberal stance, but it was in the 1920s that women began to widely open the door to reform.

The 1920s presented no panacea for the issues facing women, but they were an important turning point in shaping future discussions and developments. While Edward Bernays was clearly cynical and condescending in his use of cigarettes to epitomise female liberation and progress, it is true that he was one of the few to grasp the desire of women for social progress in the period. The forces unleashed after the First World War would eventually result in the progressive opening of opportunities and rights for women that continues to the present day.

Questions

- What factors led to women's roles changing in many places around the world in the 1920s?
- How did the end of the First World War affect women's lives?

- What role did the birth control movement play in changing women's roles in the 1920s?
- Why has the image of the 'flapper' become so associated with the 1920s? How accurate was this representation of women?
- Why did women not experience further social progress in the 1920s, particularly outside Europe and North America?

Recommended further reading

Bernays, E. (1928, 2005) *Propaganda*, New York: Ig Publishing.

Bland, L. (2013), *Modern Women on Trial: Sexual Transgression in the Age of the Flapper*, Manchester: Manchester University Press.

Honey, M. (1990), 'Gotham's Daughters: Feminism in the 1920s', *American Studies*, 31, 25–40.

McCarthy, H. (2008), 'Service Clubs, Citizenship and Equality: Gender Relations and Middle-class Associations in Britain between the Wars', *Historical Research*, 81, 531–552.

Soloway, R. (1990, 1995), *Demography and Degeneration: Eugenics and the Declining Birthrate in Twentieth-Century Britain*, Chapel Hill: The University of North Carolina Press.

Zeiger, S. (1990), 'Finding a Cure for War: Women's Politics and the Peace Movement in the 1920s', *Journal of Social History*, 24, 69–86.

Works cited

Benjamin, D. (1996), 'Women and the Labour Market in Indonesia during the 1980s', in Horton, S. (ed.) *Women and Industrialisation in Asia*, London: Routledge, pp. 81–133.

Bernays, E. (1928, 2005), *Propaganda*, New York: Ig Publishing.

Bland, L. (2013), *Modern Women on Trial: Sexual Transgression in the Age of the Flapper*, Manchester: Manchester University Press.

Cashman, S. (1998), *America Ascendant: From Theodore Roosevelt to FDR in the Century of American Power, 1901–1945*, New York: New York University Press.

Davidson, M. (n.d.), 'African women', in *An African Log*, vol. 2, Appendix I, pp. 332–338, Box 1, Marshall Bond Papers, Hoover Institution Archive, Stanford University.

Fenoulhet, J. (2007), 'Is Anybody Listening? Dutch Women Writers between the Wars', in Kershaw, A. and Kimyongur, A. (eds), *Women in Europe between the Wars: Politics, Culture and Society*, Farnham: Ashgate, pp. 109–118.

Gapminder (n.d.), 'List of Indicators', www.gapminder.org/data

Honey, M. (1990), 'Gotham's Daughters: Feminism in the 1920s', *American Studies*, 31, 25–40.

Kennedy, S. (1983), 'Useful and Expendable: Women Teachers in Western Australia in the 1920s and 1930s', *Labour History*, 44, 18–26.

Kershaw, A. and Kimyongür, A. (2007), 'Introduction', in *Women in Europe between the Wars: Politics, Culture and Society*, Farnham: Ashgate, pp. 1–24.

Luddy, M. (2007), 'Sex and the Single Girl in 1920s and 1930s Ireland', *Irish Review*, 35, 79–91.

McCarthy, H. (2008), 'Service Clubs, Citizenship and Equality: Gender Relations and Middle-class Associations in Britain between the Wars', *Historical Research*, 81, 531–552.

Ponder, S. (1998), *Managing the Press: Origins of the Media Presidency, 1897–1933*, New York: St Martin's Press.

Pugh, M. (2008), *We Danced All Night: A Social History of Britain between the Wars*, London: Vintage.

Sanger, M. (1924), *Family Limitation* (36th edition), London: Rose Witcop.

Sharma, K. (1989), *Women in Africa: Their Role and Position in Society*, New Delhi: Mittal Publications.

Soloway, R. (1990, 1995), *Demography and Degeneration: Eugenics and the Declining Birthrate in Twentieth-Century Britain*, Chapel Hill: The University of North Carolina Press.

Stopes, M. (1925), *A Letter to Working Mothers: On How to Have Healthy Children and Avoid Weakening Pregnancies*, London: The Mother's Clinic for Constructive Birth Control.

Strong-Boag, V. (1979), 'The Girl of the New Day: Canadian Working Women in the 1920s', *Labour*, 4, 131–164.

West, M.O. (1997), 'Liquor and Libido: "Joint Drinking" and the Politics of Sexual Control in Colonial Zimbabwe, 1920s–1950s', *Journal of Social History*, 30, 645–667.

Zeiger, S. (1990), 'Finding a Cure for War: Women's Politics and the Peace Movement in the 1920s', *Journal of Social History*, 24, 69–86.

PART III

PART ONE

7

DEMOCRACY AND ITS MALCONTENTS

Since the collapse of the Soviet Union between 1989 and 1991, and arguably as far back as 1945, perceived wisdom in the West has been to interpret the course of human history as a relentless march towards further democratisation. Whether it be Francis Fukuyama's contention that only democracy can deliver material well-being and recognition of the self, or the cluster of academics synonymous with modernisation theory – the idea that the 'Western' path to industrialisation will be adopted by all human societies across the globe – the idea that democracy forms the perfect – or perhaps least worst – method to manage an economy is relatively ingrained (Fukuyama 1992). Yet this is a relatively new perspective, and not one that could have been advanced with this degree of confidence in the 1920s. This chapter therefore explores a particular turbulent era in the history of certain democracies, how they rode it out, and why they did not take the path walked by the totalitarian regimes outlined elsewhere in this volume.

As we will see, the prosperity of the world's largest democracy – 1920s America – was in large part based in the fact that the country had been on the winning side of the First World War, but had expended relatively little in the way of both money and blood in comparison with the European powers. Indeed, while democracy in the United States was dominated by business and moneyed interests, European democracies found themselves increasingly under threat from non-democratic ideologies as the 1920s progressed. As subsequent sections will discuss, the two emergent alternatives to democracy were communism, thanks to the active support of the Soviet Union, and fascism, pioneered in the early 1920s by Benito Mussolini's Italy. Great Britain and France were two of the few countries to maintain functioning democratic systems and vast empires in the aftermath of the First World War, while their former rivals of Germany and Austria careened from weak and largely impotent democratic states toward dictatorship. The new nation of Turkey, on the other hand, carved itself from the ruins of the Ottoman Empire and began to institute a wide range of Western reforms under the leadership of Mustafa Kemal Atatürk that created a state with the beginning vestiges of democracy.

This chapter considers these democratic powers in turn, examining first the politics of the United States in the period often referred to as the 'Roaring Twenties' for its decadence and fetishisation of wealth. In contrast, the threats posed to democracy in both Britain and France will be considered before turning to the reforms of Atatürk as an example of how democracy, admittedly with strongly authoritarian aspects, was introduced in a defeated power situated between Europe and the Middle East. Together, these sections illustrate the tenuous status of democracy in the 1920s, even in its traditional strongholds, and provide background for the rise of non-democratic alternatives.

The eagle looks to its nest: American power in the 1920s

In January 1920, the United States Senate returned from its winter recess with one of the world's most pressing questions high on its agenda: the fate of American participation in the League of Nations. Since President Woodrow Wilson's extraordinary role in the negotiations over the Treaty of Versailles the previous year, the Senate had been unable to muster the necessary two-thirds vote to secure its ratification. The sticking points were many and varied: Republicans, who held the majority after the election of 1918, believed that American membership in the League of Nations would impinge on the country's sovereignty and ensure an endless commitment to foreign entanglements, embodying a traditional isolationist sentiment. Other members of the 'Irreconcilables', as the group of Senators who would oppose the Treaty's ratification under any circumstances became known, feared the expansion of British power and still others feared that the treaty would amount to an unjust peace. Other Senators had been willing to consider ratification if the Treaty were modified, but Wilson himself had shown an unwillingness to negotiate. On 19 November 1919, the Treaty came closest to passing the Senate but failed to garner the necessary votes.

Some hope still remained for the Treaty and the League as 1920 dawned. If Wilson proved himself to be more flexible in allowing the reservations expressed by the Republicans to be addressed, he might be able to gather enough votes for ratification. Behind the scenes, though, Wilson was in no way capable of conducting these types of negotiations. In September 1919 the President had suffered a stroke during a visit to Colorado and been rushed back to Washington. In the months since, his wife and aides had systematically concealed the fact that he was barely in control of his faculties by isolating him from nearly all visitors. In February 1920, Wilson sacked his Secretary of State for holding Cabinet meetings without his permission – the functioning of government had to go on, after all, and Wilson's leadership was questionable – further damaging his ability to conduct foreign affairs. The following month, the Senate rejected the Treaty for the last time. Technically speaking, having rejected the peace treaty the United States remained at war with Germany and her allies until 1921, when President Warren G. Harding signed an act simultaneously ending the state of war and reiterating American non-participation in the League of Nations (Cashman 1998: 177–8).

The American repudiation of Wilson and his policies would not stop here, however. In the presidential election of 1920, the Democratic Party nominated James M. Cox, the Governor of Ohio, and the Assistant Secretary of the Navy (and future President) Franklin D. Roosevelt. Cox attempted to hedge his rhetorical bets on the League of Nations but was surprised to find that many Americans he encountered were simply indifferent to the issue. The Republican Party, in contrast, nominated another Ohioan, Senator Warren G. Harding, and Calvin Coolidge, the popular Governor of Massachusetts. While Cox and Roosevelt campaigned across the country, Harding and Coolidge focused their efforts on campaigning from Harding's own front porch in Ohio, attracting crowds by promising a 'return to normalcy' after the international crises of the Wilson years. When Election Day came, the result was nowhere near close: Harding and Coolidge won more than 60 per cent of the popular vote, while Cox and Roosevelt received a mere 34.2 per cent. The Democrats won no states west of Texas and nothing north of Virginia, relegating them to their traditional stronghold of the South. To make matters worse, the Republicans picked up another ten seats in the Senate and a stunning 63 in the House of Representatives. The Democratic leader in the House, Champ Clark, lost his own seat. Republican control of the US government was now firmly entrenched and would last for more than a decade. Politically and physically broken, Wilson died in 1924 (ironically, as will be seen, outliving his successor in the Oval Office) (Cashman 1998: 185–6).

The United States in the 1920s was thus a country intrinsically conflicted about its identity. Wilson had forced a new international role on the country, yet that vision now seemed to have been repudiated. Harding's 'return to normalcy' was as much a return to the political ideas of isolationism – the notion that the United States should look exclusively to its own affairs and those of the Western Hemisphere, spurning interference in European affairs, in accordance with the Monroe Doctrine of 1823 – as it was a return to the economic policies that preceded the war. The election of 1920 was itself unique for a number of reasons. It was the first election in which all women in the country could vote, thanks to the ratification of the Nineteenth Amendment to the US Constitution, and it was the first election to be reported live on radio. The American electorate was bigger and more diverse than ever before, and it seemed to endorse the Republicans' isolationist views. This general mentality prompted one English MP, Edward Spears, to comment that 'America knows nothing of Europe – or indeed of the world at large – and cares less' (Spears n.d.).

That said, the American people seemed to agree, at least for now, with the Republican view that the country should focus on the development of its own economy rather than foreign affairs. The Republican Party itself had received extensive support from big business in the election, and with its recent victories corporate interests expected to have their investment repaid. In 1921, the Republican-dominated Congress removed an excess profits tax that Wilson had imposed to raise revenue during the war and the following year voted to hike tariffs to protect American manufacturers (Cashman 1998: 226). As President Calvin Coolidge would later proclaim, in the 1920s the 'chief business' of the United States was business itself. F. Scott Fitzgerald would argue that business so dominated the American landscape of the 1920s that the country 'has no interest in politics at all'. Writer and theatre critic George Jean Nathan was more direct when he proclaimed that 'What concerns me alone is myself, and the interests of a few close friends. For all I care the rest of the world may go to hell at today's sunset' (Hart 1967: 2).

Warren G. Harding himself was in many senses the embodiment of the country's prevailing mentalities in the period. As a former journalist, he possessed an astute sense of how to manage the press for his own purposes. He became the first President to regularly answer questions from reporters in scheduled press conferences, and his wife Florence pioneered the modern role of a First Lady by making public statements supporting her husband's candidacy and then allowing herself to be photographed voting (a direct appeal to female voters across the country who were themselves casting ballots for the first time that day). Harding himself was considered handsome and had little hesitation taking part in photo opportunities that produced images for nationwide consumption (Ponder 1998: 110–13).

There was a less-than-savoury aspect to these efforts, however, for Harding and his wife realised that by befriending the press and creating the illusion of a new openness in the White House they could simultaneously influence the stories being reported. Indeed, in exchange for access and 'scoops' from the Administration, Harding expected loyalty and discretion when it came to less favourable stories. It was a shrewd strategy, for the Administration's scandals were myriad and often stunning in their audacity. Harding himself was well known for his womanising and adultery, carrying on affairs with numerous women, many of whom were married. For nearly 15 years, Harding conducted an affair with Carrie Fulton Phillips, a married woman who threatened to go public with their relationship when Harding secured the Republican nomination. Fearing the impact of the scandal, the Party paid for her and her husband to leave the country on an extended 'trip' to Asia with a hefty monetary 'gift' in their pockets. In 2014, a series of explicit letters – sometimes on government stationery, suggesting that they had been written from his Senate office – between Harding and Phillips were released by the Harding family, revealing that Harding used the code word 'Jerry' in reference to his penis and the euphemism 'climbing Mount Jerry' to denote sexual intercourse (Smith 2014: passim). Small wonder, indeed, that the Republican Party had been willing to pay Phillips and her husband to prevent their release.

Personal scandals were only the beginning of the Harding Administration's indiscretions, however. While Prohibition was the law of the land thanks to the ratification of the Eighteenth Amendment, Harding had no personal hesitation in both consuming and serving alcohol in the White House, often to newspaper correspondents who seem to have been more flattered than outraged to share a tipple with a politician who had been a long-time supporter of making alcohol illegal (Ponder 1998: 118–19). Far more serious were the Administration's financial

FIGURE 7.1 President Warren G. Harding (centre) was popular with not only his terrier Laddie Boy, but also with the White House press corps. The corrupt machinations of the Ohio Gang surrounding him eventually brought his administration into widespread disrepute, though the worst scandals were not revealed until after Harding's death.

corruption scandals, however, many of which were committed by a group of Harding's associates known as the 'Ohio Gang'. The head of the Veterans' Bureau, an important government agency tasked with providing assistance to the country's burgeoning population of war veterans, resigned in disgrace after being accused of embezzling nearly $2 million, taking bribes, and selling hospital supplies intended to treat wounded veterans. As the investigation unfolded, his legal assistant shot himself (Cashman 1998: 287; Ponder 1998: 115). Harding's Attorney General, Harry Daugherty, was allegedly part of a scheme to sell bootleg liquor that had been seized by government agents from a house in Washington D.C., in addition to other forms of financial malfeasance and fraud. His assistant, Jesse Smith, committed suicide as the inevitable investigations unfolded, with the allegation that he had been murdered to ensure his silence circulating even in the Senate (Cashman 1998: 227–8).

Turning to golf, booze and gambling to assuage his worries as the Administration fell apart under the weight of its own malfeasance, Harding's health collapsed in early 1923. During an August trip to San Francisco the President died in the suite of a luxury hotel, possibly of a heart attack, in the middle of a conversation with his wife. Florence Harding subsequently forbade an autopsy of the President's body and burned many of his papers (Smith 2014: passim). The Vice President, Calvin Coolidge, was sworn in as President by his father at his family farmhouse in Vermont after being woken in the middle of the night. Personally speaking, the new President could hardly have contrasted more with his predecessor. While Harding had been a larger-than-life figure who dominated nearly any room he entered, Coolidge was a short, soft-spoken man who nonetheless shared Harding's pro-business views. Much of Coolidge's early Administration was preoccupied with addressing the corruption scandals that seemed to be unending, and, indeed, the most significant scandal had not yet even reached public consciousness when Harding died.

The 'Teapot Dome Scandal', as it became known, epitomised the corruption of US politics in the 1920s. In typically American style, it focused on a Wyoming oilfield, nicknamed the Teapot Dome because of a nearby natural formation, and was one of several fields designated for use by the US Navy. With the fleet converting from coal to oil, such fields arguably carried national security implications. Rather than leave the oil in the hands of the Navy, however, Harding's Secretary of the Interior, Albert B. Fall, secretly leased two fields to the Mammoth Oil Company and the Pan American Petroleum and Transport Company after convincing the Secretary of the Navy to transfer control over the fields to his agency. Fall subsequently received sizable 'gifts' from both corporations. Once the scandal broke, Senate hearings revealed the extent of the corruption. Criminal trials of Fall and his two business co-conspirators stretched on throughout the decade, with the eventual result that Fall was convicted of taking a bribe, but, bizarrely, the head of the Pan American Petroleum and Transport Company was acquitted of offering

FIGURE 7.2 President Calvin Coolidge came to office following the abrupt death of his predecessor in 1923, and soon had to contend with the less savoury aspects of Harding's legacy.

that same bribe. No one received a sentence of more than a year in jail. Even more damning was the fact that the press had known about the Teapot Dome allegations since at least 1922 but had published almost nothing about them prior to Harding's death (Cashman 1998: 228–9; Ponder 1998: 116–17). The camaraderie that Harding had cultivated in his late-night illicit drinking sessions with Washington journalists had protected him from the worst of his administration's scandals until the end of his life.

Facing the continued scandals that had largely been the makings of his predecessor, Coolidge cultivated his own reputation for personal discipline and conservatism. Nicknamed 'Silent Cal' for reputedly saying little in social settings, Coolidge continued to hold regularly scheduled press conferences but gave the reporters present few stories they could use. While he became the first President to make regular use of the radio to reach mass audiences, his speeches were generally short but often witty (Ponder 1998: 120–5). Coolidge's image as an 'everyman' who could relate to the average American but seemed vaguely uncomfortable in the public eye did much to bolster his popularity, and in 1924 he was easily re-elected as President. In this he was helped in part by the implosion of the Democratic Party at its 1924 national convention, when the party proved unable to pass a motion condemning the racist Ku Klux Klan due to the support of many Southern Democrats for the organisation. Democrats outside the South were outraged, and the party suffered a serious split (Cashman 1998: 230).

Coolidge's policies reflected the pro-business attitudes of his predecessors. Regulation was kept to a minimum, as was taxation, while protective tariffs remained high. Industrial production remained high, thanks in part to efficiency improvements and investment, through the mid-1920s. It was only in 1929 that the true weaknesses and flaws of the economy were revealed, and in the meantime Wall Street could hardly have been happier. A bull market in 1924–5 drove up stock prices considerably, and while relatively few Americans were actually investors, those that were tended to be wealthy and higher prices gave them the ability to spend cash freely and often wildly. The reputation of the decade as the 'Roaring Twenties' was directly linked to the fact that the wealthiest Americans were making huge amounts of money for doing nothing beyond having their brokers manage a portfolio (Cashman 1998: 237–40).

The election of 1928 proved to be the decisive referendum on American politics in the decade. There was no legal impediment to Calvin Coolidge seeking more than two terms as President (and he had not actually served even two full terms) so many were shocked in 1927 when Coolidge circulated a message to assembled reporters that stated simply, 'I do not choose to run for President in 1928'. The wording of the statement led some to speculate that Coolidge was hoping to receive the Republican nomination regardless (be 'drafted' onto the ticket, to use political parlance) but he subsequently took steps to prevent this from taking place (Ponder 1998: 140). His heir apparent was his Secretary of Commerce, Herbert Hoover, who had a reputation for not only having heavily pro-business attitudes but also being pro-British. Newspaper magnate William Randolph Hearst insisted on referring to Hoover as a 'loyal and law-respecting subject' of King George V, calling his loyalties into question at a time of increasing tension between the United States and Britain (Moser 1999: 66). Hoover's running mate was Charles Curtis, the Senate Majority Leader from Kansas and one of the few prominent politicians with Native American ancestry.

Still reeling from their internal conflicts with the Klan, the Democrats nominated Al Smith, the anti-Prohibition governor of New York who had a strong base of support among the working class. However, Smith was Catholic, and would be the only major party Catholic presidential nominee until John F. Kennedy successfully sought the presidency in 1960 (at the time of writing, Joseph Biden, elected in 2008, is the first Catholic Vice President in American history and Kennedy remains the only Catholic President). Indeed, Smith's religion became an integral part of the campaign, and he faced opposition from Klan members across the country, from anti-immigration activists who argued that much of his support came from Irish and Italian Catholics in East Coast cities, and from Protestants who believed in the continuation of Prohibition (Cashman 1998: 234). The outcome was again a disaster for the Democratic Party, with Smith taking just 40 per cent of the vote and Hoover netting nearly all of the rest. Smith lost even his home state of New York. Americans once again embraced the apparent prosperity that the Republican Party was offering.

Hoover would continue the pro-business policies of his predecessors and the American economy continued to boom for the time being. In March 1928, a bull market began on Wall Street that sent prices soaring. Many interpreted the boom as an endorsement of the Republican Party's policies, and it surely helped Hoover win the election later that year. Unknown to all, however, was the fact that just a year later, in October 1929, the stock market would suffer one of its greatest crashes in history, sending the world economy into a tailspin (Cashman 1998: 239–40). Rumours circulated on exchange floors that some ruined traders had resorted to throwing themselves out of their office windows rather than face penury. Whether these rumours were true or not, the decade that had been epitomised by the vagaries and corruptions of mammon ended in an economic collapse that reverberated worldwide, as the final chapters of this book will discuss.

The lion approaching winter: Britain and the Empire in the 1920s

Just as American politics were completely dominated by the Republican Party and business interests through the 1920s, the decade saw three major trends in British politics. The first was the clear dominance of the Conservative Party, which successfully took on the role of the major anti-socialist force in the country. Throughout the interwar period, the Conservatives would be in government for over 18 of the 21 years that separated the two world wars. In the 1920s they secured powerful governing majorities in 1922 and 1924 and, under the leadership of Stanley Baldwin from 1923, repositioned themselves as a calming force of stability after the maelstrom and destruction of the First World War. Baldwin in particular has been positively reinterpreted by recent historians: moving from a historiography in the 1950s which painted him as aimless and inert in the face of external threat to a more thoughtful politician who sincerely believed the nation had suffered a trauma beyond all previous instances between 1914 and 1918 and needed a more ruminative form of leadership (Williamson 1999: passim). The Conservative Party also managed to capitalise on the experiences of ex-servicemen by tailoring its campaign rhetoric to the experience of the trenches and the camaraderie of combat.

That being said, the 1920s also saw the rise of a new force in British politics: the Labour Party. Founded as a democratic socialist party before the First World War, Labour had broken its ties with the Liberal Party and begun to define its own political identity. The Party took power as a minority government (with Liberal support) for the first time in 1924, led by Ramsay MacDonald (and would indeed govern again between 1929 and 1931). Throughout this period Labour had a difficult line to walk, however. With the Liberal Party suffering under an alliance with the Conservatives brokered through a Coalition government which lasted from 1915 to 1922, Labour had to maintain its traditional left-wing policies in part to differentiate it from the other two major parties. At the same time, however, any suggestion that Labour was sympathetic to the Soviet Union and wanted to replicate its draconian and dramatic form of politics would have been electoral suicide. In 1924 the Conservative Party brandished with relish a letter supposedly from Soviet Foreign Minister Zinoviev to the British Communist Party urging its members to infiltrate Labour as a fifth column and thus push the party to the left. Stanley Baldwin duly won a landslide for the British right. Following the 1929 US stock market crash and the imposition of austerity measures to counter the downturn, Prime Minister Ramsay MacDonald stunningly abandoned the Labour Party to form a new party – National Labour – which he pledged would go into a coalition with the Conservatives. MacDonald subsequently won the election of 1931 (with a total of 13 National Labour MPs), remained Prime Minister, and the Labour Party was wiped out and lost 231 of its 287 seats. While the 1920s had been the era for the party to find its voice for the first time, Labour would have to wait until 1945 until the tectonic plates moved decisively in its favour.

The third big shift in 1920s politics was the collapse, which quickly became permanent, of the Liberal Party. The Liberals, who had won a thumping majority in the famous election of 1906 – delivering a welfare state through a new unemployment insurance, old age pensions and a system for free school meals – were caught in a pincer movement between Labour on the one hand and the Conservatives on the other. Too timid for the working class that wanted more for their suffering in the war, too radical (and led by the generally mistrusted David Lloyd George) for some in the polite middle classes, the 1923 election would be the last in British history in which the Liberals would win over 100 seats in a General Election. Given the House of Commons contained over 600 seats, they were not likely to form a government any time soon. As Ross McKibbin has observed, in the 1920s the Liberals were reduced to the role of a special interest party rather akin to the parties then catering to the German *mittelstand* (McKibbin 1990: 276).

These three trends combined to produce a phenomenon not always remarked on: the regular lack of a parliamentary majority in Great Britain. As noted, between 1915 and 1922 Britain was governed by a coalition, and in the elections of 1923 and 1929 no party was able to gain the required 50 per cent of seats in the House of Commons to be able to govern without reaching accommodation with others. It is frequently asserted that the nature of Weimar Germany's and pre-fascist Italy's system of proportional representation undid their democracies through what Bismarck had called 'the nightmare of coalitions'. But the British electoral system of First Past the Post – with all its misalignments and favouring of the big establishment parties – was often unable to deliver stable government either. In 1920s democracies, the default position was compromise, backroom deals and often coalition. This was as true for Britain as it was for the surviving democracies of France, the Netherlands and Sweden (none of whom saw single-party majority government in the 1920s), and indeed for the collapsing equivalents in Germany and Italy.

Whoever held the reins of power however, any British policy maker in the 1920s would have faced a number of almost insurmountable problems. Like most combatant states, a large collection of war debts (£1.3 billion in Britain's case) hampered what the British government could do financially in the post-war years. Indeed, the fact that such borrowing, about $10 billion when war loans to all nations were combined, was owed to the United States significantly helped the American treasury, and in fact the United States was actually running a budget surplus and paying off its national debt by the early 1920s (Cashman 1998: 185, 226). From interest rate payments covering about 2–3 percent of annual UK GDP before the war, by the late 1920s the figure was nearer 9 per cent. Attempting to pay down debt was a standard part of interwar British public policy.

Yet it was not just that Britain was spending money in an unproductive manner, it was also not making enough. With public opinion turning against the use of force to enforce British rule in imperial possessions (typified by reactions to the Amritsar Massacre in India in 1919 and the use of paramilitary 'Black and Tan' troops in Ireland before 1921), the old model by which Britain had made its money – buy raw materials from the colonies, manufacture them into a saleable product in British factories, and then sell them back to the Empire at a strong mark-up – was in tatters. Key markets like coal (Germany), financial services (the United States) and cotton (Japan) were also rapidly being taken over by foreign competitors. While much of the globe still remained under British rule, it was increasingly unclear how much longer that political dominance could be maintained when the country was mired in debt and the economic doldrums.

A natural consequence of all this was high unemployment. The 'intractable million' was a phrase used by many British policy makers to describe the high numbers of people kept out of work throughout the decade (Skidelsky 1967). The fact that more than six in ten unemployed men in the early 1920s were veterans of the First World War did not reflect well on a political class which had promised 'homes for heroes to live in' – which broadly interpreted meant not only homes but jobs and a decent standard of living too. The fact that the post-war Liberal–Conservative coalition undershot its target of 500,000 new homes by half did not do it total credit either. And, on wages, as the British coal mines (privatised after being taken over by the state during the war) saw their profits squeezed in the face of international competition, they took the decision to pass on such losses to their workforce. A direct consequence of this was the General Strike of May 1926, when 1.7 million workers went on strike in protest at wage cuts. The second instance of major industrial unrest in the decade – the first occurring in 1921 – it ended in failure when, under the pressure of the press, the government and public opinion, the Trades Union Congress acquiesced to more than a 13 per cent cut in wages. The 1927 Trade Disputes Act, passed by the then Conservative government, subsequently declared a General Strike to be illegal, further eviscerating the power of organised labour.

Throughout the decade the First World War remained a constant reference point for politicians. The 'million dead' of Britain and her empire were represented by new war memorials in every town across the UK, with the national memorial – the Cenotaph – placed yards away from the Foreign Office in Whitehall, London. Armistice Day on 11 November and the Tomb of the Unknown Warrior in Westminster Abbey were, from 1920, equally prominent reminders of the losses so many in Britain had suffered. It is frequently said that British politics remained demilitarised. By European comparison that is certainly true. Yet in the election of 1924, 200 MPs sat on the Conservative benches in Westminster who had performed uniformed service during the war (Carr 2013). These included famous names such as Anthony Eden and Harold Macmillan, both subsequently to serve as Prime Ministers in the 1950s. In political terms, the war came home.

With Labour back in office in 1929, it would be Britain's left who would have to deal with the consequences of the Wall Street Crash. Lacking a parliamentary majority and reliant on Lloyd George and the Liberals on a vote-by-vote basis, Ramsay MacDonald was always hamstrung. Yet his response to the steadily rising unemployment that Britain saw (rising to three million by early 1933) was disputed by ministers such as his successor as Labour leader George Lansbury and the future fascist Oswald Mosley, the latter of whom resigned from the government in May 1930. What was true for Britain was also true of several of her colonies – Australia briefly toyed with the Keynesian alternative of increased governmental spending to address the economic slump but, like the mother country, reverted to orthodox financial methods soon enough. Britain entered the 1930s with democracy far from a racing certainty to be its political system for the foreseeable future. As will be discussed, the fact that Britain's relations with the United States would face rapid collapse over economic rivalries at the end of the decade would do little to help the country's overall situation either.

Imperial peak: The survival of French democracy

The greater British Empire suffered about 1.1 million casualties in the First World War, representing less than 1 per cent of its overall population. Great Britain itself had taken the majority of the losses, totalling nearly 2 per cent of the country's overall population. As horrifying as these numbers were, they paled in comparison to figures in a number of the other combatants in the conflict. Devastatingly, the tiny country of Serbia lost nearly a quarter of its overall population and the Ottoman Empire almost 15 per cent. France, which had been in a bloody and often desperate fight to prevent the capture of Paris since almost the first days of the war, lost 1.3 million men on the battlefield, representing over 4 per cent of the country's overall population. Another 3–4 million had been wounded, often with debilitating injuries. Among the victors, France had paid one of the highest prices.

It is thus little surprise that the French Third Republic, which had been founded in 1870, faced a series of immediate challenges. However, in many ways the Treaty of Versailles had provided a foundation for the French government to begin rebuilding from its wartime losses. Subsequent negotiations had increased the scope of the French Empire by handing the country mandates for both Syria and Lebanon in the Middle East (Britain had received Mesopotamia, among other concessions) and creating a framework in which its closest rival, Germany, could not militarily rearm for the time being. In addition, German financial reparations payments began flowing into the French treasury, giving the country a source of regular income as long as the Germans remained compliant with the reparations system. When Germany defaulted on its payments in 1923, French and Belgian troops marched into the industrial Ruhr Valley. Other areas of the Rhineland remained under French occupation until 1930.

As elsewhere, French politics in the 1920s was defined by a stark opposition between the left and the right, but with the added aspect of anticlericalism playing a major role. Right-wing Catholic parties largely found themselves excluded from politics, and the main political competition took place between socialist and communist parties of varying degrees of radicalism and the republican parties of the right. Many elites remained suspicious and outright contemptuous of the working classes and sought to maintain a democratic system that disenfranchised most of the population (Passmore 2003: 40–2). From 1919 to 1924, France was governed by a coalition of right-wing parties known as the National Bloc – a pragmatic alliance of pro-army, pro-church and anti-communist forces. In 1923, however, a group of socialist and communist-leaning left-wing parties and radicals formed the *Cartel des gauches* (Left-Wing Coalition) and managed to gain a majority in Parliament despite receiving a minority of the public vote. Only two years later the Cartel collapsed and the right subsequently returned to power, this time themselves joined by the radicals, in no small part because of the fear of communist influence in the government (Passmore 2003: 52–7). In a period when political radicalisation was spreading across the Continent, France's political system appeared to weather the storm particularly well despite the political uncertainties of the early years of the decade.

This apparent political success was in no small part due to the relative strength of France's economy, even as the American economy began to collapse in 1929. With the French empire expanded beyond its previous borders by the Treaty of Versailles, it was inevitable that imperial trade would expand, at least initially. A sharp drop in commodities prices around the Empire after the end of the war – there was far less need for raw materials once the fighting stopped – was quickly overcome. While there would be no dramatic increase in imperial trade during the 1920s, there was a modest improvement and, more importantly, a number of French industries were propped up by the availability of imperial markets. Economic historians have identified industries as varied as cotton-weaving, sugar refining and copper smelting as those more or less sustained by exports to French colonies in the interwar period (Thomas 2005: 105). By 1928, decreased access to foreign markets had made the empire France's most important trading partner (Thomas 2005: 118). The 1920s thus saw the height of French power beyond the continent of Europe (Agulhon 1993: 204).

Indeed, this ready access to markets kept France's economy relatively strong when the US stock market crashed in 1929, the franc maintained its value at a time when other currencies were being devalued or collapsing. This, of course, had the natural effect of making French goods more expensive in foreign markets, which then began to take a toll on the economy. Having avoided the initial economic downturn, France now began to suffer because of its relative strength. By the early 1930s, a strong franc coupled with international decline in demand for the luxury products that France specialised in producing had begun to damage the economy (Thomas 2005: 104–6). The country would soon face a political crisis not unlike those being experienced elsewhere on the Continent, but it would only be with the invasion of France in 1940 that the Third Republic would meet its end. In many senses, France's democratic system had weathered the political storm of the post-war world remarkably well, but there would ultimately be no avoiding the crisis. In the longer term, the fact that France had relied so heavily on its empire for economic stability – and the fact that the colonies themselves had not been allowed to diversify their industries beyond those that met the immediate needs of the wider imperial situation – would have devastating consequences.

As seen in chapter 1, the fact that France itself was a democracy did not mean that its imperial possessions were themselves governed democratically. As was the case with the British Empire, there was an intrinsic contradiction between the democratic ideals championed at home and the realities of governing a vast and diverse empire, often through the use of force. These contradictions would become increasingly significant as the European empires would be faced with increasing challenges to their legitimacy – and their economic underpinnings – in the years after 1929. We deal with examples of such contradictions later in this chapter.

Building a new 'democracy': Atatürk and the creation of Turkey

The first three democracies considered in this section have the distinction of having been established prior to the outbreak of the First World War and having survived the conflict politically intact. As noted, however, this is not to say that any of these political systems were guaranteed to survive the Great Depression. Unlike these previous cases, the final example of 1920s democracy comes from a country that did not even exist in 1914, let alone as a democracy: Turkey. Prior to the 1920s, the territory that would become Turkey was part of the vast, multi-ethnic, multi-religious Ottoman Empire, known before the war as the 'sick man of Europe' for its endemic problems and instability.

Stretching from the Black Sea in the North to the bottom of the Arabian Peninsula in the South, the Ottoman Empire was huge geographically, beset by ethnic strife and was increasingly becoming a pawn of foreign powers, especially Germany, by the outbreak of the war. In 1908, a revolution by a group known as the Young Turks had established a form of constitutional monarchy with parliamentary aspects, but was dislodged in a coup a few years later. A number of Balkan states took advantage of the situation to revolt against Ottoman rule, ending in the loss of significant territory in Europe. In 1913, another coup brought three powerful and autocratic leaders – nicknamed the 'Three Pashas' – to power. They would retain nearly dictatorial control over the country until the end of the First World War.

The Ottoman Empire was thus already perceived as being in its death throes when the First World War broke out. Centuries of religious rule had held the country's economic development back in a myriad of ways. Automobiles were forbidden as potentially un-Islamic until 1908 and it was estimated that there were only 500 of them in the country five years later (as noted previously, the United States already had around 1 million automobiles on the road in the same period) (Russell 2015). The Ottoman Empire's military capacity was therefore nowhere near that of its European allies in 1914, though it had the advantage of massive manpower and a thorough disregard for casualty figures. The Arab and Armenian minorities in the Empire soon became problematic for the regime: the former revolted against Ottoman rule in the wider Middle East, while the latter were conspiratorially believed to be in league with the allies, not least because they were Christian rather than Muslim, and were subjected to extermination on a mass scale in the Armenian Genocide. At the end of the war, France and Britain became the biggest beneficiaries of the Ottoman defeat. Britain was given a Mandate over Palestine (composed of modern-day Israel, the Palestinian territories and Jordan) along with Mesopotamia (Iraq), while France demanded a Mandate over modern-day Syria and Lebanon. The Arabian Peninsula was left to the local leaders who had rebelled against Ottoman control to sort out, and after a period of instability, discussed in chapter 1, the Kingdom of Saudi Arabia was formed in 1932.

This state of affairs left the Ottoman Empire in shambles: the capital of Constantinople was occupied by an allied army, the Empire's leaders were driven from power, two of the Three Pashas were assassinated by Armenian nationalists in retaliation for the mass killing of the Armenian Genocide and the third died violently in battle. Into the vacuum stepped one of the Empire's greatest military leaders: Mustafa Kemal, a venerated hero of the First World War. Kemal had been a military attaché in Sofia in 1913 and with the outbreak of the conflict had been sent to the strategically critical Gallipoli peninsula, where he had previously been stationed. As a result, he was in command of Ottoman forces when they successfully repelled the disastrous 1915 British invasion of Gallipoli and prevented the capture of Constantinople (later Istanbul), ensuring his promotion and his popularity along with the honorific title of Pasha. At the end of the war, Kemal Pasha had been sent to Syria and Palestine and returned to Istanbul to assume a position in the Ministry of War (Lewis 1955: 68–9). He was thus one of the most popular leaders in the Ottoman Empire when the allies began to dictate their peace terms to the surviving members of the government.

In some senses, the allies attempted to treat the Ottoman Empire in the same way as they were simultaneously treating Austria–Hungary and Germany: by dismantling their empires. However, in the Ottoman case this was a particularly difficult proposition given the degree of religious and ethnic diversity present. In March 1920, an allied army occupied the capital and arrested key political figures. In retaliation, the popular Kemal announced the formation of a 'National Assembly' in Ankara as a 'temporary measure' until free governance could be restored. Elections were held for representatives to this body across Anatolia and non-Muslims were banned from taking part. Kemal had embarked on the road to creating a new state with a distinct identity in the ruins of the Ottoman Empire (Zürcher 2013: 31).

The fact that there remained an allied-dominated 'legitimate' government in Istanbul would soon become a point of serious contention, however, as would the machinations of the allied powers themselves. Seeking to forcibly dismantle the Empire for their own gain, the British, French and Italians encouraged uprisings and warfare in all directions: by Greece in the West, Armenia in the East, and Arabs and Kurds in the South. Amidst a series of military setbacks, Kemal was appointed commander-in-chief of Ottoman forces in 1921. The tide immediately began to turn and in September 1922 Turkish troops entered the Greek-held city of İzmir. As Kemal marched north towards the city of Thrace he encountered the multi-national Allied Army of Occupation. French and Italian divisions were withdrawn, leaving the British to face off alone against the Turks. With the prospect of a major war if either side fired on the other, an armistice was signed on 11 October. The Treaty of Lausanne the following year formally created the Republic of Turkey as the successor to the Ottoman Empire and formalised its borders (Lewis 1955: 82–4).

Kemal was now faced with the task of forming a government for the new state he had managed to salvage amidst allied machinations and ethnic violence. The capital was moved to Ankara from Istanbul, illustrating the radical break Kemal intended to make with the Ottoman past. In October 1923, the Grand National Assembly voted to declare a republic with Mustafa Kemal as its first president. While Islam would be the official religion of the Turkish state, at least initially, the supreme Muslim religious position of Caliph, discussed previously, would have no place in the state. The Caliph was theoretically the leader of Muslims worldwide and since the fourteenth century the position had been held by Ottoman sultans who variously ignored the title or used it to motivate Muslim resistance to foreign interference in the region (Lewis 1955: 93–4). Kemal's view was that too much Turkish blood had been shed in the service of Muslims beyond Anatolia's borders at the behest of the Caliphate and, as a result, the Caliph presented a political threat to the new state he was establishing. In 1924, the Grand National Assembly formally abolished the Caliphate and banished all members of the Ottoman imperial family. The last Caliph lived out his days in Europe and died in 1944, and while various claimants have emerged since, there has been no unified effort to revive the position. As Geoffrey Lewis has observed, Kemal's efforts were motivated by his desire to 'make Turkey into a modern state fit to take its place among the civilized countries of the Western world ... The primary task was to sever the bonds between Islam and the state, and then to replace Islamic by western civilization' (Lewis 1955: 92).

The first task accomplished, Kemal now turned to the second. In 1925, the Grand National Assembly passed a law banning the wearing of the fez, a traditional form of headwear that lacked a brim. Instead, Turkish men would now wear Western-style hats. Similarly, the traditional wearing of the veil by women was discouraged. The following year, the traditional calendar was officially replaced by the Gregorian calendar, bringing Turkey in line with the Western standard. A new civil code and other pieces of legislation based on European models were passed, creating a new legal code and giving women a host of new rights that put them on an even standing with men in a number of key areas (Lewis 1955: 105–6, 129). In 1928, Western numerals officially replaced traditional Arabic characters and in 1929 all government departments were required to use the new Turkish alphabet rather than Arabic script. The new alphabet was based on the Latin letters used in European languages, and in addition a new form of Turkish that dispensed with many of the linguistic styles of the past was developed (Lewis 1955: 108–10). In the course of a few years, Kemal had turned Turkey into a country that increasingly resembled its European counterparts more than the former Ottoman imperial possessions in the Middle East. In 1936 the BBC in London even ran a series of radio programmes on 'European Exchanges', one of which dealt with Turkey and which commented on such changes. The host, Elizabeth Pakenham, noted that

> Turkey is still rather mysterious ... Not that English people imagine Turkey is a country of veiled women and men with fezzes. We know that sort of thing's been swept away ... For many people over here your bowler hats, your Latin script instead of Arabic, and your corporation buses have taken the glamour out of the country.
>
> (The Listener, 1 January 1936)

As could be predicted, none of this was accomplished without opposition. Rioting accompanied the banning of the fez and other measures, leading to an official crackdown on protests. A rebellion in 1925 led to the closing of the only opposition party contending against Kemal's Republican People's Party while an attempt to assassinate Kemal in 1926 was followed by executions, banishments and further repression. Kemal himself attempted to create several opposition parties in an effort to bring true multi-party democracy to the country, but these efforts failed when the parties appeared to be moving toward the undoing of the Westernising reforms Kemal had championed. It would only be after the Second World War that truly free elections between multiple parties would take place.

In 1934, Kemal was given the title of 'Atatürk' (translated as 'Father of the Turks') in recognition of his accomplishments. While truly liberal democracy remained beyond Atatürk's powers to achieve, his reforms had placed the country on a road that led to Western institutions. He would remain president of the republic until his death in 1938. As Andrew Mango has noted, Atatürk's accomplishments had come at a time when democracy itself appeared to be in widespread retreat worldwide and particularly in Europe. The fact that an empire formerly renowned for its alleged backwardness and despotism could be partially transformed into an increasingly Western republic, with the beginnings of democratic institutions, in the course of less than a decade was nothing less than remarkable (Mango 2002: 20). That being said, Turkey at the end of the 1920s was a one-party state ruled by a charismatic leader with nearly dictatorial powers. The fact that its leader hoped to base the country's future development on the model of Western democracies rather than the fascism or communism that were becoming increasingly popular in those same democracies was the source of its hope for the future.

The limits of democracy: Liberia, Fiji and India

As noted, 1920s American democracy was less perfect than its self-proclaimed image suggested. Since the First World War had involved hysterical, and slightly hypocritical, calls to 'democracy' against 'tyranny' perhaps this was no surprise. It was certainly difficult to live up to such grandiose hype, particularly when Germany had operated a democratic system (with a welfare state) of sorts. The language of 'national self-determination' used by Woodrow Wilson in 1918 and 1919 of course ratcheted up matters further (though his recommendation for the United States to relinquish control over its own colony, the Philippines, was soundly rejected by later Republican administrations). And yet the actions of the United States in Liberia were clearly indicative that democracy was only to be invoked when it suited the major powers, and could be ignored when it did not.

Liberia had been settled by former African-American slaves in the first half of the nineteenth century and, by the 1920s, was the only African territory outside of Ethiopia (then Abyssinia) that was not part of an empire. Given the previous ties between the countries, the United States had strongly resisted Liberia's submission to European control in the Scramble for Africa in the 1880s, but this did not mean it was unwilling to exercise its own more informal form of control.

In 1920 Charles D.B. King was elected President of Liberia. Although nominally a supporter of democratic reform and a Whig, his administration would be marked by a decidedly corrupt electoral system and economic interference from the United States. In 1927, King secured a clear re-election victory over his opponent, Thomas J.R. Faulkner. King's securing of 234,000 votes was certainly an impressive tally but it suffered a slight legitimacy problem since only 15,000 Liberians were actually registered to vote at the time. Despite the election having been quite obviously stolen, King remained in office partly because his American sponsors decreed this was optimal. In the early 1920s Liberia had been heavily indebted and needed an urgent dose of cash for debt consolidation. This the United States granted, and after a trip from King to plead his country's case in Washington, the House of Representatives agreed to extend a $5 million loan to the African state. The US Senate however did not, which left Liberia further in financial limbo.

This brought the Liberians to the table again. The year before King's dubious re-election victory, the Firestone Rubber Company of Ohio obtained a concession to lease land in Liberia for the purposes of harvesting rubber for the burgeoning automobile industry. Firestone agreed to lease one million acres for 99 years at an annual rate of six cents per acre, including a clause that the company would be able to keep any gold, diamonds or other precious metals. In return, Firestone agreed to meet the terms of the $5 million loan that Congress had rejected, albeit imposing a clause whereby Liberia was forbidden from borrowing any more from the international markets. Some Liberian elites made a killing from this venture, but most of the country suffered as Firestone reaped huge profits (Christy 1931: passim).

When the League of Nations published its Christy Report of 1930 on the nature of forced labour in Liberia (used to construct new roads and infrastructure, in part to project an image that the West could buy into), it became even clearer that this supposed beacon of African democracy was anything but democratic. Cuthbert Christy, a British physician and explorer who developed an expertise in the region, himself remarked that 'during his many speeches the backward, moneyless, undeveloped negro Republic of Liberia was so camouflaged with prosperity and enlightenment that she could scarcely be recognized' (Christy 1931: 525). He later observed of the capital Monrovia that its

> good people ... have only oil lamps, and at night the streets are in darkness. Having no theatres, picture palaces, or hotel bars, only an occasional newspaper of foolscap size, and few books, they seem to devote their whole attention to local politics.
>
> (Christy 1931: 532)

Such isolation from the global community was exacerbated when the British Bank of West Africa, located in the country, closed its head office in December 1930 due to unsanitary living conditions and the death of two of its employees from yellow fever. What financial services there were now became the sole preserve and operation of the Firestone Rubber Company.

Such ambivalence towards democracy in dependent states was hardly the United States' sole preserve, however. In 1874 the UK had taken formal control over the islands of Fiji in the Pacific. In 1904 the previously advisory Legislative Council had its remit extended into a formally elected governing body. This however was a heavily gerrymandered process – of the 19 councillors, six were to be elected by Europeans, two to be appointed by the colonial governor (from a list submitted by the Great Council of Chiefs), and a further eight were to be formally appointed by the Governor himself. During the First World War the Indian community (mostly from the Gujarat) were given a nominated appointee – extended to an electable post from 1929. But there was no great rush from the British to impose the righteousness of democracy. The main source of the wish to not rock the boat, most likely, was the sugar industry. In 1913, Fiji surpassed the West Indies as a contributor to the British Empire in this regard (Knapman 1985: 66). In the case of Fiji, the British were perfectly willing to fall back on the argument of the 'White Man's Burden': Fiji was not yet ready for Western democracy and thus they must remain in control until it was. Under-development of the country's financial system had a further benefit during the war: profits were usually invested in British, Australian or New Zealand stocks for lack of local issues (Knapman 1985: 78). Democracy had its clear limits, even in colonies run by nominally democratic countries.

That was distant and small Fiji, but even in the 'jewel in the crown' of India the franchise was only expanded reluctantly. In 1919 the spirit of the Montagu Declaration two years earlier had produced a Government of India Act which created a diarchy for the major provinces involving the separation of powers between local leaders (the 'transferred list' of responsibilities included agriculture, health and education) and the British-appointed Viceroy (who retained defence, military and foreign affairs). The Imperial Legislative Council – which had only in 1909 begun to allow the election of Indians to its membership – was expanded and became a bicameral chamber, but the Viceroy could sign off any expenditure of money for 'ecclesiastical, political and defence purposes, and for any purposes during "emergencies"'. He could also veto, or simply stop debate on, the passage of any bill. If one chamber of the Council approved of a bill but the other did not, he could order passage of the bill. Initially the Indian National Congress refused to take part in the first elections under this new system in 1920 whilst the pro-British National Liberal Party was more amenable to the spirit of Montagu. Turnout was poor, with only one in four eligible voters casting a provincial vote. Partly this represented antipathy towards the British per se, but it also stemmed from general disenfranchisement. Even in a more stable atmosphere in 1925, fewer than one in ten of the Indian adult male population were entitled to vote at any level. Powers had been devolved (albeit in the heavily caveated manner indicated above), but to an electoral vacuum. Such devolution appeased liberal British sentiment, allowed them to nominally believe the 'Gandhi problem' was being dealt with, but it did little for genuine democracy.

Consider also the case of the French. During the 1920s the French Empire was still capable of formidable propaganda exercises. Throughout the decade the French undertook the third largest earth-moving exercise in human history (after the canals of Panama and Suez) to dredge and clear the Mekong Delta in southern Vietnam. As Tony Ballantyne and Antoinette Burton note, 'this undertaking was designed to improve coastal agriculture and facilitate more effective communication, but it was also celebrated by the French as evidence of the improving power of colonial rule in the face of rising anticolonial sentiment' (Ballantyne and Burton

2012: 43). If the French were capable of such a *grand projet*, after all, why would anyone want rid of them? The answer, of course, lay in the repression that went alongside such feats. But the key to unlocking the gap between rhetoric and deed often lay in outlining the plight of the white man in such circumstance. Amidst the type of collective 'White Man's Burden' thinking illustrated by the British in India, it was often the only way to achieve cut-through for the other side of the coin. In 1924 the investigative journalist Albert Londres published his work *Au Bagne – In Prison* – on the conditions in the French penal colony Devil's Island in French Guiana (the same prison colony that had once held wrongly convicted military officer Alfred Dreyfus). The book was a commercial smash hit which prompted the colonial authorities to look again at conditions on the island, which eventually ceased to serve as a prison colony in the late 1930s.

The International Labour Office served as another means of self-criticism, though here there was something of an anomaly. Since 1848 the Four Communes of Senegal had been entitled to elect a Deputy to represent them in the French Parliament in Paris. Throughout the 1920s this was Blaise Diagne (who in 1916 had helped pass a law in the Assembly to give full citizenship to all residents – black and white – of Senegal). Diagne was also active in the ILO and rose to become French representative to the body in 1930, before becoming Under-Secretary of State for the Colonies in January 1931. Diagne was a powerful advocate for black rights, but he was also someone prepared to make accommodation with the colonial regime. By the end of the 1920s colonial nationalism had arguably moved beyond the Diagnes and beyond the point where Mekong Delta-esque schemes could hold back the march to liberty. Since democracy could mean the removal of their own influence, Western powers judged it was often best applied sporadically.

Conclusion

As the 1920s dawned, the future of democracy could hardly be assured. The First World War had devastated the demographics and political systems of virtually every democratic country, with the notable exception of the United States. Having profited substantially from the war itself through armaments sales and lending money to the combatants, the United States was uniquely well positioned to come out ahead when peace was made. Indeed, American businesses reaped impressive profits for most of the 1920s. Politically, the Republican Party openly allied itself with this prosperity, benefitting electorally from the Democratic Party's internal divisions and general unpopularity in the aftermath of the Wilson Administration. Even the remarkable corruption of Warren G. Harding's administration was unable to shake the GOP's stranglehold on power. The overwhelming victory of Herbert Hoover in 1928 was greeted by a surge on the stock market and the widespread support of business leaders for a continuation of the decade's policies. Ironically, the fact that Hoover's predecessor, Calvin Coolidge, chose to not run for re-election in 1928 when he was nearly assured of victory meant that Hoover would bear the brunt of the stock market crash the following year. Hoover's political reputation would be rapidly destroyed, and despite winning a massive victory in 1928, he would receive less than 40 per cent of the popular vote in 1932. The Republican Party would not win the White House again until 1952.

The United States' debtor countries were much less fortunate in the 1920s. Having suffered shocking casualty rates in the trenches of the First World War, British voters were increasingly torn between the major pre-war parties – the Liberals and the Tories – and the upstart Labour Party that shared more than a few of its ideas with the Russian Bolsheviks. The threat of communism itself was omnipresent, and the fact that the Labour Party was incorrectly accused of taking instructions from Moscow was enough to temporarily doom its electoral prospects. By the end of the decade, however, Labour had twice been in power and, unfortunately for its leaders, was in power when the economic crash of 1929 began. The resultant split in its ranks, coupled with the outbreak of the Second World War, would ensure that the party remained out of power until 1945. On the other hand, Winston Churchill's wartime government of national unity included the Labour Party's leader, Clement Attlee, as his Deputy Prime Minister. The 1920s had been the formative decade for Labour, and despite short-term setbacks the party was positioned for future success. More menacingly to conservative voices, however, was the damage that the war had done to Britain's democratic institutions themselves. Bemoaning the prospect of a future socialist state that dispensed with electoral politics entirely, William Ralph Inge, the conservative dean of St Paul's Cathedral, remarked in 1926 that, 'The Great War seems to have given all authority a shake, and to have increased the hopes of the enemies of society' (Inge 1926: 264). For those on the right, democracy's hold looked decidedly shaky.

French democracy was in similar straits. Both right- and left-wing coalitions were able to take power at various points throughout the 1920s, unified primarily by their distaste for the Catholic and clerical parties that seemed to present a challenge to the republican principle of *laïcité* (secularism). Both communism and fascism would present themselves as threats to the existing system as the decade continued, but in comparison to many of its European rivals the French system endured remarkably well. The 1920s were also the peak of French power beyond Europe's shores, thanks in part to the massive mandates it received in the Middle East. While this had obvious benefits, France's reliance on imperial markets for its goods would initially insulate the country from the effects of the Great Depression but ultimately expose its lack of international competitiveness. In addition, France's political obsession with keeping German power in check – though understandable given the shocking bloodshed that was still fresh in the public imagination – helped give apparent legitimacy to German grievances and ultimately paved the way for Adolf Hitler's government to capitalise on these complaints. Ultimately, the weaknesses of the Third Republic would be exposed in the Second World War when France proved unable to stand up to the German military onslaught.

While democracy was at best on metaphorical life support in much of Europe throughout the 1920s, Mustafa Kemal Atatürk embarked on one of the most remarkable political campaigns of the modern world. Enraged by the treatment of

Anatolia by the victorious allies, he proved able to capitalise on this resentment to not only expel the armies occupying the country but also carve out the state of Turkey. The country Atatürk envisioned would be a modern, Westernised nation, purged of its Islamic elements and ready to compete on an equal footing with its former rivals. Though Turkey never advanced past a single-party state in his lifetime, the institutions he created would prove to be a workable basis for future reforms. Further, the rapid social and civil progress created by his laws on issues ranging from women's rights to styles of dress and calendar systems quickly made Turkey a more European-style country than would have been possible to imagine in 1914. The introduction of the Turkish alphabet and Latin numerals marked the ultimate break with the Ottoman past, as did the expulsion of the Caliph. True democracy remained a hope for the future, but this was a hope in Turkey that existed in few other countries in the period.

The world's democracies were thus in an increasingly perilous position as the 1920s came to a close. In economic dependencies such as Liberia they overlooked anti-democratic activity if it suited their economic ends, in many formal colonies such as Fiji they continued to default to the argument that such areas were not ready for democracy. The turmoil created by the economic downtown of 1929 would expose even more of the cracks in their facades. American attempts at arms-length economic intervention through the Dawes (1924) and Young (1929) Plans failed to stem the anti-democratic tide in Germany, and as the 1920s ended many were justifiably worried about democracy's future, when even this drawbridge was removed as the United States became ever more entrenched. It would only be with the defeat of fascism in 1945 and, ultimately, the end of the Cold War in the 1990s that democracy would become the world's dominant political system.

As the 1930s began, this could hardly have been further from a certainty. In November 1930 the dashing young Conservative Anthony Eden stood up in the House of Commons and implored his fellow MPs to

> make a close study of the causes of the collapse of parliamentary government in Europe since the war. It has not been because these countries are temperamentally unfitted to work the parliamentary machine. It has been for a far simpler reason, because Parliament has failed.
>
> *(Carr 2013: 86)*

Many were reaching similar conclusions even if, as yet, they lacked the solutions to address this quandary.

Questions

- What factors led to the United States becoming so isolationist in the aftermath of the First World War?
- What country had the most stable democratic system of the 1920s, and why?
- What factors led to countries turning away from democracy in the 1920s? Why did some do so, while others did not?

- Why did Turkey begin to adopt secular democratic institutions at a time when democracy was arguably on the defensive elsewhere?
- Were the world's democracies well positioned to survive the economic collapse that began in 1929? Why or why not?
- What were the major differences between Western conceptions of what democracy should be in their own country, and those other states where they had an economic interest?

Recommended further reading

Cashman, S. (1998), *America Ascendant: From Theodore Roosevelt to FDR in the Century of American Power, 1901–1945*, New York: New York University Press.

Fitzgerald, F.S. (1925), *The Great Gatsby*, New York: Charles Scribner's Sons.

Lewis, G. (1955), *Modern Turkey*, London and Tonbridge: Ernest Benn.

Thomas, M. (2005), *The French Empire between the Wars: Imperialism, Politics and Society*, Manchester: Manchester University Press.

Williamson, P. (1999), *Stanley Baldwin: Conservative Leadership and National Values*, Cambridge: Cambridge University Press.

Works cited

Agulhon, M. (1993), *The French Republic: 1879–1992*, Oxford: Basil Blackwell.

Ballantyne, T. and Burton, A. (2012), *Empires and the Reach of the Global 1870–1945*, Cambridge, MA: Harvard University Press.

Carr, R. (2013), *Veteran MPs and Conservative Politics in the Aftermath of the Great War*, Farnham: Ashgate.

Cashman, S. (1998), *America Ascendant: From Theodore Roosevelt to FDR in the Century of American Power, 1901–1945*, New York: New York University Press.

Christy, C. (1931), 'Liberia in 1930', *The Geographical Journal*, 77/6, 515–540.

Fukuyama, F. (1992), *The End of History and the Last Man*, London: Free Press.

Hart, K. (1967), 'Republican Internationalism in the 1920s', Unpublished MA thesis: Fresno State College.

Inge, W.R. (1926), *England*, New York: Charles Scribner's Sons.

Knapman, B. (1985), 'Capitalism's Economic Impact in Colonial Fiji, 1874–1939: Development or Underdevelopment?', *The Journal of Pacific History*, 20/2, 66–83.

Lewis, G. (1955), *Modern Turkey*, London and Tonbridge: Ernest Benn.

Mango, A. (2002), 'Atatürk: Founding Father, Realist, and Visionary', in Heper, M. and Savari, S. (eds), *Political Leaders and Democracy in Turkey*, Oxford: Lexington Books, pp. 9–24.

McKibbin, R. (1990), *The Ideologies of Class: Social Relations in Britain 1880–1950*, Oxford: Oxford University Press.

Moser, J.E. (1999), *Twisting the Lion's Tail: American Anglophobia between the World Wars*, New York: New York University Press.

Passmore, K. (2003), 'Politics, 1914–1945', in McMillan, J. (ed.), *Modern France*, Oxford: Oxford University Press.

Ponder, S. (1998), *Managing the Press: Origins of the Media Presidency, 1897–1933*, New York: St Martin's Press.

Russell, G. (2015), 'Jihad: The Lessons of the Caliphate', *The New York Review of Books*, 7 May 2015. Available online: www.nybooks.com/articles/archives/2015/may/07/jihad-lessons-caliphate

Skidelsky, R. (1967), *Politicians and the Slump: The Labour Government of 1929–1931*, Oxford: Pelican.

Smith, J.M. (2014), 'All the President's Pen', *The New York Times Magazine*, 13 July 2014, MM31.

Spears, E.L. (n.d.), *America and the Next War*, Journals held at Churchill College, Cambridge, SPRS 7/2.

Thomas, M. (2005), *The French Empire between the Wars: Imperialism, Politics and Society*, Manchester: Manchester University Press.

Williamson, P. (1999), *Stanley Baldwin: Conservative Leadership and National Values*, Cambridge: Cambridge University Press.

Zürcher, E.J. (2013), 'Reflections on Millets and Minorities: Ottoman Legacies', in Kastoryano, R. (ed.), *Turkey between Nationalism and Globalization*, Abingdon: Routledge.

8

COMMUNISM

To borrow the title of a famous book by leftist American journalist John Reed, in late 1917 Russia experienced 'Ten Days That Shook the World' (Reed 1919: passim). Indeed, the capture of government buildings and the Winter Palace in Petrograd by the Bolshevik Red Guard presaged the advent of a communist regime that would not fall until the early 1990s. This clearly had a tremendous impact inside the borders of Russia and, from the early 1920s, the wider Soviet Union, but it also changed the way many viewed the world beyond those confines. Along with the collapse of monarchies in Germany and Austria–Hungary, the age of the King and the Tsar was over. International diplomacy would no longer be monarch talking to monarch (in many such cases, cousin talking to cousin) but democratic politician trying to understand communist dictator, and vice versa. To put it mildly, this was not always smooth sailing. Symbolically, for one, the Soviet Union shifted its capital away from Westernised and Europe-facing Petrograd (modern-day St Petersburg) to the old capital of Moscow, located in the Russian interior, in 1922. Therefore, if we judge the 1920s as an increasingly global age it is important to qualify this assertion: the earth's most territorially large country, Russia, would look inward, and not outward, for much of this period. Winston Churchill may only have uttered his famous aphorism in the shadow of the Second World War, but for many in the 1920s Russia was indeed 'a riddle wrapped in a mystery inside an enigma'. Recognition of the new communist regime did not come from the British until 1924, and the Americans until 1933.

Perhaps because of such ambiguity, the Soviet Union became a source of fear and inspiration for many across the globe. Far-flung Persia (1920), New Zealand (1921) and South Africa (1921) were all early adopters of communist parties. By 1922 Guatemala had followed suit, and even though formed in exile the 1920s saw the formation of a communist party for Korea. And, as Mark Mazower notes, 'nowhere was the dazzling Soviet achievement watched with more concern than in central and western Europe' (Mazower 1998: 128). So-called Red Scares occurred in many territories including America, the UK and Australia. For Maurice Dobb, in 1920 a young economist in Cambridge, 'the signposts of economic and social evolution point inevitably *from* Capitalism *to* Socialism and Communism' (Overy 2009: 65). By 1924 the Communist Party was propping up the *Cartel des gauches* administration in France, and over three million Germans were voting for the KPD (Communist Party of Germany) in 1928 – before the Wall Street Crash, discussed later, increased the apparent validity of the critique of capitalism the communists were proffering. Prior to the global financial crisis of October 1929 indeed, Germans were voting communist over national socialist by four to one. The inspiration for all this, other than the nineteenth century theoretician Karl Marx, was the very contemporary Vladimir Lenin.

Lenin

Vladimir Ilyich Ulyanov was born in April 1870 in Simbirsk, Southern Russia. His brother Sacha, a member of a socialist revolutionary group in St Petersburg, was executed for plotting to assassinate the Tsar in 1887. That same year, young Vladimir began studying at Kazan University where he first read Marx's *Das Kapital*. Rebuffing his mother's attempts to launch him into a middle-class agricultural career, he instead performed various legal assistant jobs, all the while taking part in radical discussion groups. Travelling across France, Switzerland and Germany, he attempted to rally social democratic allies (often Russian exiles) across Western and Central Europe all the while avoiding the clutches of the Russian secret police. He would eventually be exiled to Siberia for three years in 1897 – a common fate for the would-be revolutionary of this era.

In 1902 he published the influential pamphlet *What Is to Be Done?* using the 'Lenin' sobriquet. This pamphlet argued that economic strife and individual disputes would not alone lead to a politicised working class. Instead they needed to form a movement – a 'vanguard' – in which to take on the capitalist order. Three years later an abortive revolution – the Bloody Sunday massacre of protestors in St Petersburg – was met with a call from Lenin for violent insurrection. This in turn produced the great split between the Mensheviks – whom Lenin considered bourgeois social democrats who would be bought off by trifling reforms such as the creation of a constitutional monarchy – and the Bolsheviks for whom only a peasant-proletarian takeover of power would do. The October Manifesto of 1905 to some degree delivered the former – strengthening the power of the Russian Parliament (the *Duma*), introducing universal male suffrage, and granting increased civil liberties. But the great revolution would have to wait.

For much of the period after the failure of 1905 until the First World War, Lenin, like Mussolini, was abroad – it is a feature indeed of the key figures of our *Global 1920s* that their decades preceding fame and power were often spent globe-trotting (Service 2000: chs 8–14). Lenin passed through Capri in Italy, London (where he used the facilities of the British Library to pen *Materialism and*

Empirio-criticism), Copenhagen (venue for the 1910 Congress of the Second International) and Paris. Until 1916 he was resident in Switzerland where he wrote his
famous *Imperialism: The Highest Stage of Capitalism* (discussed later), which argued
that the Great War itself was merely an instance of capitalistic powers seeking fresh
markets and greater profits. To preserve themselves, business interests would ultimately
force war upon the world to protect their investments and seek new ones. In this
interpretation the First World War was less about autocracy versus democracy or
even the battle of different patriotisms, but rather more simple notions of rubles
and francs. Many later communist parties took this line regarding the selfish futility
of the war and its eventual conclusion. Upon its formation in Shanghai in 1921,
the Korean Communist Party not only denounced its own country's occupation
by the Japanese, but the 'deceptive propaganda ... such as Wilson's Fourteen
Points'. To it 'the Versailles Peace Conference is nothing but a meeting of hungry
wolves to divide the territory of the defeated and collect reparations' (Korean
Communist Party 1921: passim).

In any event, in February 1917 the protracted and dire nature of the First
World War forced Tsar Nicholas II to abdicate as revolution swept across Russia. The
government that emerged in his stead was not stable, nor was the path Russia would
take from this point exactly clear. The Provisional Government, under the leadership
of Alexander Kerensky, managed to form a semblance of weak, ostensibly democratic,
government institutions, yet insisted on continuing Russia's involvement in the war.
The outcome of this state of affairs was uncertain: as Mark Mazower has contended,

> for much of 1917 it seemed that Russia would be the site of the first triumph
> of Europe's democratic revolution ... The Left, including Lenin, was pressing
> for the creation of a Constituent Assembly in order to usher in the period of
> 'bourgeois rule' which according to Marxist theory was now needed.
>
> *(Mazower 1998: 8)*

Sensing the moment was ripe for some form of change, Lenin arranged with the
German authorities to allow his passage through the country in a sealed train carriage
in order to foment a further, communistic revolution. Passing through Sweden and
Finland, Lenin arrived in St Petersburg (Petrograd) in April 1917. The leftist Petrograd
Soviet established in the city competed with the provisional government to govern
Russia, eventually winning out in November 1917 and executing most of the
former government's ministers, as well as forcing Kerensky into exile, where he
remained for the rest of his days. The dramatic spectre of an overthrown Tsar (who
had been executed, along with his family, in July 1918), much bloodshed and the
storming of symbolic Russian buildings like the Kremlin produced a fascination
with the new regime and its leader.

Reflecting on this moment in the mid-1920s in *Mein Kampf*, Adolf Hitler was
not alone in comparing the events of 1917 to those of the French Revolution in
1789. Although he detested the politics of the revolution, Hitler was prepared to
praise their oratory:

It is out of the question to think that the French Revolution could have been carried into effect by philosophizing theories if they had not found an army of agitators led by demagogues of the grand style. These demagogues inflamed popular passion that had been already aroused, until that volcanic eruption finally broke out and convulsed the whole of Europe. And the same happened in the case of the gigantic Bolshevik revolution which recently took place in Russia. It was not due to the writers on Lenin's side but to the oratorical activities of those who preached the doctrine of hatred and that of the innumerable small and great orators who took part in the agitation. The masses of illiterate Russians were not fired to Communist revolutionary enthusiasm by reading the theories of Karl Marx but by the promises of paradise made to the people by thousands of agitators in the service of an idea. It was always so, and it will always be so.

(Hitler 1941: 711)

Lenin's promise to the Russian people during the revolution had been 'Peace, Land and Bread', and now he intended to deliver on this pledge. With much of the country under Bolshevik rule – though large areas remained under opposition 'White' control and would only be conquered by the Bolsheviks years later – Russia now exited the First World War by conceding huge swathes of territory to Germany in the Treaty of Brest-Litovsk (albeit to receive much of it back – at least on paper – upon the collapse of the German Army in November 1918). The Bolsheviks were now faced with a civil war in which several allied powers including the British, French and Americans armed the anti-Communist White forces attempting to overthrow the regime. This dramatic series of events gave the new government a roller-coaster start that veered from looking like being 'strangled in the cradle' – as Winston Churchill hoped – to eventual triumph. In October 1919, White forces were closing in on Moscow and Petrograd, but were staved off by a key totem of the new regime – Leon Trotsky's Red Army (created in January 1918). By 1920, the allies had pulled the plug on their support for the anti-communist forces, and the Poles, who had attempted their own invasion, were being pushed back into their own territory. Though Josef Pilsudski would eventually achieve his aim of expanding the borders of the new Poland eastwards, the Soviet regime was able to survive this conflict too.

Part of the explanation for this success lay in the fact that Lenin the glorious revolutionary was also Lenin the consummate, pragmatic politician. This even extended to the diplomatic sphere and dealing with the capitalist powers. Because of such flexibility, at the Treaty of Rapallo in April 1922 the Soviets were able to broker a treaty with the Germans under which they each renounced territorial and financial claims on the other. This agreement was all the more remarkable for it occurred as a breakout of a much wider gathering at Genoa, at which the Western powers had hoped to see the Soviet regime accept its responsibility to meet the financial obligations to France, Britain and others incurred by the Tsar. Lenin (and in particular his foreign minister Georgi Chicherin) had successfully sidestepped that economic question and forged their own path, but there were certainly other questions to be answered. Though the civil war was finally won in 1921, rapid inflation was imperilling the new state. With prices rising ten-fold each year between 1917 and 1921, peasant uprisings were commonplace as a cost-of-living crisis gripped the nation. Partly by consequence, at Kronstadt, near the border with Finland, the crews of two Soviet warships (the *Petropavlosk* and the *Sevastopol*) moved and approved 15 resolutions all denouncing the Soviet regime in one way or another. These included the notion that 'no political party should have privileges [in the army] for the promulgation of its ideas', calls for the 'liberation of all political prisoners', demands for freedom of speech for the press, and the holding of new elections. This was a call for pluralism unwelcome for a government predicated on glorious revolutionary action. The regime responded by denouncing Kronstadt as the work of French intelligence and the previous leftist (but non-Bolshevik) force, the Social Revolutionaries. Troops were sent into the city in March 1921, and over 1,000 supporters of the declaration were killed, with around 6,500 captured.

The sheer statistics of this period are extraordinary. In the winter of 1921–2, in large part due to both sides in the civil war having lived off the produce of the land they conquered, a staggering five million people died in a famine which swept Southern Russia at the conclusion of the conflict. This caused millions to take to the road – or dirt-track – in search of food. Around seven million orphans wandered around the country in search of anything resembling nutrition. In Omsk 20,000 refugees were arriving each and every day seeking such basic necessities (Mazower 1998: 118). These were the birth pains in which the regime struggled for life. Initially aid from the American Relief Association was refused though, partially due to developments outlined below, this position was eventually reversed. The new organisation Save the Children contributed much from the British side too.

Lenin had to react to this challenge, and the path he took led the regime, for a few years, away from the pure communist ideal. The introduction of the New Economic Plan (NEP) from 15 March 1921 involved the legalisation of a limited private sector, the free movement of prices, and the replacement of simple state requisition of agricultural goods in a de facto enforced tithe with a progressive tax rising from 5 per cent to 17 per cent. Large-scale industry – including the banks and transport – remained under national control but the NEP did intend to liberalise aspects of Soviet economic policy. It was a pragmatic response from an ostensibly dogmatic set of revolutionaries. So-called 'Nepmen' were emblematic of a potentially new turn for the regime which, by 1922, had introduced paid holidays, an eight-hour working day and a welfare state. This was not yet Joseph Stalin's USSR of collectivisation and the state exercising complete influence in almost every aspect of everyday life.

Part of this was mere necessity, but there was also a broader debate taking place in the early 1920s over what communism should be in practice. Indeed, as Robert Service has shown, throughout its history there were almost as many variants of communism as there were communist countries (Service 2007: passim). For those on the Soviet left, such as Trotsky, the NEP agenda should be only a short-term necessity. Industry should be modernised but brought under state auspices and, crucially, the revolution should not end in Russia. Marx had called for 'workers *of the world*' to unite – and this meant the goal should be communism for all, not just those within the Greater Russian sphere. But many disagreed. For those on the Soviet right – the Bukharinite gradualists, so called after Nikolai Bukharin, their most prominent leader – the NEP was a long-term cause. To Bukharin, Alexei Rykov and their supporters, the Russian peasant should be appeased through market reforms which meant they could sell their goods to organisations other than a state which would inevitably enforce a low price upon the producer. The revolution should consolidate itself without thinking of immediate expansion: 'socialism in one country' – a phrase associated with Stalin and Bukharin in the mid-1920s – was sufficient for now.

The story of left versus right was resolved, in part, by human frailty. From early 1922 Vladimir Lenin was gravely ill after surviving an assassination attempt – suffering three strokes, paralysis and eventually losing the ability to speak. He died in January 1924. The power struggle for his succession we consider shortly.

The Red Scares Worldwide

Ideologically, the person who succeeded Lenin was of the utmost importance for communism worldwide. Whereas Mussolini would declare fascism as 'not for export', many on the Soviet left very much predicated themselves – at least theoretically – on global expansion of their ideology. The Communist International (known as the Third International, but more commonly as the Comintern) was formed in 1915 to 'fight by all available means, including armed force, for the overthrow of the international bourgeoisie and for the creation of an international Soviet republic'. Its founding Congress was held in Moscow in 1919 and attended by workers' groups from the United States (the Socialist Labor Party), the Italian Socialist Party, British socialists, Japanese leftists and others. The Second Congress, held across July and August 1920, was a rather less convivial affair. There Lenin argued that, in order to shake off the yoke of imperialism, communist parties should support liberal revolutionary independence movements in colonial countries. Many, however, disagreed and argued that they should only support truly communist revolutionaries. Here again the pragmatism versus ideological purity debate loomed over proceedings. It would play out in China later in the decade, as we will note.

On the other hand, all were agreed that another breakthrough would be welcome, even if they disagreed on the timing. In 1919, abortive communist revolutions in Bavaria and Hungary produced conservative and autocratic rises to power respectively. Rather more unlikely, and within the confines of our decade, on 2 August 1920 *The Times* of London reported of 'our bolshevists' – the plucky few gathered at the first congress of the British Communist Party. As with the later formation of the British Union of Fascists in 1932, many attendees – *The Times* put it at three or four hundred – attended simply to witness the spectacle. The paper reported that

Communists in conference declare for the Soviet (or Workers' Council) system as a means whereby the working class shall achieve power and take control of the forces of production; declare for the dictatorship of the proletariat as a necessary means for combating the counter-revolution during the transition period between capitalism and communism; and stand for the adoption of these means as steps towards a system of complete communism wherein all means of production shall be communally owned and controlled.

The Conference also agreed to join the Third International. Perhaps most interestingly however, the notion of seeing a Labour-led government elected as a Kerensky-type administration which would inevitably be swept aside by a communist takeover was also debated. Through the Zinoviev letter of 1924, the British Conservative Party was able to transfer such talk into its own electoral fodder. 'Vote Tory get stability, Vote Labour get Marx' played rather well for Prime Minister Stanley Baldwin, as we noted in chapter 7.

That said, the chance for communism to succeed in a democratic system was always more likely to the South-east of the North Sea than it was to its West. After the failure of left-wing revolution in January 1919 in Berlin (and subsequently in Munich), and the deaths of Rosa Luxemburg (who had actually criticised the 1917 Bolshevik revolution) and Karl Liebknecht at the hands of the counter-revolutionary Freikorps, German communism assumed a parliamentary form in the shape of the KPD. As Russel Lemmons has shown, one of the key interwar communists from this point was KPD leader Ernst Thälmann, who became the face of German communism. For Lemmons,

although party leaders assured that no German figure would come to eclipse either Lenin or Joseph Stalin in importance among the KPD's rank and file, party propagandists touted Thälmann and his movement as the only alternative to a Nazi dictatorship and years of oppression and warfare ... He was, in the eyes of KPD propagandists, a true *Arbeiterführer*, a 'leader of workers'.

(*Lemmons 2013: 3*)

This quote gets to the heart of the non-Russian communist movement's dilemma: how to reconcile national sensibilities with the glorious nature of the Soviet example. And as Lemmons argues, 'when opponents accused the KPD of being nothing more than a tool of the Soviet Union and its leader a mere lackey of Stalin, they were not far off the mark' (Lemmons 2013: 12). 'Orders from Moscow' was a perennial refrain for communist movements from Berlin to Beijing.

Since our next chapter on fascism will remark on the famous Munich Putsch of November 1923, it is worth contextualising that this attempted right-wing revolution in the German South occurred less than a month after an attempted communist insurrection in Hamburg in Germany's North-west. There a radical KPD sect – the KP *Wasserkante* – received orders from the local leadership to begin a rebellion. Around 300 Hamburg communists stormed 26 precincts, managing to extract weapons from 17 of them. From a local membership of some 14,000, this was a limited rebellion indeed. Most of it fizzled out rather quickly – the whole affair lasted less than a day and in many parts of Hamburg it was over before noon. All told, over 100 activists were killed during an uprising for which the exact motives remain unclear to the present day. Its major effect, as Lemmons observes, was 'in catapulting Thälmann to prominence in the KPD and help to secure him a position first on the Central Committee, then as party chairman' (Lemmons 2013: 31). When Thälmann was temporarily ousted from this position for covering up the embezzlement of a friend, Stalin stepped in and demanded Thälmann's reinstatement. By the late 1920s Thälmann – and through him Stalin – had developed a personality cult in German communism.

Around this period, ironically like the Nazis, the parliamentary route became the modus operandi of choice. There were still street battles with the right, but these were held within the context of trying to convince the masses of communism's overall righteousness. To some degree this strategy seemed to bear fruit. In 1925, Thälmann gained almost two million votes in the Presidential election that propelled Hindenburg to power, whilst the number of KPD Reichstag deputies rose from just four in 1920 to 62 in May 1924. As with the Nazis, they suffered a dip in the second election of 1924. They similarly found it difficult to make the case for a worker's revolution in the late 1920s as democratic capitalism seemed to be producing rather successful results for German citizens. Yet, as the economy collapsed from 1929, they too re-emerged as a serious political force. As the Nazis became the second largest party in the Reichstag from September 1930, the KPD managed to rise to third place by the November 1932 election. By this stage, however, the Nazis were able to use the threat of a communist takeover for their own ends. On 3 March 1933 Thälmann was arrested by the Gestapo and would be imprisoned for 11 years before he was executed at Buchenwald concentration camp in 1944.

Across the Atlantic things could also be dramatic. For one, Brazilian politics had long been dominated by *coronelismo* – the rule and patronage of the *coronel*, a dominant local oligarch. Throughout the Old Republic (1889–1930), *coronelismo* saw rural businessmen – principally coffee planters – at the top of most local state political structures. In São Paulo in particular the landed gentry's politics of *café com leite* ('coffee with milk') involved dairy and coffee barons monopolising local influence at the expense of the ordinary worker. This provided a platform for the charismatic leader Luís Carlos Prestes to lead the so-called *tenentes* revolts in 1922 and 1924. Born to a military father and a teacher mother in 1898, Prestes was not yet formally a Marxist (he would only go over during an exile in Bolivia and then Buenos Aires in the early 1930s), but the 1922 and 1924 insurrections were staging points along his transition. The first revolt in 1922 was a largely middle-class band of ex-servicemen revolutionaries angry at the *café com leite* local politics. But by 1924 the Coluna Prestes (Prestes' Column) had morphed into a social reform movement of the left. Although the Brazilian *tenentes* would split between the moderates who would install Getulio Vargas as President in 1930 (leading to a quasi-fascistic experiment with so-called integralism) and the radicals under Prestes, the chance for violent leftist insurrection marked Brazilian politics in the interwar period (Macaulay 1974: passim).

The fear of communist revolution was also felt widely in the most free-market capitalist country on earth, the United States. The prospect of communist revolution breaking out in a country in which the President would openly declare that the primary business of his country was business itself – as per Coolidge – was unlikely to be the next step in the advance of the flame of revolution. This fact, however, did not stop some from trying, and it certainly did not prevent the government from worrying about the possibility. In the midst of the First World War, Congress had passed the Espionage Act, which made it illegal to obstruct the war effort, and the following year passed the Sedition Act, which explicitly made it illegal to use 'disloyal, profane, scurrilous or abusive language' to insult the United States or its Constitution. This clear violation of the First Amendment was justified on the grounds of national security, and prosecutions soon resulted. Socialist and Industrial Workers of the World (IWW) leader Eugene V. Debs was arrested and imprisoned for allegedly encouraging obstruction of conscription. He ran for President in the 1920 election from his prison cell in Atlanta. In 1919, the Supreme Court ruled in the case of *Schenck v. United States* that it was constitutional for the government to intervene against speech when it presents a 'clear and present danger' – a test that remains in place to the present day (Cashman 1998: 161–4).

There was more drama to come. In April 1919, dozens of mail bombs addressed to key public officials were found by postal officials. Among the intended victims was Attorney General A. Mitchell Palmer, who was convinced that the plot was the beginning of an attempt at revolution. Soldiers and police stormed left-wing newspapers and made arrests, and in June a bomb exploded at Palmer's Washington D.C. home. Raids around the country arrested thousands of leftists, and those found to be foreign born were swiftly deported. Left-wing union leader Big Bill Haywood was arrested and fled to Moscow, where he soon died, as did John Reed, the journalist who had written a compelling account of the Russian Revolution and been open about his increasingly communist views. He soon died in the Soviet Union as well (Cashman 1998: 178–9). The Communist Party of the United States (CPUSA) was forced to move its operations underground and would eventually be banned in a number of states.

The Palmer Raids and the First Red Scare, as the period became known, had effectively broken the power of the radical left in the United States, from which it would never truly recover. Organised-labour leaders would henceforth go to great lengths to disassociate themselves from socialism and communism in their pronouncements, lest they become associated with radicalism in the public eye. Fears over communism and communist infiltration would again come to the forefront of American politics in the aftermath of the Second World War. While Soviet agents and communist sympathisers were certainly gathering information in the United States throughout the twentieth century, the country's domestic communist movement was nowhere near as strong as its foreign counterparts. As the century continued however, the United States would be increasingly occupied by the push to stop communism from spreading elsewhere – particularly under the Soviet leadership of Joseph Stalin from the mid-1920s.

Stalin

Ioseb Besarionis dze Jughasvili was born in the South of the Tsarist Empire in 1878 in modern-day Georgia (Service 2010: chs 2–3). He was a sickly child born with two conjoined toes, had a face permanently scarred by the effects of childhood smallpox, and an injury to his left arm rendering it shorter than its counterpart. His father was an abusive drunk – at one point young Joseph is said to have thrown a dagger at him – and his childhood generally very difficult (Montefiore 2003: ch. 1). A clever boy, he entered Tbilisi's Russian Orthodox seminary only to be expelled at the age of 21 when he was absent from his final exams. It was at this point he first encountered the work of Vladimir Lenin – his friend and rival. Involved in several of the early insurrections of the 1900s, he was frequently exiled to the frozen plains of Siberia, only to escape and find his way back to European Russia. In the early 1910s he began to permanently use the alias of Stalin.

Initially supportive of Kerensky's provisional administration as editor of *Pravda*, Stalin shifted to out-and-out opposition once Lenin prevailed at the Communist Party conference in 1917. Appointed People's Commissar for Nationalities' Affairs in 1917, he opposed Trotsky's leadership of the army, ordered the executions of former Tsarists, and adopted a scorched earth policy towards occupied villages. In the war against Poland he was blamed for failing to take Warsaw and Lvov, and returned sheepishly to Moscow. Trotsky took his chance and at the 1920 Party Congress openly denounced his actions. Stalin survived this criticism and plotted how to exact his revenge. But he was not yet in a position to make all the running and would have to react to events. As it transpired, he

FIGURE 8.1 Following Vladimir Lenin's death in early 1924, Joseph Stalin (left) rapidly consolidated his influence in the Communist Party and eliminated his opponents.

was a master at the Machiavellianism needed to advance up the ranks of the 1920s Soviet Union.

In 1922, already a dying man, Lenin penned a document he wished to be read out at the Twelfth Congress the next year. This explosive tract – known as Lenin's Testament – recommended the removal of Stalin from his position as General Secretary of the Party. Whilst describing Trotsky as the most able man in the party, it also claimed he was fundamentally arrogant. For the up-and-coming Bukharin, Lenin further claimed he could be called 'a Marxist only with great reserve'. In denouncing so many key figures this created something of a problem after Lenin's death. Certainly it was not in Stalin's interests to have the document read out to the entire party, but it was also not the done thing to refuse Lenin's wishes (especially since his widow was so eager to see them enacted). At the Thirteenth Congress of 1924 the document was eventually read out, but with the proviso that the taking of notes was prohibited and it would not be referred to at the major plenary meeting that year. The lack of circulation for its recommendations became a point of fissure during the quarrel between the Stalin–Bukharinite gradualists and Trotskyite Left Opposition that followed Lenin's death (Service 2009: ch. 32).

Some of this was ideology (the 'socialism in one country' of Stalin versus Trotsky's desired global revolution), but much was down to Stalin's political trickery. Telling Trotsky the wrong date for Lenin's funeral was indicative of what was to come. As incumbent General Secretary of the Party, Stalin used his patronage to build his power base and utilise the secret police, and the outlawing of factionalism by Lenin in 1921 played into the hands of those holding official party roles. That the interests of 'the party' and 'the revolution' were always those of Stalin was of course no coincidence. The so-called *troika* of rightist leaders – Stalin, Bukharin and Rykov – marginalised Trotsky and his supporters through 1925 and 1926, and saw Trotsky removed from ministerial office before being expelled from the party in 1927. At the Fifteenth Congress of 1927 Stalin removed all Left Opposition members from the party and assumed total power. There would scarcely be better reward for Stalin's erstwhile collaborators, and both Bukharin and Rykov were shot for allegedly conspiring to overthrow the state in March 1938.

For the newly empowered Stalin the events of the 1930s – the great purges of potential rivals and impending alliance then war with Hitler – were far on the horizon. Instead, perhaps the key challenge in the late 1920s – particularly given the famine of 1921–2 – was to keep agricultural production efficient. Here, in a sense, the functioning New Economic Plan had actually begun to solve the problem: as one witness put it, 'in the food products trade the private trader held almost a monopoly; no efforts on the part of co-operative shops could avail against his flexibility, his spirit of enterprise and his trading skill' (Solonevich 1935: 83). During the 1920s the flexibility of the NEP had created three types of Soviet farmer (as defined by the regime) within the supposedly uniform communist paradise. First there was the *bednyak* pauper, usually regarded (not universally accurately) as loyally pro-Soviet. Secondly sat the *serednyak* in the middle who perhaps had a small private concern doing relatively well under the New Economic Plan – and thus could be regarded as a temporary ally at best. And thirdly, critically, came the *kulaks* – who had prospered under the NEP and were thus to be stigmatised as class enemies. Here ideology clashed with practice. In *practice* the kulaks could turn out the grain and corn the regime needed, but this bumped up against the communist *theory* that private industry along the capitalist line did not, indeed could not, work. As Ivan Solonevich (a pro-monarchist who escaped from a Soviet prison camp in 1934) argued, this produced a situation where the regime was forced to say to itself, 'Yes, we want corn, but we want Socialist corn. We do not want the kulak corn'. 'But where', this begged, 'shall we get the Socialist corn from?' (Solonevich 1935: 84).

The need to resolve the kulak question and the nature of agricultural production per se became ever more acute during the grain shortage that hit Russia from 1927. Stalin had broadly been caught completely unawares by what he was soon attempting to rebrand as a 'peasants' strike' (Solonevich 1935: passim). Doubtless there was sporadic evidence of such hoarding of produce, but climatic conditions (mostly drought) in the Middle Volga and Kazakhstan had played a far larger role in limiting production of both grain and wheat. In any event, in the face of what Stalin claimed were recalcitrant kulak elements he soon led the regime back away from a tolerated – if small – private sector towards War Communism and the collection of grain by force. With two million tonnes of grain estimated to be the shortfall, the Politburo set out to confiscate two and a half million tonnes on behalf of the people. To do so Stalin set out on a new policy of collectivisation – the parcelling up of individual farms into larger, communal areas of land where, supposedly, decent bednyak could till the land together, working co-operatively for the good of the regime.

This collectivisation spelled serious trouble for the kulaks. All told, it led to the deportation of ten million Soviet citizens (often from west of the Ural mountains to far-flung areas of Siberia), with over 30,000 summary executions. The hoarding of grain became a crime against the regime as party activists urged others not to 'think of the kulak's hungry children; in the class struggle philanthropy is evil' (Mazower 1998: 121). As with the fascist principle of 'working towards the Führer' – taking a vague desire of Hitler's and pursuing it to a radical degree – 'the national collectivization targets for 1929–30 were progressively raised ... [and] even the higher targets of October 1929 and January 1930 were eclipsed by the actual collectivization rates' (Bernstein 1967: 1). Small mercies including allowing peasants access to municipal tractors, thus increasing output in some areas. But across the board, replacing relatively efficient kulak farms with collective, sometimes poorly tilled areas meant lower output, an almost 50 per cent reduction in the number of livestock, and the removal of a system of farming that had existed for centuries. As a result of this reform, around 11 million people died in a further famine in 1932–3. Many of these were in the Ukraine – previously deemed the agricultural 'breadbasket' of Eastern Europe.

This fell under the broad spirit of the regime's first Five Year Plan, framed in 1927 (for the 1928–32 period). Amidst a brief but significant fear that Western powers, fuelled by perceived anti-Soviet feeling in Britain, were preparing to attack the Soviet Union the new plan set the regime on a path of collectivisation and modernisation. Concurrent with the aforementioned agricultural reforms, the latter would see the number of industrial, construction and transport workers within the USSR rise from under five million in 1928 to over 12.5 million by 1940. With war supposedly in sight, staggering targets were set for industrial production, and new industrial centres such as Dnieper and Nizhny Novgorod were constructed at lightning speed. Capital plant, however initially rickety and dehumanising, was the new watch-word. Indeed, with the establishment of the economic advisory agency Gosplan (initially staffed by non-communist technocrats) in the early 1920s, there had always been elements within the regime seeking to unleash the potential of centralising and expanding industry. Until this point, Gosplan had few powers of compulsion or decree. But the new Five Year Plans which continued throughout the dictatorship – the last of which was set to last from 1991 until 1995 – would henceforth fall under their remit. Under this new Gosplan–Five-Year-Plan model, ever more dramatic targets and efficiencies would become the communist norm. The *Brave New World* Aldous Huxley would satirise in literary form in the early 1930s had in many ways arrived.

Solidifying the regime in the late 1920s

This desire for ever more grandiosely titled agencies and programmes indicated the contemporary importance of propaganda. As Matthew Lenoe has observed,

> between 1925 and 1930, Soviet newspapermen, under pressure from party leaders to mobilize society for the huge task of industrialization, moulded a new master narrative for Soviet history and a new Bolshevik identity for millions of novice Communists. They began to present everyday labor as an epic battle to industrialize the USSR, a battle fought against shirkers and saboteurs within and imperialist enemies without.
>
> *(Lenoe 2004: 1)*

This was about reducing nuance and drawing the world in black and white. For Lenoe, issues of state newspapers *Pravda* and *Izvestiia* in the early 1920s at least maintained efforts at some form of objectivity, replete with editorial commentaries and mildly satiric pieces about the grumbles of everyday living. Within a few years, 'the shrill declamation of the same newspapers in the early 1930s, by contrast, seems alien and bizarre' (Lenoe 2004: 11). In terms of presentation, this shift included 'exclamation points, commands, military metaphors, and congratulations from party leaders to factories for surpassing their production plans' (Lenoe 2004: 11). As Golfo Alexopolous shows, the notion of 'the family' was dragged into this too – from an initial fear that loyalty to relatives would undermine loyalty to the regime, by the late 1920s Stalin had become the father and grandfather of the nation (Alexopolous 2008: passim). In broad terms, simplicity was generally the watchword.

As noted, part of this was about highlighting the 'good' and 'bad' peasant. As Lynne Viola, Denis Kozlov and V.P. Danilov note, there was a demarcation of the peasantry according to political priority:

according to Lenin, the poor peasantry was an ally of the urban proletariat; the middle peasant 'wavered' in class (and by implication, political) loyalties between the proletariat and the bourgeoisie (or kulak); and the kulak remained, inherently according to socioeconomic definition, the enemy of Soviet power.

(Viola et al. *2005)*

To some degree, this would have made at least theoretical sense: the vehicle of Marxist power was, after all, the proletariat. But, as these authors argue,

the actual definition of the kulak remained amorphous and slippery, given to politicization if not demonization, in Marxist–Leninist thinking throughout the post-revolutionary years. Starting with the policy of the Committee of the Village Poor, the kulak became a figure of opprobrium in the Marxist–Leninist pantheon of enemies and, more often than not, a category defined by politics rather than by actual socioeconomic standing.

(Viola et al. 2005: 9)

To survive in the Soviet Union of the 1920s, not being a kulak would have been high up the priority list. But then this was not always a condition the individual was able to set for themselves.

All this was curious to the outsider at the very least. One international witness to the new regime was the British trade unionist Walter Citrine. Citrine's 1925 visit to the Soviet Union has been somewhat underexplored by historians until a recent article by Jonathan Davis, but it has much to tell us about the way the USSR attempted to manage Western perceptions of itself, and how Westerners felt when confronted with the reality of Soviet rule. For context, Citrine was a critical yet ultimately somewhat sympathetic source. Responding to Lenin's view that 'communism is Soviet power plus the electrification of the whole country' he noted that he had been 'enthused' by this picture of a republic 'organized on such lines as would ensure every citizen, however humble, the advantages of a planned economy'. Citrine's visit was an exercise in public relations for the regime and, as Davis notes, 'the Soviet authorities were very good at ensuring that foreign visitors saw what the government wanted them to see' (Davis 2013: 148). This produced a quasi-comic game of cat and mouse, when Citrine and his travel companion – the future Labour MP George Hicks – would attempt to spring their desired visits on their tour guide at the last possible moment to prevent any stage management of the spectacle put in front of them.

In any event, short of sealing the carriage *à la* Lenin, there was little the regime could do to stop Citrine staring out of the window on his train into the Russian heartland. Gazing out, he could not help but feel 'a sense of despondency' the further he went into Russian territory. Everything, he claimed, seemed 'sordid' and living standards appeared 'lamentably low'. To the Citrine of 1925 'it looks … as though it will take many years to bring these peasants up to a really decent standard of living' (Davis 2013: 151). There was worse, as we have noted, to come. Yet this must be tempered by the generally low expectations many had of Russia in the first place. As Davis sets out, 'while Citrine could be critical of certain Soviet practices', particularly the lack of concern shown towards the homeless and the rather shunned position enjoyed by the trade unions, 'he was enthusiastic about the modernisation of what was always seen as a backward, undemocratic country' (Davis 2013: 159). For many beyond the borders of the USSR, replacing Tsar and serf with communist bureaucrat and dispossessed kulak did not amount to a particularly dramatic change.

Other hardly dispassionate observers were also globe-trotting in this period too. Indeed, it was the early life of a future communist leader, the later Vietnamese Prime Minister, Ho Chi Minh, that perhaps most strongly demonstrated the global nature of the burgeoning communist movement (for related issues see Marr 1984: passim). Minh had been born Nguyen Sinh Cung in 1890. His father was a Confucian scholar and sent young Nguyen to a French *lycée* based in Vietnam. This French education would serve him well, as in 1911 he boarded a steamer bound for Marseille – his first encounter with the country that would form his political education in the 1920s. After working in New York and London in various restaurant and hotel roles (in London he was a pastry chef at the then-grandiose Carlton Hotel), he arrived in France in 1919 where his socialism came to the fore. In Paris he joined a group of Vietnamese nationalists centred around Phan Chu Trinh. Using the American Declaration of Independence as his model, Trinh argued that Wilsonian self-determination should include the French colonial territory of Indo-China (Vietnam). The young Nguyen imbibed these arguments – though also developed a strong Francophilia, even arguing that French sportswriters should refrain from using English derivatives such as 'le manager' or 'le knock-out'. Increased technological and transport links meant Nguyen was hardly alone in experiencing such a 'global' political education. According to one measure recorded by David Marr,

> there were 1,556 Vietnamese students in France in early 1930. Although scattered in nine locations around the country, students were increasingly choosing to concentrate in Paris. A significant minority was already very much involved in left-wing activities, including participating in diverse French organizations, meeting with Vietnamese sailors stopping off in Marseilles, Le Havre, or Bordeaux, and smuggling printed materials back to Vietnam.
>
> *(Marr 1984: 40)*

Nguyen was particularly fleet of foot, however. In 1923 he followed the spirit of communism to its new home, Moscow, studied at university in Russia, and was paid by the Comintern for his troubles. The next year he moved to China, settling briefly in Guangzhou where he gave a series of socialist lectures and married a local woman. When Chiang Kai-Shek took up arms against the Chinese Communist Party, Nguyen left China via Russia and Paris. He would then spread the gospel of communism through Thailand, India and back in China. This, in short, was an international communist indeed – and one who as leader of the Viet Minh independence movement from the early 1940s would come to French, American and finally global attention as the century progressed.

The second communist breakthrough? China in the 1920s

The Vietnam War of the 1960s was indeed a later situation where the Cold War threatened to blow hot, but the more immediate question in the 1920s was whether communism could make its second big breakthrough. Was socialism really just for one country, as Stalin had stated, or was this a worldwide revolution? Much would depend on China. Just as with Tsarist Russia, rural China was hardly the most obvious ground for Marx's idealised industrial proletariat to cast aside their shackles. But, partially because of actions taken by Moscow, there was a chance that Russia's Eastern neighbour could follow her lead in this regard.

As Adam Tooze has recently noted, 'the fact that the centuries-old Ch'ing dynasty [in China] finally collapsed in February 1912 to be replaced by a republic marks one of the true turning points in modern history' (Tooze 2014: 89). By contemporary standards the new Chinese state was certainly on the democratic side: a franchise limited to men over the age of 21 with elementary education still allowed over 20 million Chinese to vote in the 1913 election. At this election the leading republican party, the nationalist forces of the Kuomintang (KMT), achieved a clear majority – only to be forced from office by the assassination of its leader by forces linked to President General Yuan Shi-kai. Yuan attempted to install himself as monarch, only to be met with a national revolt, and eventually appointed the German-schooled military official General Duan as his Prime Minister. With Yuan's passing in June 1916 a further opportunity presented itself – President Li Yuanhong came to power and sought to reinvigorate the spirit of 1912–13, and tilt China in a more pro-allied direction – yet he himself would be overthrown by the pro-German General Zhang in 1917. In the decade prior to that considered here, therefore, China was undergoing its own period of crisis, revolution and counter-revolution every bit as dramatic as that seen in its neighbour Russia. As Anthony Joes notes,

> the death of Yuan in 1916 inaugurated the chaotic warlord era, in which provincial military governors exercised semi-sovereign powers in accord with or in defiance of the central Peking [Beijing] regime, making alliances with one another, often under the tutelage of foreign governments.
>
> (Joes 2010: 8)

By the early 1920s around one and a half million Chinese were under arms, by far the majority in the service of the various regional warlords.

In part in response to this instability the Communist Party of China (CPC) was formed in 1921. Building on the anarchical legacy of the May Fourth Movement of 1919, both leading lights of the new CPC – Li Dazhao and Chen Duxiu – believed the Russian revolution had changed history forever. Gone was monarchical or tribal dominance and in was a new, glorious era for oppressed peoples across the globe, including, they hoped, the Chinese. The first Congress of the new party was modest indeed – with police interruptions meaning it took place on a boat on Jiaxing South Lake, attended by just 12 delegates. Chen was soon elected leader – an important moment given that he and Li differed on the degree of co-operation that should be afforded to the nationalist KMT. From an initial membership in the low hundreds, by 1927 there were 93,000 members of the CPC (Joes 2010: 8). A potential vanguard to take power in this destabilised state had emerged.

That said, the politics of this period in China were more ambiguous than elsewhere. Formed in 1912 and, after the aforementioned coups, re-formed in 1919 after several of its leaders fled to Japan, in 1923 the 'bourgeois ... nationalist' KMT received aid from the Soviet Union after the West had denied it formal recognition (Joes 2010: 8). This was perhaps slightly curious for, as Anthony Joes argues, the KMT was about 'effective central government, one that could maintain order and collect taxes ... [it stressed the need to] modernize the country under the direction of the educated classes ... and wanted, in short, a political revolution and not a social one' (Joes 2010: 10). It was also not entirely clear that Leninism would afford in practice the goals it professed to offer in theory. Intellectual father of the Chinese Republic and KMT leader Sun Yat-Sen's view was that the West had actually had much right – and the separation of powers between judiciary, executive and legislature was a sound principle on which to base a democracy. Yet he argued the democratic revolutions in Britain or America were not fully convertible to the Chinese experience. In his 1924 work on *The Principle of Democracy* therefore, Sun demanded that 'the power of censorship [in the new China] includes the power to impeach. Foreign countries also have this power, only it is placed in the legislative body and is not a separate governmental power'. In addition to this, he believed that 'the selection of real talent and ability through examinations [which] has been characteristic of China for thousands of years' should be restored (Sun Yat-Sen 1924). Merit should mark the new Chinese government – though his allusions to the success of the British civil service in this regard may have conflicted with the left-wing Fabian thinkers we encountered in chapter 2.

Although both CPC and the KMT wanted to reform the status quo the KMT was about urban, maritime and international-facing China whilst the CPC stressed the role of the rural peasant and the need to re-calibrate the idea of a workers' revolution to the countryside. Still, under the 1923 agreement which provided aid to China the CPC was instructed to co-operate with the KMT by Moscow and many members, including Mao Zedong, joined the KMT that year. A united front was declared between the two parties which were nominally separate but enjoyed much crossover. Since Mao was a member of both organisations he was able to lead the KMT's Peasant Movement Training Institute. In that role he trekked through rural Hunan to appraise the lay of the land. There he noted the 'colossal event' of the 'present upsurge of the peasant movement' in early 1927. In a short while, he argued, 'they will sweep all the imperialists, warlords, corrupt officials, loyal officials and evil gentry into their graves'. For any potential vanguard he believed

> there are three alternatives. To march at their head and lead them. To trail behind them, gesticulating and criticizing. Or to stand in their way and oppose

them. Every Chinese is free to choose, but events will force you to make the choice quickly.

(Mao Zedong 1927: passim)

By the time Mao was writing, history was already on the move. Part of the initial early 1920s spirit of CPC–KMT co-operation involved dispatching the military leader Chiang Kai-Shek to Moscow to learn from the Soviet economic, political and military systems. There he met Trotsky but emerged broadly unimpressed with what he had seen – Soviet communism was not, he thought, for China. Upon the death of the more pro-Russian KMT leader Sun Yat-Sen in 1925, Chiang became head of the National Revolutionary Army and swiftly moved the KMT in a less-Soviet-aligned direction. A conflict between the nominal allies was moving ever closer and eventually arrived.

Through 1926 and 1927 war duly broke out across China between the rightists under Chiang Kai-Shek and those who desired a full-blown communist revolution. On 7 April 1927 leaders loyal to the KMT, including Chiang, debated the communist agitation that was occurring across the Chinese territories. Most around Chiang were agreed that the communist elements within the KMT should be removed, and by execution. Hundreds of members of the Chinese communist party were arrested and shot in what was dubbed the 'Shanghai Massacre'. This caused a split in the KMT which boiled over a few months later. At the beginning of August that year Chinese Communist forces revolted against the Nationalist government in Nanchang, Jiangxi. This immediately followed a call from the Soviet Third International for a general strike 'to compel the Imperialists to stop the war against China, and to avert a war against the Soviet, which would synchronise with the 13th anniversary of the Great War, which gave the world Mussolini, Hindenburg, and Pilsudski' (*New Zealand Herald*, 1 August 1927).

The news worried many in the West. The Paris correspondent of the British *Daily Mail* reported how

> Chinese secret societies were enrolled by the Bolsheviks to fight Western civilization. He says the Reds, aided by the Cantonese at Hankow, have now joined the Moscow Reds. Each member must undergo forty days' sacred exercise when he is beaten with bamboo canes to test his physical resistance. The tests are supposed to show a candidate for full Bolshevik honours is worthy to be a soldier of the Red Army.
>
> (New Zealand Herald, 3 August 1927)

All this was a truly global affair. As Adam Tooze argues,

> in 1926–7, through their sponsorship of the Great Northern Expedition, the Soviet [Union] delivered the first truly telling blow to the post-war order, making painfully obvious the failure of Japan and the Western Powers to come to terms with Chinese Nationalism.
>
> (Tooze 2014: 511)

Trotsky had cautioned against this approach – believing the USSR should renounce the KMT and back a full workers' revolution. But Stalin again won out. Chiang was backed by the big Chinese merchants, he seemed to lead an efficient military machine that looked likely to win, and was, in short, useful. The revolution could wait.

For some, the violence seen throughout the Northern Expedition fed into notions of an 'Asiatic' Bolshevism – a strain of political thinking that was alien to Western, European thinking. But whilst the West could dismiss Bolshevism they could not ignore the effects of the ongoing conflict. Through *Pathe News* the war was brought to European audiences more generally, with scenes of peasants carrying barricades of furniture, women holding helpless children, and military inspections demonstrating the militarisation of everyday Chinese society. Despite such action, success was by no means certain for the communists. The rebel communist army – later the People's Liberation Army (PLA) – initially met with a firm rebuff: KMT forces retook Nanchang and forced the remaining rebels into the countryside. Sporadic penetration occurred in the South of China but the conflict was long and arduous – interrupted only by a temporary unity intended to repel the Japanese invasion in 1936.

All told, the Great Northern Expedition, which concluded in 1928, saw Chiang Kai-Shek win a series of important strategic victories. But this came at a cost to China's territorial integrity. Indeed, China was divided in more ways than one in this period. The Communists maintained their capital as Beijing whilst the KMT were undecided as to the location of their alternative. Left wingers pressed for Wuhan, whilst the right favoured Nanjing. But in June 1928 Beijing was itself captured by KMT forces, and as time went by the Eastern seaboard would almost entirely be controlled by the nationalists. With seeming victory came further disunity however. Nationalist forces could not agree on what a (re-)unified China should look like, both in terms of its tribal composition and military make-up. Later conflicts within the nationalist forces, particularly the Central Plains War of 1930 fought between Chiang, Yan Xishan, Feng Yuxiang and Li Zongren, would take these onto the battlefield. All told, seven and a half million people would die in the civil war which would last until Mao Zedong proclaimed the new People's Republic in 1949. The 1930s, so synonymous with civil war in Spain, actually began with it still raging in China.

Conclusion

The 1920s started with a Soviet regime in Moscow under threat of defeat from White Russian opponents of the regime and potentially losing huge swathes of territory to Poland. It ended the decade firmly in power in Moscow, with the KPD pushing for elected office in Germany, and with an economic crisis brewing in the capitalist West that seemed to provide an imminent opportunity in a number of states. Given this, it is difficult to judge the 1920s as anything other than a success for global communism. Of course, the military reckoning with Hitlerian fascism from 1941 and the diplomatic travails against the United States from 1945 were yet to come. But by 1929 the USSR had reasons to be optimistic.

By the middle years of the decade, the communist state that Lenin had established was being run by Stalin, a far different kind of ruler. Brutal in his methods, Stalin first solidified his power and then turned to forcing his will on the country. Having taken power promising to do away with the dehumanising aspects of Tsarism, by the late 1920s the Soviet regime was arguably condemning huge swathes of the population back to serfdom in the form of collectivisation. 'For the people' had replaced 'for the motherland' as the rationale behind such actions, but the consequences were often similar. As Ivan Solonevich put it in 1935, 'a hundred years ago military settlements were set up in the name of world counter-revolution; today, collective farms are set up in the name of world revolution' (Solonevich 1935: 82). And, he continued,

> the results are more or less the same. Instead of a revolution in agriculture, there is no stop to famine in the country; instead of the strengthening of military power, the regular army has to face a rear turned against the Government and, therefore, against itself.
>
> *(Solonevich 1935: 82)*

Karl Marx had never predicted that communism would emerge in a single country, indeed believing that it would inevitably sweep across the globe. He, among many others, believed that Germany would be the first to light the revolutionary flame, and while that belief was belied by the 1917 Russian Revolution, Germany did appear to be a likely place where the revolution could next break out. On the other hand, by the early 1920s the Soviet Union was increasingly boxed in by its enemies. The United States and Britain had failed in their efforts to aid the White cause during the civil war, but now they denied the state diplomatic recognition and thwarted its plans to spread the revolution abroad. In the United States, the Red Scare gave the government power to shut down most aspects of the organised left and forcibly deport its representatives in many cases. Anti-communist rhetoric and action were so effective in the United States that a 1936–7 poll found that if forced to decide between the two, 38.8 per cent of Americans would have preferred to live under a fascist government while only 25 per cent would have preferred communism. The Soviet system simply had little to no appeal for Americans even as they lived through a crisis of capitalism. Other than the potential for the Soviet Union to expand its own frontiers militarily, communism's future increasingly appeared to lie in Africa, Asia and Latin America, where the struggle between the Warsaw Pact and NATO would unfold in the post-Second-World-War world. That, however, would require Western withdrawal and inflows of communistic funds and weaponry. For now, socialism would concentrate on its leading bastion.

Questions

- What were the conditions necessary for a communist uprising in the 1920s?
- Where and how would the next major breakthrough occur for communism?
- How Marxist was the Soviet Union?

- Did the likelihood of a worldwide communist revolution increase or decrease through the 1920s?
- What looked the strongest by the end of the 1920s: capitalism, fascism or communism?

Recommended further reading

Davis, J. (2013), 'An Outsider Looks in: Walter Citrine's First Visit to the Soviet Union, 1925', *Revolutionary Russia*, 26/2, 147–163.

Mazower, M. (1998), *Dark Continent: Europe's Twentieth Century*, London: Allen Lane.

Montefiore, S.S. (2003), *Stalin: The Court of the Red Tsar*, London: Phoenix.

Service, R. (2007), *Comrades. Communism: A World History*, London: Pan Macmillan.

Works cited

Alexopolous, G. (2008), 'Stalin and the Politics of Kinship: Practices of Collective Punishment, 1920s–1940s', *Comparative Studies in Society and History*, 50/1, 91–117.

Bernstein, T.P. (1967), 'Leadership and Mass Mobilisation in the Soviet and Chinese Collectivisation Campaigns of 1929–1930 and 1955–1956: A Comparison', *China Quarterly*, 31, 1–47.

Cashman, S.D. (1998), *America Ascendant: From Theodore Roosevelt to FDR in the Century of American Power, 1901–1945*, New York: New York University Press.

Davis, J. (2013), 'An Outsider Looks in: Walter Citrine's First Visit to the Soviet Union, 1925', *Revolutionary Russia*, 26/2, 147–163.

Hitler, A. (1941 edn), *Mein Kampf*, Boston, MA: Houghton Mifflin.

Joes, A. (2010), *Victorious Insurgencies: Four Rebellions that Shaped Our World*, Lexington: University Press of Kentucky.

Korean Communist Party (1921), 'Manifesto of the Korean Communist Party in Shanghai', abridged via http://afe.easia.columbia.edu/ps/korea/korean_communist_party.pdf

Lemmons, R. (2013), *Hitler's Rival: Ernst Thälmann in Myth and Memory*, Lexington: University Press of Kentucky.

Lenoe, M.E. (2004), *Closer to the Masses: Stalinist Culture, Social Revolution, and Soviet Newspapers*, Cambridge, MA: Harvard University Press.

Macaulay, N. (1974), *The Prestes Column: Revolution in Brazil*, New York: New Viewpoints.

Mao Zedong (1927), 'Report on the Investigation of the Peasant Movement in Hunan', abridged via http://afe.easia.columbia.edu/ps/china/mao_peasant.pdf

Marr, D.G. (1984), *Vietnamese Tradition on Trial, 1920–1945*, Berkeley: University of California Press.

Mazower, M. (1998), *Dark Continent: Europe's Twentieth Century*, London: Allen Lane.

Montefiore, S.S. (2003), *Stalin: The Court of the Red Tsar*, London: Phoenix.

Overy, R. (2009), *The Morbid Age: Britain Between the Wars*, London: Allen Lane.

Reed, J. (1919), *Ten Days That Shook the World*, New York: Boni and Liveright.

Service, R. (2000), *Lenin: A Biography*, London: Pan Macmillan.

Service, R. (2007), *Comrades. Communism: A World History*, London: Pan Macmillan.

Service, R. (2009), *Trotsky: A Biography*, London: Pan Macmillan.

Service, R. (2010), *Stalin: A Biography*, London: Pan Macmillan.

Solonevich, I. (1935), 'Collectivisation in Practice', *Slavonic and East European Review*, 14/40, 81–97.

Sun Yat-Sen (1924), 'The Principle of Democracy', abridged via http://afe.easia.columbia.edu/ps/cup/sun_yatsen_democracy.pdf

Tooze, A. (2014), *The Deluge: The Great War and the Remaking of Global Order*, London: Allen Lane.

Viola, L., Kozlov, D. and Danilov, V.P. (2005), *Annals of Communism: War against the Peasantry, 1927–1930, Volume 1: The Tragedy of the Soviet Countryside*, New Haven: Yale University Press.

9

FASCISM

While European fascism would in many ways meet its end in a Berlin bunker in 1945, its birthplace was more than 1,000 miles to the south, in Italy. In the early 1920s, fascism was a new political force in a relatively new country, with Italy only having unified in 1861. For all its sudden emergence, it would prove to be a reactive and dynamic force that, along with communism, would shape twentieth-century history irreparably. The 1920s saw the triumph of fascist power in Rome, the growth, decline and re-emergence of German Nazism, and through the Wall Street Crash of 1929 outlined later in this book, laid the groundwork for a further rise in the 1930s. The 1920s, in short, made fascism, and, for a period of time, it appeared to be *the* future form of governance for a Europe struggling to adapt to the modern age. As Mark Mazower notes, while in 1921 it was possible for the British scholar James Bryce to claim the 'universal acceptance of democracy as the normal and natural form of government', this was a fleeting moment. 'By the 1930s, parliaments seemed to be going the way of kings' (Mazower 1998: 2). The leading figure in this shift would be Benito Mussolini.

Italy

Benito Mussolini was born in Milan in 1883. His father Alessandro, a blacksmith and socialist, named his son after Benito Juarez, the progressive and reforming Mexican President of the nineteenth century. His mother, a devout Catholic school teacher, seems to have found her husband's anti-clerical socialism rather difficult. Young Benito was sent to a boarding school run by monks, but he would not be baptised until 1927, nearly five years into his premiership – an action clearly linked to political considerations rather than personal religious commitment. This parental compromise was actually rather symptomatic of the type of middle path Mussolini would himself, for all the bluster, walk in later life.

In 1902, partly motivated by the desire to avoid impending military service, Mussolini emigrated to Switzerland and undertook various forms of low-paid, short-term manual work. Whilst in Switzerland he read Nietzsche's work on the *übermensch* and that of the French syndicalist George Sorel which both had a profound effect on the way he viewed the world.

We know this from his conversations in the 1920s. In November 1924 Mussolini was interviewed by Oscar Levy, the translator of German philosopher Friedrich Nietzsche's works into English, for *The New York Times*. The then Prime Minister remarked to his guest that

> in the letter which you wrote me you alluded to the Nietzchean color of my speeches and writings. You are quite right ... Fifteen years ago when I was quite a young man and was expelled from one Swiss canton to the other. I came across his books. I have read them without exception. They made the deepest impression on me. They cured me of my socialism. They opened my eyes about the cant of statesman such as the 'consent of the governed' and about the inner value of such things as 'parliament' and 'universal suffrage.' I was also deeply impressed by Nietzsche's wonderful precept: 'live dangerously.' I have lived up to that I think.
>
> (New York Times, *9 November 1924*)

Yet for all Mussolini's protestations of being 'cured' of leftist sympathy, and as much as it also relied on ideas of 'the nation' traditionally associated with the nationalist right, fascism did indeed attempt to adopt aspects of pre-First-World-War socialism. Sorel's views on the moribund nature of parliamentary democracy made a lasting impression on the future fascist leader. In 1932 Mussolini remarked that 'in the great stream of Fascism are to be found ideas which begin with Sorel' (Delzell 1970: 97). The belief that liberal democracy could not solve contemporary ills, and that only radical action could plot a new course gave fascism its driving principle. As 1920s French fascist Georges Valois put it, 'the state as it is constructed today, compared to the State which is needed, resembles a horse-drawn carriage compared to a 40-horsepower motor vehicle, or a candle compared to an electric lamp' (Delzell 1970: 97). The theme that democracy was outmoded and unfit for the modern age would unite many a fascist thinker across Europe and beyond.

Later to speak of the *irredenta* – Italian speaking territories that lay outside that country's national borders – much of Mussolini's early career was shaped outside of Italy itself. One of his first politically active positions was as Secretary of the Italian workers' union in Lausanne, Switzerland and, subsequently, in 1909 he took a job as Secretary of the Labour Party in Trento, then part of the Austro-Hungarian Empire. This gave the future Italian nationalist a crudely accented knowledge of German, which he would later augment with almost indecipherable attempts at English. Returning to Italy, he quickly rose up the ranks of Italian socialism. His editorship of the left-wing newspaper *Avanti!* (*Forward!*) was boosted by its opposition to the Italian invasion of Libya in 1911. The future fascist Mussolini was a skilled and charismatic propagandist for revolutionary socialism and the Italian Socialist Party (PSI) in particular.

Although initially he favoured Italy remaining neutral, by 1915 Mussolini came out firmly for intervention in the First World War in the pages of his own newspaper, *Popolo d'Italia* (*People of Italy*). A police report in 1919 summed up his wartime activities:

> he undertook a very active campaign in behalf of Italian intervention, participating in demonstrations in the piazzas and writing quite violent articles in *Popolo d'Italia*. Called into military service, he was sent to the zone of operations and was seriously wounded by the explosion of a grenade.
>
> *(Delzell 1970: 4).*

The war shifted Mussolini's worldview. Instead of a proletarian uprising, he now believed that a revolution could – and should – ensue through the combined effort of men of all classes. Returning home from battle after his injury, Mussolini – oddly given later events – was paid a stipend of £100 a week (around £6,000 today) by the British intelligence agency MI5 to propagandise for Italy's continued fighting for the allied cause. Enlisting such a skilled propagandist was a reasonable move, for Italy's continued presence in the war was far from a racing certainty. In April 1917, German and Austro-Hungarian troops inflicted a heavy defeat on Italy at Caporetto in which 10,000 Italian troops were killed. 'Caporetto' would become a euphemism for the inability of liberal democracy to secure the national good after 1918 – a watch-word for defeat and wider decline.

And yet, just about, Italy emerged on the winning side in the First World War. She took her place at the winning table at Versailles, and expected to be rewarded for her efforts assisting the allied war effort. Under the terms of the Treaty of London in which Italy had entered the war in 1915, renouncing her previous alliance with Austria-Hungary and Germany, she had been promised large territories on the Adriatic coast and it was expected that Prime Minister Vittorio Emanuele Orlando would now deliver these. The port city of 'Fiume', Orlando pointedly remarked of the then-Austrian possession in late 1918, 'is more Italian than Rome'. The results were less than expected, however, and Orlando fell from power nine days before the Treaty was signed. Rather than Fiume and the other territories he hoped to annex, Orlando received only slivers of territory on the Dalmatian coast that were not enough to assuage Italy's expansionary desire, nor the price she felt she had paid in the blood of battle.

When the Versailles terms were announced, the poet and war veteran Gabriele D'Annunzio described the peace as a *'vittoria mutilata'* – a mutilated victory. Subsequently, on 12 September 1919 he led over 2,000 troops into Fiume, forcing out the Anglo-American and French occupying forces, and declaring the territory as annexed to the Kingdom of Italy. Although D'Annunzio was ultimately forced to leave in 1920 when the Italian navy itself bombarded Fiume, his escapade provided two important examples for 1920s fascism: firstly, that bold action outside the democratic system could be popular and receive mass support, and, secondly, it instituted the broad architecture – corporatism and the division of society into diverse 'corporations' which would all cohere towards the national good – of what later became the Italian fascist state. D'Annunzio was talked up as a future national leader, but day-to-day administration was hardly his interest or expertise. The romantic inclusion of 'music' as a fundamental principle of the breakaway Fiume state did not make it into Mussolini's fascist platform; the wearing of black shirts and utilisation of the stiff-armed Roman salute, both features of Fiume, however did. After the fascist seizure of power in 1922 D'Annunzio wisely retired to his literary career.

Six months prior to Fiume, on 23 March 1919, Mussolini announced the creation of the *Fasci di Combattimento* at a Milan meeting attended by around 120 people. The term *fasci* derived from the ancient Roman symbol of bundle of rods tied together, with an axe blade sometimes attached, called a *fasces*. The axe symbolised power over life and death: during the Roman Republic the lictors carrying *fasces* for a magistrate were only allowed to attach the axe when outside the sacred precincts of Rome, signifying that inside the city the people rather than the magistrate held those powers. The only exception was a dictator, appointed in a time of crisis, who took on exceptional powers and thus symbolised them by having his lictors attach the axe head inside the precincts of the city to represent the extraordinary powers of the office. Similarly, the rods represented the fact that even if an individual stick could be broken by some external force the structure would still stand – a metaphor for the unity and order a fascist state would bring. Like the inclusion of the axe head on the symbol of the *fasces*, the word *combattimento* (combat) within Mussolini's new alignment also stood as evidence that, as Richard Griffiths has noted,

> the First World War [had] added some new characteristics to the profile of the radical Right. The first of these was the myth of renewal through war. Most of the new movements that arose in the immediate post-war period found much of their popular appeal in the cult of the ex-serviceman.
>
> *(Griffiths 2000: 29)*

Right from the outset, Mussolini was clear that fascism was a rather vague phenomenon. He told his audience that in Milan 'we dare not bog down in details; if we wish to act, we must grasp reality in its broad essentials without going into minute details' (Delzell 1970: 8). By April of that year a party programme was produced which suggested that what 'details' there were would be significantly derived from the ideas of the left: an eight-hour working day, minimum wage scales, and 'a heavy and progressive tax on capital which would take the form of a meaningful partial expropriation of all kinds of wealth' (Delzell 1970: 13). Compromises would have to be made on this agenda in the early 1920s, however.

In the Milan elections of November 1919, the fascists gained just 5,000 votes out of 270,000 cast. This was initially a locally specific movement that was unable to make significant inroads even in that locality. And yet, as with Germany after 1929, crisis would intervene to propel fascism to power. As a 1930s fascist, the British leader Sir Oswald Mosley, wrote in his autobiography, the rise of new parties on the [European] continent during the twenties and early thirties coincided exactly with the decline of economic prosperity. Both Germany and Italy suffered economic collapse, accompanied by an acute inflation which dislocated industry, caused widespread unemployment, and ruined the middle class. The Italian disintegration, economic, political and psychological, was extreme, and brought Mussolini and the fascists to power in Italy almost as rapidly as the collapse of the war brought Lenin and the communists to power in Russia.

(Mosley 1968: 278–9)

In the summer of 1919 the new Italian Prime Minister, Francesco Saverio Nitti, had to deal with rising inflation, an inability to acquire foreign credit and, by 1920, the very real possibility that the country was about to face bankruptcy. Strikes and violence broke out across the country throughout 1919 and 1920. In the wake of November 1917 these took place, as Griffiths notes, 'amid fears of a Bolshevik revolution' (Griffiths 2000: 35). The notion that fascist movements of the 1920s and beyond were a bulwark against communism was a crucial one.

There is an important debate here. The Marxist–Leninist thinker (and later British Labour Party minister) John Strachey argued in his 1932 book *The Menace of Fascism* that the triumphs of figures such as Mussolini were the last throes of the capitalist system determined to preserve itself against an impending communist takeover. In this way, as historian R.J.B. Bosworth argues, he was essentially parroting the old views of the Italian Communist Party: 'the party line was that Fascists were mercenaries working in the cause of those commanding the ruthless heights of the capitalist world' (Bosworth 2005: 150).

In some ways this argument suited both sides. Though Mussolini balked at being a stooge of big business, it was certainly in his interests to play up the communist threat to attract those self-same sources. Fascists were instrumental in crushing left-wing agitation, most famously at the Alfa Romeo car factory in Milan in August 1920 and in the Po Valley a few months later. Alongside such street violence, however, there was clearly a degree of compromise to the supposedly revolutionary fascist movement the nearer it came to actual power. Fascists learned to wear suits and ties as well as black shirts and uniforms. In 1921, Mussolini negotiated an electoral pact with liberal Prime Minister Giovanni Giolitti and gained 36 seats under Giolitti's 'National Union' ticket at the May election that year. The fascists did not so much storm the establishment citadel as they were ushered into the corridors of power. In November 1921 a National Fascist Party was formed, thus confirming the parliamentary origins of a future fascist regime. For all the symbolism, the fascists would seek power in the same manner as the liberals or any other politician before them.

But this does not suggest that fascism was purely a product of aristocratic con-venience. Ordinary people backed Mussolini and many believed in him fervently. In 1921 the fascist functionary Umberto Pasella analysed the profiles of more than 150,000 members of the growing fascist movement. He reported that 24.3 per cent were peasants of one form or another, 15.4 per cent were workers, 13 per cent students, 12 per cent landowners, 9.2 per cent traders and artisans, 6.6 per cent lawyers, doctors and other professionals, 4.8 per cent bureaucrats, 2.8 per cent big businessmen, 1.1 per cent teachers and 1 per cent seamen (Bosworth 2005: 151). These categories, as Bosworth notes, 'hide as much as they reveal'. 'Peasants' and 'workers' were ill-defined, and it is difficult to make a class reading of support based on them. Certainly by late 1921 62 per cent of fascist members were based in Italy's more prosperous North compared to just 19 per cent in the poorer South (Bosworth 2005: 153). But, at the very least, what is clear is that it was not *just* a movement of high finance and their useful idiots.

By August 1922, Italy was in full-fledged economic chaos. The left demanded a general strike and the liberal government was in no place to deal with the prospect of unrest that a major industrial action would carry. Mussolini issued a demand stating that the government had 48 hours to address the situation or the fascists would 'supplant the state'. The crisis was narrowly avoided, but by this point Mussolini was very much the coming man. And, as power came nearer, so too did increased levels of compromise. A few weeks prior to becoming Prime Minister, Mussolini dropped his opposition to the continuance of the Italian monarchy, a key strategic concession on the road to power. Unless he was willing to risk civil war, the King, after all, would have to appoint him to office.

In October 1922 that moment arrived. Addressing 60,000 supporters in Naples in the Italian south on 24 October, Mussolini declared that

> we don't believe that history repeats itself; we don't believe that after democracy must ensue super-democracy! If democracy was useful and profitable for the nation in the nineteenth century, it may well be that in the twentieth century some other political system will give greater strength to the national community.
>
> *(Delzell 1970: 42)*

As it transpired that political system was but days away.

Around 25,000 men made the famous 'March on Rome' – though not including Mussolini himself, who remained in Milan lest anything go wrong. Hearing the fascists were on their way, the Prime Minister Luigi Facta drafted a military order denoting Rome as being in a state of siege. The King, however, refused to sign the order, closing the door to a violent confrontation between the fascists and the Italian state. Instead, on 29 October, King Vittorio Emmanuel appointed Benito Mussolini Prime Minister of Italy, a process helped by Mussolini appointing only four fascists to his first 14-man cabinet. Just over ten years later Adolf Hitler would come to power in Berlin with his deputy, the conservative Franz von Papen crowing about having 'hired him'. In both cases, fascist regimes started through nominal coalitions with the traditional right. In Hitler's case, the dangerous delusion of von Papen and other conservatives that they could 'control' the National Socialist Party and its leaders would lead to precisely the opposite outcome.

In order to break the deadlock resulting from the extant Italian political system and build up his own base of support, Mussolini now embarked on changes to the country's electoral system. In the next election, it was decreed, the largest party (provided they gained over 25 per cent of the vote) would be awarded two-thirds of the seats in Parliament outright. In the event, around 61 per cent of those who took to the polls voted for Mussolini's National Bloc, but many, interestingly, did not vote at all: of Italy's near 12 million electorate, it is worth recording over seven million did not vote for Mussolini. However, the new parliamentary arithmetic delivered what Mussolini desired; a stable governing majority.

Third place at that election was taken by Giacomo Matteotti's United Socialist Party. Matteotti was a committed anti-fascist and published a book entitled *The Fascisti Exposed* denouncing the regime. On 16 August 1924 his corpse was found twenty miles outside of Rome. He had been stabbed several times with a carpenter's knife – a brutal end and a harbinger of things to come. Was Mussolini directly responsible? It has long been debated, but the case remains open. What is clear is that the murder had significant consequences for the still nominally parliamentary dictator. The opposition demanded Mussolini's resignation and boycotted Parliament, but Mussolini did not offer to go nor did the King pressure him to do so. The issue rumbled on for months before Mussolini gave perhaps his most famous peroration: his parliamentary address of 3 January 1925.

On that date, frequently asserted to be the beginning of the Italian dictatorship, Mussolini declared that 'if all the acts of violence have been the result of a particular historical, political and moral climate, well, it is my responsibility'. Having referenced the Matteotti murder, he then issued a chilling warning for the future: 'Italy, gentlemen, wants peace, wants calm, wants stability which allows work to continue. This calm, this stability, we will give her with love and, if necessary, with force' (Griffin 1995: 50). Mussolini later claimed the revolution had ended with the creation of the Grand Fascist Council in 1923 (subsequently merged into the governmental structure in December 1928), but the Matteotti affair and its aftermath put the cap on any imminent prospect of regime change (the Grand Council would eventually vote for Mussolini's removal from power in 1943). Fascism was backed by legal statute, but it ultimately rested on violence. As Mussolini himself acknowledged in 1925: 'I had obtained plenary powers, but I thought it better to reinforce them with 300,000 bayonets' (*The Times*, 25 June 1925). This would be a perennial refrain. Thousands of Italian communist leaders were arrested during the late 1920s, many faced internal exile to remote Italian villages which suddenly expanded by up to three times their previous sizes to cope with such Siberian-style internal banishment (Ebner 2011: 75 and 108).

For their part, in 1925 in the august surroundings of King's College Cambridge, that college's Political Society voted by six votes to five that they would prefer to be governed by Mussolini rather than nineteenth-century Italian liberal Giuseppe Mazzini. Lenin gained only three supporters (Political Society 1925). Fascism, it appeared, was in Italy to stay. The question soon became where it would next appear and make a bid for power?

What was fascism?

If historians are generally agreed on the degree of violence (or threat of it) needed to uphold such regimes in the 1920s and beyond, they are less decided about its ideology. Certainly the Janus-faced nature of fascism is often remarked upon, and with good reason. One half of this involved invoking the mysticism of days gone by, and Ancient Rome and its leaders were a constant reference point under the Italian regime. Attempting to gee up his supporters for the March on Rome, Mussolini declared that

> the Roman Empire was and is a spiritual creation, since it was the spirit of the Roman legionnaires that ordered their physical arms to thrust out the spears. Now, therefore, we want the greatness of the nation to exist in both the material and the spiritual senses.
>
> (Delzell 1970: 43)

Indeed, Mussolini's obsession with Ancient Rome translated into practical action when his government sponsored vast excavations and restorations of archaeological sites around the country, including the famous ancient forum in Rome. Many of these became associated with Mussolini's new national mythology when they were used as the backdrop for mass rallies and parades by the fascist regime.

Similarly, Hitler – other than invoking the Germanic heroes of Frederick Barbarossa, Frederick the Great and Otto von Bismarck at various points – claimed to answer to 'the external Court of History' during his trial for the Munich Putsch. Fascist leaders often did not talk in the here and now, instead comparing their actions to an often-imagined or idealised past. Like Mussolini's appropriation of ancient Roman sites to bolster the perceived legitimacy of his regime, Hitler's Nazi Party made use of the Externsteine, a rock formation in Westphalia that was allegedly an ancient pagan religious site, as a backdrop for its propaganda. The more ancient and romantic the site, the more useful it could be to the fascist propagandist.

Yet allied to such vagaries and nostalgia was a forward-looking, very practical dimension of fascism. Fascist economic doctrine was heavily predicated on using new technology to create jobs for the unemployed, ideally to the point of achieving full employment (a near impossibility under free-market capitalism). The fascist view was not just that democracy was innately unnecessary, but that it was singularly unfit to deal with the problems of the modern age. In 1930s Germany, famously, the National Socialist response included projecting the building of the network of *autobahns* (highways) using public funds as creating vast numbers of jobs (though sources such as Ritschl 2000: passim, dispute whether this actually worked). The first major scheme was in Italy in the 1920s, however. In May 1924, the decision was taken to press ahead with a mass programme of land reclamation. Reclamation consortiums – funded and overseen by the state – were created to channel the waters of rivers and reclaim swamp land. In September 1929 Mussolini announced a two billion lira scheme 'which would be a monument to the ever-lasting glory of the fascist regime'. As the British press reported at the time, 'through the work provided *men* would be reclaimed, and through them the race' (*Manchester Guardian*, 15 September 1929). Fascism attempted to project vigour, manliness and innovative thinking. Mussolini posed himself the question, 'are we reactionaries? No. We are pioneers, anticipators. Men who are realising a new form of political and social life'. Many democratic politicians – including David Lloyd George in the UK who built Mussolini-esque public works schemes into his unsuccessful Liberal Party manifesto in 1929 – looked on enviously. One such man who did make the jump was W.E.D. Allen, a Conservative MP who later joined Oswald Mosley's British Union of Fascists. In a 1930 article before his full conversion, the voice of the future fascist can be heard:

> The old men stand for things we cannot accept; they stand for fixity, institu-tionalism; they have a philosophy of continuity, of 'gradualness' ... And to us, the young men, change is the very breath of life. The rhythm of change throbs through the blood of the young men of today. In this glorious year of 1930, youth has the ball at its feet, and the ball is the world. In the next twenty years anything may happen; but we must be the young men who make things happen, not the old men who ask 'what will happen next?'.
>
> *(Allen 1930)*

Such prose is useful in helping codify what fascism actually was – no easy task. For the historian Richard Griffiths, the three major intellectual tenets behind fascism were firstly anti-rationalism, secondly the belief that corporatism would better serve the community than out-and-out capitalism, and thirdly anti-Semitism (Griffiths 2000: 11–16). As to the first Mussolini remarked that, 'for us, the nation is not just a territorial thing; above everything else, it is a spiritual thing' (Delzell 1970: 42). Fascist intellectual Giovanni Gentile argued that fascism went beyond politics and into every facet of one's life:

> like the Catholic invests with his religious feelings the whole of his life ... so the Fascist, whether he is writing in newspapers or reading them, going about his private life or talking to others, looking to the future or remembering the past and the past of his people, must always remember he is a Fascist!
>
> *(Griffiths 2000: 54)*

Similarly, Roger Griffin has argued that the core of fascism amounts to a mythology about the need for the radical rebirth of the state – what he calls palingenetic ultranationalism – in the wake of its past decadence and destruction. Fascism therefore focuses on a return to a semi-mythological 'golden age' from the past, but coupled with modern technology and a radical overcoming of the recent past (Griffin 1993: passim). To these we may also add economic autarky – the belief that a state insulated against the vicissitudes of global capitalism would better serve the people than seeking refuge in the international markets. Domestic, inflationary capital investment and a tightly controlled set of economic levers rather than a more transnational, trade-based approach by public and private sector alike was in a sense fascism's big economic offer. To these economic drivers Robert Paxton has proffered further underpinnings, including the primacy of the group above the 'selfish' individual, the desire for authority from an (exclusively male) leader, and the beauty and desirability of violence in a supposedly noble cause (Paxton 2004: 41). All this was the positive case, of sorts, for fascism.

In the case of German Nazism, the negative enemies being presented as the opponents of this vision were clear. Communism, internationalism, and Judaism were all viewed as intrinsically opposed to the fascist worldview and system. The Jew was held to be pulling the strings in both Wall Street and Moscow. In the 1933 propaganda film *Hans Westmar*, the eponymous character – a fictionalised version of Nazi martyr Horst Wessel – is taken in a taxi through 1920s Berlin where signs such as 'Hungarian Cuisine', 'Italian Restaurant' and 'U.S.A. Tea-room' flash by the window. Maude, his German-American love interest, remarks that 'Oh! This Berlin is indeed international'. Her chaperone father replies that 'you can find everything here, just nothing German'. For Westmar, things are portrayed as only getting worse. Entering a nightclub, the three encounter black-coated attendants, a band singing in English, and a refusal to serve beer from Munich: 'we only serve English beer'. Seeing all this, the young lady asks 'so, Papa, our papers seem to tell the truth about how well the Germans are doing?'. Westmar leaps in: 'the Germans? Maybe a few pushers and swindlers. All the others drown in misery'.

The notion that previous sacrifice had given way to utter decadence was writ large through the film, and Nazi dogma per se. When the club's band starts to play 'Die Wacht am Rhein', a song popular in the trenches of the First World War, Westmar finally explodes: 'You will not be allowed to play this song here!'. Storming out he declares 'my dear Maude, that is not Germany, Germany is somewhere else!'. A shot of the bawdy nightclub dancing, where black men mix freely with white women, dissolves into the heroism of the Western front. It was this view of Weimar Germany (pointedly, a leading communist in the film is also portrayed as stereotypically Jewish) that informed the Nazi's *weltanschauung* in the 1920s, and their concrete policies after 1933.

Germany

While Mussolini had lived outside of Italy for several years, Adolf Hitler was actually born and grew up outside the German Reich. This was far from unique amongst leading Nazis – Deputy Führer Rudolf Hess was born in Egypt, the ideologue turned foreign policy adviser Alfred Rosenberg grew up in Estonia, and Walter Darré – later a leading *blut und boden* (blood and soil) Nazi theorist – spent his first years in the outskirts of Buenos Aires, Argentina. For the future Führer himself, it was only at the age of 24 that he settled in the land he would eventually rule. Having left his boyhood home of Linz and a tramp-like bohemian existence in Vienna, he moved to Munich in 1913 – ostensibly to avoid serving in the Austro-Hungarian army which he considered a 'Babylon of races'. A year later, he would don the German uniform in the trenches of France and Belgium.

The First World War was everything to Hitler. It took a life that was meandering along aimlessly and injected meaning. In *Mein Kampf* – the autobiographical tract written during his period of incarceration after the failed Munich Putsch of 1923 – he described the dramatic reaction to its onset:

> to me personally those hours appeared like the redemption from the troubling moods of my youth. Therefore I am not ashamed today to say that, overwhelmed by impassioned enthusiasm, I fell on my knees and thanked Heaven out of my overflowing heart that it had granted me the good fortune of being allowed to live in these times.
>
> *(Hitler 1941: 210)*

His fellow soldiers may have regarded him as something of an oddity, but generally he seems to have found something of a comradeship that had eluded him to that point.

Having served bravely and won the Iron Cross, Hitler's war ended in a military hospital where he was recovering from the effects of an allied mustard gas attack in 1918. There he heard of Germany's defeat, and began considering the 'stab in the back' explanation of Jewish and communist treachery having led to his nation's decline. He was not alone on the right in propagating such views. According to Hitler,

> Kaiser Wilhelm II was the first German Emperor who extended his hand to the leaders of Marxism without guessing that scoundrels are without honour. While they were still holding the imperial hand in their own, the other was feeling for the dagger. With the Jews there is no bargaining, but only the hard either – or.
>
> *(Hitler 1941: 270)*

This was a major early difference between the German and Italian fascist movements – indeed when Italy passed its own race laws in 1938 it emerged that over 10,000 Jews were members of the PNF. The Jews were never 'the issue' with Mussolini as they were with Hitler. Indeed, Hitler recounted that it was when he was brooding on the Jews in the corridors of Pasewalk Military Hospital in November 1918 that he 'resolved to become a politician'.

In 1919, Germany had embarked on an equally novel experiment: parliamentary democracy. Under the new Weimar Republic – named after the Thuringian city where the new constitution was signed – Germany had one of the most democratic electoral systems in the world. Women's suffrage, proportional representation, a voting age of 20 and the ironing out of previous electoral rotten boroughs were features of the burgeoning new democracy. Germans also made the most of their – in some cases new – vote, with turnout for federal elections never dipping below three-quarters and sometimes reaching as high as 83 per cent. The new democracy simply lacked one major feature: total legitimacy from the outset.

The arguments against the Weimar regime from the German right were not over specific matters of policy but its very existence. As Hitler told a sympathetic audience at the Kindlkeller beer hall in Munich, we need some national pride again. But who can the nation be proud of these days? Of [Socialist President Friedrich] Ebert perhaps? (*laughter*) Of the Government? We need a national will just as much. We must not always say: We can't do that. We must be able to do it. In order to smash this disgraceful peace treaty, we must regard every means as justified.

(*Noakes and Pridham, 1983: 17*)

The 'loud applause' this police report records the last sentence as receiving was a key point. In the early years of the republic this anti-democratic undercurrent was dangerous background noise, but politicians were still able to keep it in the background.

Many were thinking similarly. Even when he stumbled across a small meeting of Nazis in a Munich beer hall – 'club life of the lowest form', as he later wrote – Hitler was not the only, nor the most likely, right-wing leader looking to make a stir in post-1918 Germany. As Richard J. Evans notes, whilst

military models of conduct had been widespread in German society and culture before 1914 ... after the war they become all pervasive; the language of politics was permeated by metaphors of warfare; the other party was an enemy to be smashed, and struggle, terror, and violence become widely accepted ... Uniforms were everywhere. Politics, to reverse a famous dictum of the early nineteenth century military theorist von Clausewitz, became war pursued by other means.

(*Evans 2004: 72*)

In March 1920 a right-wing military coup – often referred to as the Kapp Putsch – attempted to overthrow the Weimar regime (and succeeded in forcing the government to flee from Berlin) but, under the pressure of 12 million workers striking in protest, it collapsed quickly. One incredulous witness was Hitler himself. Flying from Munich to Berlin with the aim of taking part in the putsch, Hitler was met by the sight of strikers at the airport. Pretending to be an accountant and armed with a stick-on beard, Hitler managed to pass through the strike barriers but by the day he arrived the coup's prospects were all but over.

The Kapp Putsch, though ultimately a failure, simply highlighted the weakness of the Weimar state in the eyes of its citizens. This was not without cause: between 1919 and 1930 there were eight Chancellors of the German Reich and a dramatic economic crisis, described in later chapters, that further undermined the perceived competence of the democratic government. In contrast, the UK, itself undergoing more political changes than usual due to the ousting of one Prime Minister and the terminal illness of another, had just four Prime Ministers during the same period. Weimar democracy thus became a game of musical chairs in which a constant cycle of elections produced a series of inconclusive election results where horse trading – and thus squabbling – between the parties to achieve a workable number of votes became commonplace. A variety of SPD, Centre Party and technocratic-led governments passed through the decade, but, for those on the political fringes, it was easy to point to all such forces and call a plague on all their houses.

This method of denouncing the Weimar state's unstable nature and the vagaries of its politics appeared to be particularly successful amongst the young. Historian Juan J. Linz has demonstrated that nearly 60 per cent of Nazi members prior to the November 1923 putsch were under the age of 31 (Linz 1991: 3–121). The party was young even by the standards of European fascism: 55 per cent of the top-tier of National Socialists leaders had been born in the 1890s, with 42 per cent of the second-tier likewise. This put the party at significantly younger than their SDP socialist opponents – of whom 60 per cent of their leadership had been born in the 1880s – and indeed than Italian fascism, which itself mustered 40 per cent of leaders, included Mussolini, born in the 1880s. Fascists per se emerged from a relatively poorly educated, relatively rural background. Compared to 51 per cent of socialist and 48 per cent of Christian leaders, only 31 per cent of interwar European fascists had been to university. Half the NSDAP (National Socialist German Workers' Party) top brass were born in rural areas and villages, though a quarter, including Hitler, came from provincial cities. None, interestingly, were born in Berlin.

As Anthony McElligott has recently argued, 'the authority of the [Weimar] republic hinged to a large degree on its ability to ensure … material security' (McElligott 2013: 69). In Germany a key issue in this regard was hyperinflation, as the economics chapters of this book consider in greater detail. One witness to this phenomenon was the then-student Albert Speer, later Hitler's architect and Armaments Minister, who took a cycling holiday through the Black Forest in September 1923. He sarcastically wrote home that it was 'very cheap here! Lodgings 400,000 marks and supper 1,800,000 marks. Milk 250,000 marks a pint'. Six weeks later, he remarked, 'a restaurant dinner cost ten to twenty billion marks, and even in the student dining hall over a billion' (Speer 2002: 37–8). Speer was a (self-professed) example of the middle-class, relatively apolitical type inclined to give Nazism a hearing for primarily economic motives. He 'did see quite a number of rough spots in the party doctrines. But I assumed they would be polished in time' (Speer 2002: 50). The financial upheaval of 1923 forced the Speers to sell the old family firm and factory to another company at 'a fraction of its value in return for "dollar treasury bills"' (Speer 2002: 38). The fascist offer of stability above all things played to such ears.

The hyperinflation described by Speer, and discussed in detail elsewhere in this book, was exacerbated by the French occupation of the Ruhr in 1923 in protest at Germany's non-payment of the terms imposed on it at the Treaty of Versailles. The *Ruhrkampf* became a new low for a nation already on its knees. More than 100 Germans were killed by the invading French, and the passive resistance of the Germans to the incursion won international sympathy. Under pressure from international finance the French withdrew, a new repayments plan was produced (financed by American capital), and the crisis passed.

As already mentioned, during the Ruhr episode the use of French African colonial troops in the occupation particularly rankled with those on the right. As Hitler wrote in *Mein Kampf*, it was and is the Jews who bring the negro to the Rhine, always with the same concealed thought and the clear goal of destroying, by the bastardization which would necessarily set in, the white race which they hate, to throw it down from its cultural and political height and in turn to rise personally to the position of master.

(Hitler 1941: 448–9)

This was another layer to the narrative of national humiliation upon which fascism was dependent. The mixed-race 'Rhineland Bastards' that were born to German women in the aftermath of the French occupation soon became a lasting obsession for the Nazis, and in the 1930s several hundred of the children were subjected to compulsory surgical sterilisation by the German state to prevent them from spreading their 'unfit' genes.

By the mid-1920s, German fascists had a ready-made template from which to gain office: Mussolini's Italy. In November 1922, Hermann Esser – one of the fledging NSDAP's leading lights – proclaimed Adolf Hitler to be 'Germany's Mussolini'. As Ian Kershaw has shown, references to Hitler as 'our *Führer*' (leader) multiplied in the Nazi press from this point. The March on Rome cemented the ideal of the visionary leader who could seize power in a single bold act. Outside the Nazis, the *Stahlhelm* (Steel Helmet) veterans association began to demand an end to 'the plague of parliamentarianism' and claimed the country needed 'a dictator, a Mussolini, who would sweep out the entire muck with an iron broom' (Kershaw 2001: 20–1).

Il Duce himself was interestingly rather sniffy toward German National Socialism at first. In 1924 he declared openly to Oscar Levy that 'I know that Hitler, Wulle and Ludendorff crew. One of them, I forget who, even came here and asked me to receive him. I refused, of course, to have anything to do with them' (*New York Times*, 9 November 1924). Partly this must have been due to the fact that, at this point, Hitler's movement looked simply incompetent for they had failed with their own 'March on Rome' – the Munich Putsch of November 1923.

Like the failed Kapp Putsch in 1920, the goal of the Munich fiasco was to overthrow the Weimar government and replace it with a right-wing government. Hitler's initial effort, however, was to ally with Bavarian State Commissioner Gustav von Kahr who had made placatory noises about taking on Berlin. Hitler, not believing he would match word with deed, now resolved to take matters into his own hands. Backed by 600 paramilitary *Sturmabteilung* (SA) troops who surrounded the building, Hitler marched into a speech Kahr was giving on the evening of 8 November. To shouts of 'theatrical! South America! Mexico!' from the stunned audience, Hitler declared that a march on Berlin would begin and invited Kahr and others to join him. Feigning acquiescence, Kahr managed to alert the authorities to the plot. The coup ended in catastrophic and dramatic failure at the *Odeonsplatz*, a large square in central Munich, with 16 Nazi supporters dying under the fire from the police. The dead of Munich, together with Horst Wessel (a National Socialist murdered in 1930 by a communist, and later memorialised in the famous Horst-Wessel-Lied), became martyrs under the Nazi regime. Party legend held that the flag carried by the Munich marchers, bearing a swastika on a white background, was soaked in the blood of the Nazi dead that day, transforming it into a swastika in a white disc on a red background. Versions of this flag – called the *blutfahne* (blood flag) and used in Party rituals and Nuremberg Rallies throughout the Third Reich – would become the Party's symbol and, in 1935, it would become the national flag of Germany.

In the short term however, there was a high-profile court case for both Hitler and his ally in the Putsch, General Ludendorff, to contend with. This provided a platform for Hitler to rant in front of a sympathetic judge, and be almost guaranteed prominent press coverage. The actual verdict of the trial (Hitler receiving a five-year jail term, but was eligible for parole in nine months) was less important than this platform. The issues Hitler talked about included his usual vagaries. Attempting to define National Socialism, he claimed that

> we want to create order in the state, throw out the drones, take up the fight against international stock exchange slavery, against the politicisation of the trade unions and above all, for the highest honourable duty which we, as Germans, knew should be once more introduced – the duty of bearing arms, military service.
>
> *(Noakes and Pridham 1983: 34–5)*

This agenda was redolent with anti-politics, but it gave those Germans who would later buy *Mein Kampf* (authored during his spell in jail) an insight into what was to come.

When Hitler was released on 20 December 1924 he was banned from speaking in public until 1927. He used this time to re-orient Nazism towards seeking power through democratic mandate rather than violent coup. Reliant on others, particularly the Strasser brothers (Gregor and Otto) and a young Joseph Goebbels to lead the fight in Germany's North, Nazism briefly looked likely to tip away from mere Hitlerism. This was partly about personality, but it was also, in short, about whether National Socialism should emphasise the 'National' or the 'Social' elements of its programme. For some, including Goebbels, the Nazi Party should be overtly anti-capitalist. Yet for Hitler himself, there was no ideological necessity to touch the private sector or business. When he was asked by Otto Strasser, 'what would you do about Krupp's [steel]? Would you leave it alone or not?' Hitler replied 'of course I should leave it alone. Do you think me so crazy as to ruin Germany's great industry?' 'If you wish to preserve the capitalist regime, Herr Hitler', argued Strasser (pointedly not addressing him as *Mein Führer*), 'you have no right to speak of socialism' (Noakes and Pridham 1983: 67). Otto Strasser would manage to escape from Germany in 1934, but his brother would be murdered during the Night of the Long Knives – when the Nazis secured their grip on power by violently settling a series of old scores. Goebbels was one of the few Nazis to express open disdain for Hitler in the 1920s but then play a prominent role thereafter as Minister of Propaganda in the Third Reich.

The problem of Strasserism was not merely about policy towards industrial elites, the very notion of socialism was at odds with the Nietzchean appeal upon which fascist leaders predicated themselves. The idea of the primacy of the leader united, and would unite, fascist forces across the globe. To questions about his own authority, Hitler was incredulous: 'you wish to give Party members the right to decide whether or not the Führer has remained faithful to the so-called Idea. For us the Idea is the Führer, and every Party member has only to obey the Führer' (Noakes and Pridham 1983: 66). The period of 1926–8 was crucial in Hitler instilling this in his party, and it also saw progress across the board.

Though the financial crash of 1929 would propel the movement from a fringe gathering to a potential party of government, the Nazis had received an earlier boost during the winter of 1927–8. During this period of relative prosperity, the Weimar Republic increased the salaries of civil servants. Pouncing on existing dissatisfaction with metropolitan elites, the Nazis used a low-tax platform to appeal to the dispossessed rural German who, as in a January 1928 meeting in Oldenburg, saw 'in the German National Socialist Hitler movement the only salvation from the parliamentary morass' (Noakes and Pridham 1983: 61). From October 1928 to September 1929 Nazi membership increased steadily from 100,000 to 150,000 people.

And then, quite suddenly, the stock exchange in New York collapsed. Having opposed the renegotiation of German war debt on the grounds that reparations should be discontinued rather than negotiated on at all, the Nazis were given a boost by the fact that the American banking system was now withholding the credit to Germany that made those debts even theoretically payable in the first place. More than one in four German workers were unemployed by 1931, a figure that increased to around a third of the labour force by 1932. From just 2.6 per cent of the vote in the 1928 Reichstag elections, the Nazis polled over 18 per cent in 1930. German National Socialism was on the march, and its consequences would be felt across the globe in the 1930s and 1940s.

Global fascism

But were the signs of a transnational advance there earlier? By the early 1930s the globe had clear examples of fascism outside of Berlin and Rome. Brazilian Integralism, Chilean National Socialism, the Hungarian Party of National Unity and the puppet Libyan Fascist Party permitted by Mussolini were all manifestations of this. But the intellectual roots of fascism had spread before the Wall Street Crash, and mostly – since German Nazism was barely in a position to influence the politics of its own nation, let alone the world – through the prism of Italian fascism. Certainly, there was a grey area here. In large part 'fascist' organisations, particularly in the early 1920s, performed several of the functions one might associate with a generic expatriate body. The nine million Italian nationals (a figure extended by Italy's looser laws on citizenship) residing abroad were a ready-made platform from which to export an ideology Mussolini had once claimed was 'not for export' at all.

Leading the charge was the *Ufficio Centrale per i Fasci all'Estero* (Central Office for the Organisation of the Overseas Fasci). For Parini, the last Secretary of the organisation, the *Fasci all'Estero* appeared in the early 1920s, with the specific intent of assisting, with discipline and dedication, the work of the consuls. They established everywhere meeting-places where Italians might nourish their spirit, remembering their faraway Motherland, join in fraternal and solidarity work, raise their cultural level, and strengthen the moral, national and fascist education of the younger generation.

This tension between whether this lobbying group was a pro-Italian or pro-Fascist organisation – and where the dividing line should be drawn – marked its activities prior to its sidelining (in a quarrel between the governmental Foreign Office and the fascist party itself back in Rome) in the late 1920s.

It all, in any case, began rather slowly. As fascism saw its first signs of a break-through in Italy across 1920 and 1921 the first branches of Fasci popped up around the Mediterranean basin and northern Europe, but this was no instant explosion of interest. As Luca de Caprariis notes, 'by 1921 the [London] branch had barely 20 members, a good half of whom "were always absent"'. One year later, on the eve of the March on Rome, membership had only grown to 30. In Switzerland and France, despite the immediate influence of Italian events and large emigrant communities, the fascist presence remained negligible (de Caprariis 2000: 152). After the embrace of what de Caprariis calls 'generic nationalism' there was a gradual increase, but it was unsurprisingly the March on Rome in October 1922 which galvanised Italian immigrant communities. The expansion from 1922 to 1925 was certainly impressive: in August 1922 the *Fasci all'Estero* had 13 branches. By the following February this had risen to 150, and by mid-1924 there were over 296 overseas branches prompting the groups' backers to claim that they were 'flourishing in nearly every corner of the world' (de Caprariis 2000: 157). By 1925 there were around 65,000 members of the bodies across the globe. Given their huge levels of nineteenth-century Italian immigration, Brazil and the United States perhaps unsurprisingly accounted for almost a third of the total foreign branches.

In Argentina, where Italian immigrants were often steeped in the liberal traditions of their nineteenth-century ancestors, the opportunities to expand appeared minimal. Despite having non-political expatriate organisations with almost 150,000 Italian nationals, Argentina only possessed eight Fasci branches, most of which were scantly populated. This was the same number as in Turkey, Australia, Egypt and, initially China (though in Peking a third branch opened in 1925). Siam maintained a slightly forlorn branch, whilst there were six branches across Africa, all told. Given the significant Italian populations in several American cities – most prominently New York – the failure of the Fascist League of North America (FLNA) to break through was particularly galling for Mussolini. The FLNA's terroristic activities of vandalising newspaper offices, engaging in street violence and even carrying out assassinations did little to engender wider appeal. Such organisations often limited themselves to indoctrinating Italian immigrants in the new ideology rather than gaining a sympathetic ear from the indigenous population and thus remained ghettoised.

The explicitly Mussolini-sponsored Fasci had their own problems, but even when nationalist parties attempted to forge their own path, success in the 1920s (and indeed the 1930s) was often limited. An important example to conclude on is France for, as Robert Paxton notes, 'the richness, fervor, and celebrity of the intellectual revolt against classical liberal values in the early twentieth century would seem, on intellectual history grounds alone, to make that country a prime candidate for the successful establishment of fascist movements' (Paxton 2004: 76). Even in the depth of the depression in the 1930s, the more a French fascist movement sought to imitate the Mussolini model, the less success it had. By contrast, Colonel La Rocque's *Parti Social Français* was able to gain more traction by tapping into republican traditions in France and remaining comparatively moderate (Paxton 2004: 68–9). Even in a global 1920s, and for all that events in Wall Street or Moscow could influence the political picture, all such movements would have to adapt to national circumstance. In the end, fascism would arrive in other countries via German or Italian invasion far more often than it did via the democratic ballot box.

Conclusion

In the shadow of the horrific events of the Second World War and, in particular, the organised slaughter of innocent civilians through the Holocaust, historicising fascism remains a difficult endeavour. But for all the challenges in doing so it is a vital task. Despite the talk of Nietzschean supermen, Hitler and Mussolini were political operators seeking to exploit the existing terrain in a way not unknown to 'ordinary' politicians of other persuasions. The status quo was unacceptable and disadvantageous to their countrymen, and they proposed to fix it. This involved the usual compromise seen elsewhere on the political spectrum – ditching anti-monarchism for Mussolini, and holding his nose and entering the democratic process of the Reichstag for Hitler – but fundamentally the success or failure of fascism depended on circumstances completely beyond its control. Rampant speculation and the eventual crash on Wall Street, and Moscow's ability to exploit its con-sequences, were not issues within the purview of Benito Mussolini or Adolf Hitler. The parlous state of the economy under democratic management and the con-current threat of communism as an alternative form of government were rhetorical framing devices to be sure, but until they became a reality few were willing to give fascism a shot: whether it be in Milan, Munich or elsewhere. As chapter 11 notes however, seemingly quite suddenly, this scenario began to play itself out.

Fundamentally, the fascist project was about the radical remaking and reimagining of the state to simultaneously restore it to a semi-mythical former entity while at the same time unleashing the forces of modernisation to achieve its aims. In both Italy and Germany, the economic and political consequences of the First World War laid the groundwork for fascism to attract supporters as democracy appeared to fail. There was no inevitability about its success in gaining power in these countries, and ultimately its perceived association with the tyranny of the Third Reich would make it unpalatable for nearly all but the most radical in other countries. Fascism was one anti-democratic approach to the challenges of modernity and the unrest of the interwar period. Like communism, its political triumph would soon result in the deaths of millions.

Questions

- What were the defining characteristics of 1920s fascism?
- Can we speak of one 'fascism' existing in the 1920s? Why or why not?
- Why did fascism emerge victorious in Italy and not, for example, Britain or the United States?
- How important was the leadership principle to fascism?
- Was fascism a left- or right-wing movement?

Recommended further reading

Ben-Ghiat, R. (2015), *Italian Fascism's Empire Cinema*, Bloomington: Indiana University Press.

Bosworth, R.J.B. (2005), *Mussolini's Italy*, London: Allen Lane.

Evans, R.J. (2004), *The Coming of the Third Reich*, London: Allen Lane.

Falasca-Zamponi, S. (1997), *Fascist Spectacle: The Aesthetics of Power in Mussolini's Italy*, Berkeley: University of California Press.

Hitler, A. (1941 edn), *Mein Kampf*, Boston, MA: Houghton Mifflin.

Kershaw, I.K. (2001 edn), *The 'Hitler Myth': Image and Reality in the Third Reich*, Oxford: Oxford University Press.

Noakes, J. and Pridham, G. (1983), *Nazism 1919–1945, Volume 1: The Rise to Power 1919–1934*, Exeter: Exeter University Press.

Paxton, R.O. (2004), *The Anatomy of Fascism*, New York: Random House.

Works cited

Allen, W.E.D. (1930), Newspaper article within Oswald Mosley Papers, University of Birmingham, OMN/B/2/3–4.

Bosworth, R.J.B. (2005), *Mussolini's Italy*, London: Allen Lane.

de Caprariis, L. (2000), 'Fascism for Export? The Rise and Eclipse of the *Fasci Italiani all'Estero*', *Journal of Contemporary History*, 35/2, 151–183.

Delzell, C.F. (1970), *Mediterranean Fascism 1919–1945*, London: Harper and Row.

Ebner, M.R. (2011), *Ordinary Violence in Mussolini's Italy*, Cambridge: Cambridge University Press.

Evans, R.J. (2004), *The Coming of the Third Reich*, London: Allen Lane.

Griffin, R. (1993), *The Nature of Fascism*, London: Routledge.

Griffin, R. (1995), *Fascism*, Oxford: Oxford University Press.

Griffiths, R. (2000), *An Intelligent Person's Guide to Fascism*, London: Gerald Duckworth and Co.

Hitler, A. (1941 edn), *Mein Kampf*, Boston, MA: Houghton Mifflin.

Kershaw, I.K. (2001 edn), *The 'Hitler Myth': Image and Reality in the Third Reich*, Oxford: Oxford University Press.

Linz, J.J. (1991), 'Some Notes toward a Comparative Study of Fascism in Sociological Historical Perspective', in Lacqueur, W. (ed.), *Fascism: A Reader's Guide*, Berkeley: UCLA Press, pp. 3–121.

Mazower, M. (1998), *Dark Continent: Europe's Twentieth Century*, London: Allen Lane.

McElligott, A. (2013), *Rethinking the Weimar Republic: Authority and Authoritarianism, 1916–1936*, London: Hodder Arnold.

Mosley, O. (1968), *My Life*, London: Nelson.

Noakes, J. and Pridham, G. (1983), *Nazism 1919–1945, Volume 1: The Rise to Power*, Exeter: Exeter University Press.

Paxton, R.O. (2004), *The Anatomy of Fascism*, New York: Random House.

Political Society (1925), Minutes 2 November, Journals held at King's College, Cambridge, KCAS/13/8.

Ritschl, A. (2000), 'Deficit Spending in the Nazi Recovery, 1933–1938: A Critical Reassessment', via https://ideas.repec.org/p/zur/iewwpx/068.html

Speer, A. (2002 edn), *Inside the Third Reich*, New York: Phoenix.

PART IV

10

GLOBAL ECONOMIC CONDITIONS IN THE 1920S

In 1916 Bolshevik leader Vladimir Lenin published his pamphlet *Imperialism: The Highest Stage of Capitalism*. In it, *contra* Adam Smith, he argued that rather than supposedly spreading wealth and prosperity capitalism would in fact inevitably result in the formation of cartels that would crush all competition, assume monopoly power and take control of nominally free markets. At that point, these monopolistic forces would have to seek out new markets to continue their growth and, invariably, begin looking at other countries to colonise for both resources and markets. Thus, he concluded, the rapid growth of empires in the late nineteenth century was the result of a 'moribund capitalism' that had grown to its greatest possible limits and was now teetering on the brink of collapse (Lenin 1917: 161–2). The First World War had therefore been 'imperialistic (that is, [an] annexationist, predatory, plunderous war) on the part of both sides; it was a war for the division of the world, for the partition and repatriation of colonies, "spheres of influence" of financial capital, etc.'. As a result, he added, 'Imperialism is the eve of the proletarian social revolution' (Lenin 1917: 4, 10). At which point in Russia, of course, enter Lenin himself as the self-proclaimed saviour.

This was the standard communist explanation for the First World War: greedy capitalists, seeking new markets and profits, had contrived to go to war for economic gain. The workers had no vested interest in the war's outcome, according to this analysis, because the true battle to be fought was between the classes, not between nations. The 1914 voting for war credits on the part of the Social Democratic Party in Germany, and indeed Labour's broad backing for the conflict in the UK (albeit with notable exceptions) had shown that even advanced, progressive capitalist opinion could not buck this overall trend. Yet if the First World War had truly been about the acquisition of resources to keep the profit machines of capitalism working, then the logical follow-up was to ask 'had this worked?'. Indeed, as our first chapter has discussed, although the victorious empires – principally Britain and

France – made major territorial gains in the war's aftermath, many of these, like Iraq, had proved expensive to maintain. The numbers did not always add up. Indeed, outside the Soviet Union (where even the reforms of the New Economic Plan were a long way off unfettered capitalism) the early 1920s saw a worldwide economic slump as wartime price levels returned to normal. Yet by the middle years of the decade, the US economy had recovered and entered the early phases of a boom that would last, with a few hiccups, until the crash of 1929. Economies elsewhere proved more unstable, but for many the decade was one of general prosperity and growth. However, whether or not Lenin's assessment of the Great War was correct, the results of the conflict were often mixed for both loser and victor alike.

This chapter considers the state of the world economy throughout the 1920s, beginning with an examination of how German war reparations affected not only that country's economy but the world economy more widely. We then turn to the underpinning of the global economy – the gold standard – and outline how what was supposed to be a force for stability was in reality a house of cards that severely restricted policy makers' options. The third section will consider the American economy, most closely associated with popular notions of the twenties' prosperity, along with the wider global picture from South American oil to intra-Asian immigration. Lastly, we then look at the impact of capital flows and trade from areas as far-flung as Nigeria and Japan. Together, these provide an account of economic conditions prior to the crash of 1929, discussed in the following chapter.

Reparations and restoring order

As the first chapter of this book discussed, the foremost economic questions for European countries in the 1920s surrounded their First World War debts, most of which were owed to the United States, and the equally, if not more, vexed issue of German reparations. As noted, British economist John Maynard Keynes had publicly argued in 1919 that there was simply no way that the Germans should be asked to pay more than 20 to 40 billion marks without risking severe damage to both the country's economy and the wider world economic system. Ignoring this advice, in the early 1920s the allies demanded 132 billion marks from the Germans. Niall Ferguson has shown that the Germans made a large effort to make these payments in the early years of the decade, and for a period turned over more than 50 per cent of the country's revenues as part of the payments in the process (Ferguson 1998: 409–10, 424–5).

The German government soon found itself in serious financial trouble. It could not both make the reparations payments and pay for the rebuilding of the country (including an expensive welfare state), and in the face of a mounting rightist challenge to the legitimacy of the Weimar Republic it was seen as politically impossible to raise taxes across the board out of fear that the government's opponents would argue that it was taxing good Germans purely for the benefit of the country's former enemies (Evans 2004: 104). Faced with an increasingly ruined economy and a pending reparations bill, the German government opted to begin inflating the mark by printing large quantities of the currency (thus making each individual mark worth less on the foreign exchange markets). From late 1921 to early 1922 this strategy seemed to work reasonably well: people who incurred debts for large purchases, for instance, found it easy to pay them off as they were quickly able to make greater sums of money. Indeed, the German economy appeared to be rapidly improving, if not booming, in mid-1922. High levels of German employment, coupled with a short recession and plunging prices for goods in Britain and the United States, led to an increase in imports (though a decline in German exports to other countries) (Ferguson 1998: 433–5). The German economy seemed to be well on the road to recovery.

Yet the situation deteriorated significantly in the second half of 1922. In early June the mark had stood at 1,200 against the British pound but thanks to the increasing quantity of marks being printed by the government by the middle of July it had fallen to 2,400 (Lamb 1989: 11). Against the weaker US currency, the mark moved from 1,000 per dollar in August to 7,000 per dollar in December (Evans 2004: 104). Inflation was beginning to spin out of control and, more devastatingly, this meant that buying gold, which was required to make the reparations payments to the allies, would be all but impossible for the German government since it had arguably lost control of its currency. It was obvious that no country would be willing to lend Germany the vast sums of money necessary to make the payment, and consequently the spectre of default loomed. In August, French Prime Minister Raymond Poincaré travelled to London to argue that German default had already de facto taken place and the industrial Ruhr region should be immediately occupied in accordance with the Treaty of Versailles. British Prime Minister David Lloyd George was sceptical of the desirability of such a plan, observing that the allies would likely face resistance from German workers in the occupied region and there would probably be little profit to be had as a result (Lamb 1989: 11).

As the crisis grew, Lloyd George fell from power and was replaced by the Conservative Andrew Bonar Law, who now had to deal with French obstinacy. In January 1923 he travelled to Paris with a plan to allow the Germans a four-year grace period to get their economy under control until the reparations continued, after which each payment would be reduced from its previous value for 10 years and thereafter the reparation amounts would be set by a tribunal. The French angrily rejected the proposal, which was pilloried in the French press, and days later Poincaré ordered French troops into the Ruhr with the Belgians following. The mark plunged to 41,000 to one British pound, and President Warren G. Harding ordered US troops out of their base in the Rhineland to show his administration's displeasure. The British, however, took no action (Lamb 1989: 12–14).

The economic damage continued to spread within Germany. American writer Ernest Hemingway recalled visiting a German town in September 1922, still the early stages of the crisis (the mark was exchanging at 800 to one US dollar), and encountering an elderly resident who could not afford to pay 12 marks – less than two cents at that point – for apples because his life's savings had presumably been invested in war bonds and had thus been wiped out by hyperinflation. Hemingway regretted not offering the man some of the apples he had himself just purchased because they were, after all, a trivial expenditure for an American carrying dollars in his pocket (Frieden 2006: 136–7). While already piteous, this scene had taken place before the French had marched into the Ruhr and the mark fully embarked on its terminal spiral.

The Ruhr occupation met with widespread condemnation. Racist American writer Lothrop Stoddard – a strong supporter of the eugenics movement, an anti-immigration activist and a Ku Klux Klan sympathiser – visited the region in July 1923 and was appalled to find that the French had used African troops in their occupation force. The Rhineland was, he claimed, full of 'the scum of North Africa; the most degraded, syphilitic lot of Arab-mulattoes you can imagine'. He continued: 'Unless something is done to get the French out, terrible things will probably happen' (Lord Strachey Papers 1923). British commentator William Ralph Inge was similarly outraged by the French actions, though on more nuanced grounds. 'No attempt was made to mitigate the insults and injuries which this aggression [the occupation of the Ruhr] caused in Germany', Inge wrote in 1926. 'The French had decided that German hatred and the desire for revenge must be accepted as inevitable; with logical ruthlessness they decided to make that hatred impotent' (Inge 1926: 153). Winston Churchill called the occupation 'the darkest moment for Europe since the fighting stopped'. 'Deep in the soul of France', he continued, 'and the mainspring of her policy and of almost her every action, lay the fear of German revenge' (Churchill 1929: 485).

At the end of the day, the occupation of the Ruhr was a disaster for both sides. All reparations payments were suspended and the German government encouraged its citizens to deny the French and Belgians any co-operation. As a result, the economy continued into a tailspin. Rather than even semi-manageable levels of inflation, the Germans now faced true hyperinflation in which the mark became almost worthless. By late in the year, one British pound was worth 250 million marks and the country began to shut down as workers could no longer be paid in a meaningful way. In the final stages of the crisis, the mark stood at 4.2 *trillion* to one US dollar. The government employed more than 100 printing plants and 30 papers mills just to keep up with the printing of cash (Frieden 2006: 135). Facing complete collapse, in August 1923, Gustav Stresemann became Chancellor of Germany and took steps to end the crisis. The resistance campaign was ended, reparations payments resumed, and, in 1924, American expert Charles Dawes proposed a new plan for reparations that included paying a non-fixed sum based on German exports. A new currency, the Rentenmark (later the Reichsmark), was introduced and placed on the gold standard, effectively ending the hyperinflation crisis (Evans 2004: 108–9; Skidelsky 1992: 129). For the millions of Germans who had lost everything, however, it was already too late.

As Adam Tooze has written, the occupation and the hyperinflation had more than just economic effects and profoundly affected the politics of the Weimar

Republic. After 1923, 'strategic debate in Germany was never the same again', and far-right nationalist parties, including the National Socialists, began to gain additional traction against the government (Tooze 2006: 2). Crime rates had skyrocketed, and workers who received their pay had immediately gone to spend the money on tangible goods, lest its value be dramatically reduced by even the end of the day (Evans 2004: 110). The hyperinflation crisis had shown not only the relative impotence of the Weimar Republic but also what might await Germany without strong future leadership. In 1929, the Young Plan further revised the reparations model and set up a system of payments by Britain and France to the United States to pay their First World War debt. While the Plan offered Germany more favourable repayment terms than the status quo, the German far right strongly opposed the measure and they were increasingly joined by other right-wing parties. Germany's politics were more and more moving toward the extremes as the decade came to a close, in large part because of the economic turmoil to which the country had been subjected (Evans 2004: 95; Cohrs 2008: 525–30).

The gold standard

Germany's woes were certainly extreme, but all nations sought a more stable currency in the 1920s. The so-called gold standard which would come to define interwar politics in this regard had first emerged in the early nineteenth century and had become standard for industrialised countries late in the century thanks in large part to pressure from the British. The theory was that a full gold standard existed when a country held sufficient gold to cover all its currency in circulation at the denoted rate of exchange. Money, in short, should be convertible for a fixed amount of gold and thereby prices should remain stable in the long run since gold was a finite commodity with a determinable value. That was the theory. In practice, the gold standard trade-off was essentially between price stability and levers of monetary policy. With a fully implemented and defended gold standard, business would be able to gain price discovery, plan for the long term with relative ease and be able to easily sell their goods overseas because nearly all currencies were convertible to gold at fixed rates (on the other hand, prices were de facto being set in gold, meaning that market changes anywhere in the world would directly affect the prices all manufacturers and producers received). Yet at the same time, governments would lack the ability to control the supply of money (unless they could acquire more gold bullion) should economies take a tumble or unforeseen events occur, as they inevitably would. As Jeffry A. Frieden has noted,

> first-class financial citizenship [before the First World War] was available only to those countries willing to subordinate the needs of their domestic econo-mies to their commitments to gold … It meant privileging the international standing of your currency over the state of the domestic economy.
>
> *(Frieden 2006: 116)*

One external shock was clearly the course of European diplomacy that faced a major crisis with the assassination of Archduke Franz Ferdinand of Austria in 1914. During this maelstrom, many nations including Britain and Germany tumbled off the gold standard in order to gain greater control over their currency. In the British case, a run on sterling meant exchange controls had to be introduced which meant that pegging the value of the pound to the nation's gold stocks was no longer viable. This pattern of multiple exit caused significant inflation across the West, though the United States itself was able to remain on the standard throughout the conflict. The new Federal Reserve (created in 1913) intervened to mitigate against the effect of gold imports from overseas which would otherwise have driven up the supply of money, which it wished to avoid.

After the war most advanced nations clamoured to once again peg their currency to gold. Restore parity, create an economic system all could buy into, and surely prosperity would follow – or so the logic went. By 1927 most had achieved their aim of rejoining, but things – as chapters 11 and 12 make clear – would not run so smoothly. Traditionally the collapse of the gold standard in the early 1930s is seen as a consequence of the events on Wall Street in October 1929 and the Great Depression that followed. In this view the gold standard was fundamentally a sound endeavour but was overwhelmed by events. Yet Barry Eichengreen has gone furthest in reinterpreting this picture. To Eichengreen, 'far from being synonymous with stability, the gold standard was the principle threat to financial stability and economic prosperity between the wars' (Eichengreen 1992: 4). To Eichengreen, its survival was dependent on two criteria: credibility and co-operation. Credibility denoted the willingness of investors to bet against the cycle when leading countries such as Britain, Germany and France showed signs of wavering on gold. When gold stocks dipped, capital would flow into such core countries in anticipation of making a killing when reserve losses began to stabilise. Because of such counter-cyclical betting such states very rarely had to meaningfully intervene – the foreign capital making its way to, for example, London would mean the British government's nominal commitment to gold would never actually have to be called on. The system was supposed to be self-reinforcing.

But the war had changed things. In instigating the type of welfare spending and fiscal redistribution discussed earlier in this volume, governments now had different challenges to the world the Federal Reserve had been created into in 1913. Cutting infrastructure or social spending to defend gold reserves became a political impossibility to the degree it had not been two decades previously. The need to divert monies to protect, in essence, business confidence rather spend it in the here and now was not something many were willing to countenance, and the 'many' now had the vote. Democracy, to some degree, killed the gold standard – or at least the necessary credibility to uphold it. But crucially it also undermined the necessary transnational co-operation. The pre-war days of one central bank or set of bankers intervening to protect the gold reserves of another country (in order to maintain faith in the system itself) had also become far less palatable an option. Monetary policy had become far too intertwined with fiscal policy for governments to ignore – central banks had lost their true independence. Thus, even had they not had their own problems, bailing out the Germans in the early 1930s would have been a political impossibility for the British or French. Although there were modes of international co-operation in the 1920s – most prominently the League of Nations – there were clear limits to what national governments could actually do in the face of their own electoral pressures.

As something of an exception to the above rule, a word must be reserved for the first Governor of the New York Federal Reserve, Benjamin Strong. Strong was a vigorous advocate of blurring the lines between monetary and fiscal policy – in practice, between government and central bank – through encouraging the use of so-called open market operations. Whilst the United States remained on the gold standard, from 1922 Strong began to press the National Reserve in Washington (New York comprising just one of 12 regional Federal Reserve Districts across the United States) to pursue a middle ground of purchasing and selling government securities as and when he felt circumstances demanded. In a sense, as Keynes noted, he invented the idea of the interventionist modern central bank which would look to maintain a delicate balance between growth and inflation. As Europe tumbled into chaos in the early 1920s, Strong became an advocate of efforts amongst its states to rejoin the gold standard. These Strong-backed policies designed to stabilise American prices had positive knock-on effects for US trade with Europe. The lowering of the Federal Reserve's interest rate in 1924 and 1927 helped divert American capital over the Atlantic – a deliberate aim of Strong, though the sub-sequent rise later in the decade had the opposite effect (Metzler 2003: 262). But in 1928 Strong died, removing him from the political scene before the turmoil of the Great Depression struck. Historians continue to speculate on whether the Federal Reserve, the United States, and in turn other central banks operating off their lead, would at the very least have had a different range of options going into the 1930s had he lived (Metzler 2003: 264). In the 1920s the gold standard appeared to some a mighty fine house of cards, but there was a strong breeze ahead.

The world economy

The country which had managed to stick with gold during the First World War was the United States and, as Frieden has observed, 'World War One and its immediate aftermath drew the belligerents out of the world economy and toward the war effort and pulled the United States into the resultant vacuum' (Frieden 2006: 129). Drawn into this new role, it is little surprise that the economy most closely associated in the popular imagination with the 'Roaring Twenties' was the United States. Though the decade began with a recession caused by falling prices at the end of the war, for most of the 1920s the American economy – and the US stock market – skyrocketed. The exception was the agricultural sector, which was in a prolonged slump throughout the decade. As the next chapter will note, seemingly favourable economic indicators, coupled with the availability of easy credit, fed a speculative boom that saw millions invest beyond their means in the stock market.

As noted, in mid-1928, a bull market drove stock prices up considerably. This would be the stock market that catastrophically crashed in late October 1929, as chapter 11 discusses. 'By 1929 everyone', Robert T. Patterson observed,

> was in the market: rich and poor, bankers and bootblacks, dowagers and scrubwomen, teachers and students, nurses and barbers, clergymen and taxi-drivers, and even the corner newsvendor. It was a new kind of democracy. The ten-share plunger and the multimillionaire operator were brothers under the skin.
>
> *(Patterson 1965: 18)*

While the US economy was doing generally well throughout the decade and booming in its last years, in part because its former European allies owed a great deal of money in war debts, it was by no means the only show in town. For most people who were not directly involved in banking or investing, local factors were far more significant than events taking place in New York City. The economy of Great Britain, discussed subsequently, was severely hampered by the decision to return to the gold standard in the middle years of the decade, effectively pegging the British pound at an artificially high price. British industry immediately began to suffer as a result, and this pain would only be exacerbated by the 1929 crash. One consequence of this we noted in chapter 7 – the General Strike of 1926.

The French Empire, in contrast, was able to prop itself up economically by using its own internal trading networks to support industries that might otherwise be unsustainable, as the country would find out in the 1930s. At the same time, political disputes between the left and the right over taxation led to uncertainty over the country's economic policy and foreign investors began to pull their assets out of the country. By 1926, the country was facing a serious inflation crisis and unemployment rose to 11 per cent, only to subside when the franc was stabilised. However, the signing of the Locarno Treaty in December 1925 by Belgium, France, Italy, Germany and the UK – which guaranteed the Western borders of Germany and in effect conceded that the Alsace–Lorraine question which had vexed Europe since 1871 had finally been solved – helped to stabilise relations in Western Europe after the Ruhr crisis. Germany even joined the League of Nations the following year. Over the short term this helped trade relations amongst former belligerent states too. The fact that Locarno said nothing of Germany's potential aims in *Eastern* Europe was one that would become increasingly important in the 1930s. But in 1929, as the next chapter will note, France was actually in a better position to initially weather the storm of the Depression than most of its European counterparts (Johnson 1997: 87, 106–7).

Both the British and the French already had their own burgeoning supply of oil thanks to their acquisition of former Ottoman possessions in the Middle East. American companies wanted their own share of this lucrative pie and seven US and British companies (the 'Seven Sisters') soon negotiated an agreement to allow them to drill in the British Mandate of Iraq in exchange for paying the government a royalty on every ton of oil. The Iraqi oil fields soon turned out to be some of the most lucrative in the world, and the Seven Sisters effectively had a monopoly on them all, much to the consternation of their competitors (and government regulators, who quickly recognized that illegal collusion was taking place between the companies) (Cashman 1998: 252–3). By the end of the 1920s, the Middle East was well on its way to becoming a collection of states dependent on their oil exports for continued prosperity.

Yet these machinations were only part of the wider economic story of the decade. We briefly remarked in our second chapter on the oil-based economic miracle experienced by Venezuela – which during the 1920s rose from fifteenth to second in terms of volume of oil produced (and to first place in terms of exports). This was dramatic indeed. By 1929, leaders in Caracas were reading about production rates of 376,800 barrels a day – about three-quarters of the total South American market. But they were not the only South American state to significantly up production in the 1920s. Between 1920 and 1929 Peru's production increased over four-fold (from c.7,700 to c.36,700 barrels a day), Argentina's over five-fold (from c.4,500 to c.25,700 barrels a day), and Colombia went from almost no production whatsoever to 55,000 barrels a day (Wilkins 1974: 426). Bolivia and Ecuador established smaller footholds in the market too. Importantly, this growth was largely based on the activity of multi-national oil companies which exercised significant control over both distribution and refining. Through the Royal Dutch Shell Company, Anglo-Persian Oil and Standard Oil, both British and American governments attempted to gain a significant slice of this new production – building on pre-war penetration into markets like Argentina.

Initially, it looked like this could get rather ugly. In 1920 the US State Department sought to try and block European influence in the areas of Latin America where it could exercise direct influence, principally around transportation through the Panama Canal. But by 1922, the United States and Europe had reached something of an understanding whereby if the Americans relaxed the economic aspects of the Monroe Doctrine in the Americas, perhaps the Europeans could allow America greater penetration into their own colonial sphere stretching from Persia to the Dutch East Indies. With something of a détente reached, and in exchange for agreeing to construct oil refineries in the various oil-producing states, South American governments began to increasingly court European and North American oil companies. One measure is that in 1920 the government-owned Yacimentos Petroliferos Fiscales controlled almost 87 per cent of the total Argentine market. By 1929 this had dropped to 58 per cent. To drill down further into a particular product – gasoline – by 1928 the American corporate giant Standard Oil held 46 per cent of the Argentine, 47 per cent of the Brazilian and 61 per cent of the Chilean markets. Shell held 28 per cent, 20 per cent and 37 per cent respectively. As Mira Wilkins states, '[by] 1929, the bulk of the oil output of South America lay in foreign hands' (Wilkins 1974: 426). With European, Japanese and American requirements for oil only set to increase under the combination of increased use of the motor car and likelihood of another world war, this would become big money in the 1930s.

More widely, Latin America was re-evaluating its relationship with the United States throughout the 1920s. By 1921, 16 of its countries had joined the League of Nations, but the regional hegemon – the United States – had not joined, harming the body's ability to mediate disputes involving the wider region. Latin America was a natural market for American investors to do business in, but the natural corollary would be that the United States would then take a direct interest in protecting the investments of its citizens. Companies had long exploited natural resources in the region and relied on its markets for American goods, and in the past this relationship had been maintained with the liberal use of US troops to settle disputes and protect American interests.

Mexico, sitting on the southern border and still recovering from the effects of the Mexican Revolution, was now particularly troublesome for the United States (and had allegedly been enticed to enter the First World War on the side of Germany by the famous Zimmerman Note). In 1923 the United States formally recognised the Mexican government for the first time since the country's revolution in exchange for concessions on oil drilling and compensation for US citizens who had lost property in the upheaval. In 1924, the United States lifted its arms embargo against Mexico in an effort to improve relations, but the Mexican government now fell and its replacement responded by passing a law declaring that the country's oil reserves could not be exploited by foreign companies without a special permit. This was an obvious blow against major American oil companies. In 1925, the withdrawal of US Marines from Nicaragua led to the outbreak of civil war and the return of US troops, ostensibly to protect the Panama Canal. The war ended in a US-negotiated truce, but damaged relations with Mexico further. By 1927, the appointment of a new US ambassador and a celebrity appearance by Charles Lindbergh had begun to thaw out the relationship and by the end of the decade the United States–Mexico relationship had been profitably repaired (Cashman 1998: 253–5).

Although it lacked both oil and proximity to the new economic superpower of America, Africa too experienced significant economic changes, readily recorded by the new International Labour Organization set up by the League of Nations. Certainly, however, there remained a divergence between different parts of the continent. In 1928 the ILO recorded that

> with its vast agricultural and mineral resources and the communications which are being created in it, the African Continent is rapidly acquiring increased importance in the world, and the experience of South Africa will be of the greatest interest for other countries.
>
> *(ILO 1928: passim)*

In terms of progressive measures that economic improvement could bring, in Kenya the various native councils were, by the end of the 1920s, seeking new powers to tax citizens to provide capital for new education programmes. The ILO further noted that among the women, social work and the influences of western thought are revolutionising tribal tradition, even though slowly. Recognising these tendencies, it seems impossible ... for Kenya to be satisfied with a labour position which discloses a reliance upon women and children.

The bigger estates of Central and East Africa – particularly the sugar industry around Lake Victoria – were also showing signs of improved working conditions (ILO 1928: passim).

And yet if there was one sign that the global 1920s were not the beacon of progress they might occasionally be portrayed as, it was the continuation of slavery in parts of Africa. In the Sudan the ILO reported that

slavery in the provinces north of Khartum is moribund, chiefly as the result of the publicity given to the possibilities of freedom and the increased opportunities for independent employment. In the extreme South, slavery may be said to be non-existent, no slave-owning communities existing there. [However], in one or two of the central provinces, notably Kordofan and Kassala, the progress of manumission has not been so rapid as might be desired.

In Sierra Leone, legislation in 1926 for the purpose of abolishing slavery saw significant legal challenge in the Supreme Court and 'the right of slave-owners to recapture runaway slaves' was occasionally recognised. A further bill was passed in 1928 to tighten the legal position, and around 200,000 slaves were – in law at least – freed on the stroke of midnight 31 December 1927 (ILO 1928: passim).

For those with more freedom to move however, many indeed did and, importantly, this trend lay beyond the so-called developed world. One measure we have here is the contemporary ILO measures of continental immigration. In 1927 285,000 Indians made the trip to Ceylon (now Sri Lanka) to look for work. Likewise, that same year 243,000 Malayans moved from India back to their homeland. These numbers far exceeded the 64,000 people moving to France or the 71,000 to Germany. Both even trumped the 147,000 people seeking a new home in the United States – though the ILO, for one, noted that the American numbers were likely an underestimation given the level of 'secret immigration from Canada and from Mexico, which is considerable'. Such movements, as ever, were largely economic. To give one example, the ILO recorded that

an interesting fact to be noted in connection with continental migration in America is the decrease, due to the crisis in the sugar industry, in migration to Cuba of negro labourers from other islands in the West Indies. There is, in fact, a considerable return movement on the part of these labourers to their country of origin.

(ILO 1929: passim)

Where they could, the global 1920s citizen was not afraid to travel to earn their corn. And, as one immigrant from India to Fiji put it, the rewards were obvious.

Ahmed Ali's travels had been, he stated 'a journey undertaken to find security in this life, an ingredient largely missing in village India. [As] a lowly peasant appearing predestined to poverty, migration offered an escape towards the enjoyment of some material benefits in the present life'. (Ali 1979: xxvii, xxix)

Capital flows and global interdependency

If citizens moved so too did capital, and with it the reach of big firms, particularly financial institutions. As Mark Metzler has observed, during the 1920s 'J.P. Morgan and Co. was at the time predominant in U.S. and global-finance in a way that no single firm had been before or has been since' (Metzler 2002: 277). The line of credit American banks had extended to the British in 1916 was crucial in the winning of the First World War. They also exercised significant influence over the French decision to leave the Ruhr in 1923. But their influence extended beyond the Western powers in the 1920s and this is important for two reasons. Firstly, it shows the sheer interconnected nature of the global economy in the 1920s. Capital flows, together with reparations and the mutual reliance on the convertibility of gold, were part of a three-fold bind that would either make or break the financial system in this decade. The international system would stand or fall as one. And, secondly, because money could often talk. One does not have to swallow a Thomas Carlylesque 'Great Man' view of history wholesale to at least be tempted to ascribe much of interwar policy making to that source: Mussolini and fascism, Chaplin or Mayer and film, Stalin or Lenin and communism, Lindbergh and aviation, and so forth. But we must qualify this for it was the interconnected nature of global finance that could often dictate policy. In 1931 the British Labour government would fall from office complaining of a 'bankers' ramp' with many of its members unwilling to take action (cutting state expenditure) they felt was being dictated by the global capital markets. In the 1920s this was essentially par for the course in Japan.

The post-war economic system really began when the United States removed its wartime embargo on exporting gold in the summer of 1919, and great amounts of it headed abroad. Much ended up in Japan – an ally during the First World War – in particular. Initially this led to a speculative boom on the Japanese markets – as in the United States itself – but a collapse in inflated stock and commodity prices in early 1920 led to over a decade of, as Metzler notes, 'falling prices, repeated banking crises, chronic trade deficits and mounting bad debts' (Metzler 2002: 279). Given this state of affairs, Japan came to depend even more on acquiring US investment and obtaining money on the New York markets (which replaced London as their principle source of investment).

The key driver here was Thomas W. Lamont of J.P. Morgan. For Lamont and like-minded figures, Japan needed a good dose of financial liberalisation. Japanese finance ministers were told that government-owned railways should be privatised and left to the free market. Ministers such as Mori Kengo (Financial Commissioner, 1911–27) were instructed that their government should reduce its dependency on borrowing, and join a gold standard which, they were assured, would eliminate most of the problems hampering Japan's path to becoming a truly twentieth-century power. This was not just modernisation in theory, but liberalisation in practice. 'Join the international system under certain conditions, and we will give you the credit to do so' essentially marked the relationship between J.P. Morgan, Wall Street per se, and the Japanese Empire. The effect of this was, as Metzler argues, to tie 'Japan's domestic monetary system to the global monetary system just as that system was beginning to collapse' (Metzler 2002: 292). We deal with the exact consequences of this in the next chapter, but it speaks to the growing question as to whether economic autarky or free trade would win the day. This has a number of intersections with other chapters in this volume. The cultural trend of anti-Westernism this imbued amongst some we covered in chapter 5. The move towards fascist autarky we also noted in chapter 9.

Japan was becoming more open to the global economy then, and part of this involved selling cloth to the then British colony of Nigeria in West Africa. In one sense the increasing globalisation of Nigeria's position reduced the levels of bad debt racked up domestically. Previously, many Nigerians traded on a sale and return basis where credit was often extended for the nominal 'sale' of a good, only to see it returned at the end of the month when a debt could not be met. But cheap cloth from Japan had an increasing effect on the local *adire* (dyed textile) industry. As export prices from Nigeria fell by half between 1920 and 1926, with another third lost up to 1932, African labourers were having to work harder and harder to make ends meet – buffeted, in part, by industries the aforementioned American credit to Japan had helped bolster. The impact was not just transcontinental however – as Nigerian immigrants to the Gold Coast and the Belgian Congo began churning out replicas of the *adire* of their native land, the forces of globalisation were clearly intensifying all over the world. As Judith Byfield argues, in Nigeria

> those sectors which were least dependent on the international economy for raw materials or markets were best able to limit the damaging consequences of the depression. However, those fully enmeshed in the international economy through markets or credit were extremely exposed and vulnerable to the cycles of the crisis … It was an economic disaster for dyers because they were so fully exposed to the international economy.
>
> *(Byfield 1997: 77)*

As in Japan, exposure to the international economy meant playing by its rules. Here it is worth noting that in the late 1920s Wall Street successfully mandated the creation of independent central banks in several Latin American nations including Bolivia, Chile, Mexico and Ecuador – all of which built on Brazil's move in this regard earlier in the decade. Giving independent (previously wholly commercial) banks the power to issue notes had an obvious advantage – whereas governments could or likely would manipulate a nation's monetary supply to suit political priority, the banks, the markets assumed, would operate in a longer-term, more-neutral manner. This was not always true. In the case of Brazil, the newly independent central bank proved so expansive with its monetary programme that its status as a bank of issue was withdrawn by the government in 1926. Still, since Brazil appeared to be high-growth territory where money could be made, such appeasing of the Western capital markets generally worked – in 1890 Brazil's foreign debt had stood at £31.1 million, but by 1930 it had grown by an additional £340 million. Throughout this, Brazil maintained a stable credit rating and generally played the game – indeed when the crash came the government's response was not to directly expand credit for fear this would affect the currency, but instead to withdraw notes from circulation to try and forestall an expected run. Under political pressure some expansion eventually came, but it took time. This was emblematic of the straitjacket of economic conditions seen in the 1920s and early 1930s.

Conclusion

In contrast to the perception that the world economy was constantly booming throughout the 1920s, particularly in the United States, the economic conditions of the decade were in fact more mixed. The United States experienced two short recessions prior to the stock market crash of 1929, and the fundamentals of the economy came nowhere near to supporting the speculative investing that became widespread by the end of the decade. Elsewhere, economies were far less explosive in their growth: the British economy was in the doldrums after the return to the gold standard, while the French economy underwent significant inflation and capital flight following political controversies. Japan experienced such difficulties that it required the input of American capital and, like Brazil, had to orient itself in the direction Wall Street demanded. In the case of Britain and France, the fact that both of these countries had large empires allowed them a degree of flexibility in their handling of economic issues, but ultimately they too would fall under the pressure of the worldwide depression. The interconnectedness of things was a boon in times good but a disaster in times bad.

The European exception to all the trends of the decade was Germany, where the government was faced with the task of paying massive sums in war reparations while facing an economy that was simultaneously in dire straits. The government's initial strategy of using inflation to make the mark less valuable and therefore easier to pay to the allies backfired magnificently when out-of-control hyperinflation took away the government's ability to control the country's economy. In the dark period of 1922–3, Germany was effectively ruined and its currency worthless, in part because one of its most profitable industrial regions was under French and Belgian occupation. It was only when the mark was abandoned and replaced with the Reichsmark that stabilisation and recovery could take place. This period of relative success was followed by the 1929 crash, which again wiped out the German economy. Ruined by an economic situation in part of its own making but also the result of external factors, the Weimar Republic itself would soon fall.

Outside Europe, the 1920s were a period of mixed growth. Latin American economies generally improved but were dependent on economic conditions in the United States. The discovery of oil in both South America and the Middle East gave both those regions new significance in the foreign policies of the major powers, with American companies proving particularly adept at getting their way in both regions. The United States made great attempts to demonstrate its goodwill toward its Central and South American neighbours, but it was clear that the ultimate guarantor of regional stability was still the US military.

As the world careened toward the October 1929 crash, the intrinsic weaknesses of the world system became increasingly apparent. With the gold standard still internationally accepted by all major powers, governments had very little flexibility when it came to the value of their currency. After 1929, the convertibility of currency into gold would lead to runs on national bullion supplies and the abandonment of the gold standard under duress. The events of that fateful period we consider in our final two chapters.

Questions

- What policy decisions led inflation to take off so dramatically in Germany?
- How did German hyperinflation affect the wider politics of the Weimar Republic?
- How did economic decisions being made in the financial capitals of New York, London and Paris affect other countries in the 1920s?
- What underlying economic factors helped lead to the crash of 1929 and the Great Depression?
- In what ways did having an empire both help and hurt countries economically in the 1920s?

Recommended further reading

Eichengreen, B. (1992), *Golden Fetters: The Gold Standard and the Great Depression*, Oxford: Oxford University Press.

Frieden, J.A. (2006), *Global Capitalism: Its Fall and Rise in the Twentieth Century*, New York: W.W. Norton.

Johnson, H.C. (1997), *Gold, France, and the Great Depression, 1919–1932*, New Haven: Yale University Press.

Patterson, R.T. (1965), *The Great Boom and Panic, 1921–1929*, Chicago: Henry Regnery Company.

Skidelsky, R. (1992), *John Maynard Keynes, Volume 2: The Economist as Saviour, 1920–1937*, New York: Allen Lane.

Wilkins, M. (1974), 'Multinational Oil Companies in South America in the 1920s: Argentina, Bolivia, Brazil, Chile, Colombia, Ecuador, and Peru', *The Business History Review*, 48/3, 414–446

Works cited

Ali, A. (1979), *The Indenture Experience in Fiji*, Suva: Fiji Museum.

Byfield, J. (1997), 'Innovation and Conflict: Cloth Dyers and the Interwar Depression in Abeokuta, Nigeria', *Journal of African History*, 38/1, 77–99.

Cashman, S.D. (1998), *America Ascendant: From Theodore Roosevelt to FDR in the Century of American Power, 1901–1945*, New York: New York University Press.

Churchill, W.S. (1929), *The Aftermath: The World Crisis, 1918–1928*, New York: Charles Scribner's Sons.

Cohrs, P.O. (2008), *The Unfinished Peace after World War I: America, Britain and the Stabilisation of Europe, 1919–1932*, Cambridge: Cambridge University Press.

Eichengreen, B. (1992), *Golden Fetters: The Gold Standard and the Great Depression*, Oxford: Oxford University Press.

Evans, R.J. (2004), *The Coming of the Third Reich*, New York: The Penguin Press.

Ferguson, N. (1998), 'The Balance of Payments Question: Versailles and After', in Boemeke, M.F., Feldman, G.B. and Glaser, E. (eds), *The Treaty of Versailles: A Reassessment after 75 Years*, Cambridge: Cambridge University Press, pp. 401–440.

Frieden, J.A. (2006), *Global Capitalism: Its Fall and Rise in the Twentieth Century*, New York: W.W. Norton.

ILO (International Labour Organization) (1928), Report of the Director Presented to the Conference, Geneva: ILO.

ILO (International Labour Organization) (1929), Report of the Director Presented to the Conference, Geneva: ILO.

Inge, W.R. (1926), *England*, New York: Charles Scribner's Sons.

Johnson, H.C. (1997), *Gold, France, and the Great Depression, 1919–1932*, New Haven: Yale University Press.

Lamb, R. (1989), *The Drift to War: 1922–1939*, New York: St Martin's Press.

Lenin, V.I. (1917, 2010), *Imperialism: The Highest Stage of Capitalism*, London: Penguin Books.

Lord Strachey Papers (1923), House of Lords, London, ST 19/5/19, 13 July.

Metzler, M. (2002), 'American Pressure for Financial Internationalization in Japan on the Eve of the Great Depression', *Journal of Japanese Studies*, 28/2, 277–300.

Metzler, A. (2003), *A History of the Federal Reserve, Volume 1: 1913–1951*, Chicago: University of Chicago Press.

Patterson, R.T. (1965), *The Great Boom and Panic, 1921–1929*, Chicago: Henry Regnery Company.

Skidelsky, R. (1992), *John Maynard Keynes, Volume 2: The Economist as Saviour, 1920–1937*, New York: Allen Lane.

Tooze, A. (2006), *The Wages of Destruction*, London: Penguin Books.

Wilkins, M. (1974), 'Multinational Oil Companies in South America in the 1920s: Argentina, Bolivia, Brazil, Chile, Colombia, Ecuador, and Peru', *The Business History Review*, 48/3, 414–446.

11

THE CALAMITY ON WALL STREET

The morning of Tuesday, 29 October 1929 began tensely on New York City's Wall Street. Just five days before, on 'Black Thursday', stocks had tumbled precipitously, putting heavy pressure on the magnates of finance and the millions of average Americans who had invested their life savings – and often borrowed money on top of their own – to get a chunk of the profits that only a few months before had seemed unending. By mid-morning, sellers desperate to get out of the market to cover their losses had overwhelmed any buyers willing to purchase their shares, and by the end of the day more than 12 million shares had changed hands, an all-time high, but prices had been temporarily stabilised thanks to the action of a group of wealthy bankers who bought large numbers of shares and the worst case scenario had been averted. The 25th had seen more losses, and on Monday, the 28th, selling had accelerated late in the day and driven prices down further. There was no telling what might happen when the Stock Exchange opened on Tuesday (Patterson 1965: 119–32; Thomas and Morgan-Witts 1979: 378–80).

When the opening gong sounded that morning, the worst fears of the traders were quickly confirmed as the phrases 'Sell at the market!' and even 'Sell at any price!' rang out across the exchange floor. Massive orders to sell quickly drove down the prices of heavyweight stocks like US Steel, the Radio Corporation of America (RCA) (which lost nearly a quarter of its value in mere minutes) and American Telephone & Telegraph (AT&T), among others. Prices fell so quickly that the ticker tape on the trading floor was unable to keep up with the actual prices at which stocks were being traded. Concerted efforts by bankers to keep prices high by continuously buying shares were nowhere near enough to stem the tide. At noon, the governors of the New York Stock Exchange briefly debated whether the trading floor should be shut down to stem the massive losses that were compounding. Full of the optimism of the 'Roaring Twenties' and convinced that the market would recover on its own if they simply allowed it time, they opted to allow trading to continue (Thomas and Morgan-Witts 1979: 392–6; Patterson 1965: 147–52).

As they met, a noontime service in Trinity Church, at the corner of Broadway and Wall Street, was filled with stock traders who put aside their individual religious affiliations for the afternoon. Some of those still at work were driven to kneel and pray on the edges of the trading floor itself while their counterparts wept nearby. Such responses were more than justified. At the end of the day, more than 16 million shares had changed hands, amounting to a staggering $10 billion in losses (Thomas and Morgan-Witts 1979: 399). The next day, London newspapers reported that Americans who were holidaying in Europe were desperate to sail back to the Unites States in the face of their fortunes literally disappearing overnight. The transatlantic telephone cables linking New York and London became so overwhelmed with call traffic to brokerage firms that their use had to be rationed (Patterson 1965: 150).

Prices briefly recovered through the rest of the week and many small investors who had taken substantial losses now tried to make their money back. Brokers' offices were now inundated with calls from clients putting in orders to buy at what many believed were discount prices. Requests for loans skyrocketed as those who had already lost their savings tried to obtain cash to invest, often borrowing against their houses, life insurance policies and even their personal belongings. Pawn-brokers in New York were hit so hard that some had to close their doors because they had run out of cash (Patterson 1965: 156–7). When the market opened on 4 November, prices collapsed again despite an initial buying frenzy. The downward trend continued until 13 November, wiping out many who had borrowed to invest and now had to sell off their stocks at a loss to cover their debt obligations and margin calls. At their lowest points in October–November 1929, AT&T had dropped from a 1929 high of 310¼ to 197¼, RCA from 114¾ to 26 and US Steel from 261¾ to 150. For anyone who had invested at the high of the market only a few months before, these drops were devastating (Patterson 1965: 155–60). Rumours began to circulate that ruined investors and bankers had begun taking their own lives by jumping out of windows in New York City, and while these stories were certainly exaggerated, there were documented cases of suicides related to the crash (Thomas and Morgan-Witts 1979: 404). In the aftermath of 'Black Thursday', 29 October became immortalised as 'Black Tuesday'.

By Saturday 2 November, *The Economist* in London was already hailing the development as 'a landmark in post-war financial history'. It continued that

> the share boom of 1926–29 originated in a period of industrial prosperity which has never been surpassed in the world's history. The stock market became a cynosure of interest for the whole American nation, high and low, rich and poor. While the boom lasted Wall Street was a market for the world's floating resources, since to speculate in that centre, or to lend to others for that purpose, afforded a higher rate of return than any other form of contemporary activity.
>
> (The Economist, 2 November 1929)

Such safe returns on capital were, for the time being, over and would not return for over two decades. The 1920s ended with perhaps their most defining moment still playing out.

Unsurprisingly, therefore, the crash of 1929, and the events that followed, became seared in the American psyche. By the mid-1930s, the country was plunging into the series of events that would become known as the Great Depression and the world would soon follow suit. But what factors had led to this catastrophic economic collapse? After all, as the previous chapter has noted, the US stock market had crashed before, only to recover in a fairly short time. There had been extended recessions – even depressions – before. Yet the 1929 crash was different – the stock market did recover, somewhat, only to plunge again and again. This chapter considers the causes and immediate effects of the 1929 stock market crash and its effects around the world. The following chapter examines both intellectual and government policy responses to the events of 1929, and while the vast majority of the Great Depression took place in the 1930s, the foundations of what would come later were laid in the final months of the 1920s.

Causes of the crash

The American stock market crash of 1929 did not happen in a vacuum and was in fact the result of long-standing factors affecting the US economy. 'In 1929', economist John Kenneth Galbraith wrote, 'the economy was headed for trouble. Eventually that trouble was violently reflected in Wall Street' (Galbraith 1961: 93). Galbraith blamed the crash on widespread speculation in stocks that exceeded all rationality, coupled with an overproduction of goods and a downturn in American agriculture. After the crash took place, he argued, it was made worse by the heavy concentration of wealth in the hands of a very few (discussed in chapter 2 on class in the present book); poor corporate practices that included regularly using income to pay off substantial debts; a weak banking structure that quickly began to fail; other countries owing the Unites States too much money (discussed in the previous chapter) and relying heavily on the US economy; and poor economic policy making ('it seems certain that the economists and those who offered economic counsel in the late twenties and early thirties were almost uniquely perverse', Galbraith 1961: 176–88).

There is little doubt that in retrospect the US economy in the 1920s was weaker than it seemed at the time. The stock market had crashed in 1920–1, causing a short recession, and 1926–7 had seen a downturn as well. American agriculture was in a serious slump for nearly the entire decade, partially as a result of having produced so many products for military use during the First World War and now effectively flooding markets with cheap goods. The value of American farm products decreased from over $21 billion in 1919 to about half that by the end of the decade, while the number of American farms that had mortgages rose from 37 to 42 per cent in the same period (Cashman 1998: 238). Also not to be ignored was the fact that Prohibition was causing ongoing harm to farmers who produced wheat, barley and other products commonly made into alcohol, and much of the normal economy that surrounded alcohol production and consumption had been put out of business or simply driven into the realm of illegal trade.

The bull market that preceded the crash began in March 1928, around the time of the inauguration of pro-business President Herbert Hoover. Stock prices rose precipitously, led in part by the technology stocks of their day: radio. As noted, RCA had skyrocketed throughout the decade and made its early investors fabulously rich. In 1921, RCA was trading at $1.50 per share, the next year it was trading at $66 after the company gave its shareholders one share for every five they held to boost the price (called a one-for-five reverse split), and by 1927 the stock was trading above $100. This was only the beginning of the boom, however, and in 1928 it was trading above $400 a share. The stock then split into five shares for every one share (reversing the previous reverse split) and eventually hit almost $115 per share. Investors who had bought the stock at the beginning of the decade had more than quadrupled their money by simply holding on to their shares (Kyvig 2004: 214). As already seen, RCA's price was hammered down to $26 per share in the opening days of the 1929 crash, wiping out virtually anyone who had bought after the middle years of the decade.

The swiftness of the crash was assuredly brought about by the prevalence of buying stocks using credit – called 'margin' – during the 1920s. With margin, investors only had to put up a relatively small amount of money to buy stocks, sometimes as little as 10 per cent of the value of what they were purchasing, while a broker or bank lent them the rest. In a period of rising prices and dividends, both sides would profit from this arrangement: the broker would make the trading fees and charge interest on the loan while the client would be able to buy far more stock than they could otherwise afford. However, the customer was also required to maintain a certain amount of actual money in the account to cover the broker's risk, so if the stock price fell too low the client would be asked to put up more money (a 'margin call') to maintain the minimum ratio. If they could not pay, the stocks in the account would be continuously sold until the necessary ratio was reached (Kyvig 2004: 214). As stock prices began to tumble, clients across the country were asked to urgently put up money they did not have, leading to even more selling and a further drop in prices. In the dramatic days of October 1929, brokers recalled taking calls from clients begging for more time to find the money to cover their margins rather than face ruin. People who had considered themselves millionaires because of the number of shares they owned on margin were abruptly wiped out (Thomas and Morgan-Witts 1979: 396).

It is worth considering the international origins of this crash and indeed the depression too. For Peter Temin, we must pay close attention to the 'diminution of capital exports from the United States to Germany in the last years of the 1920s that then spread to other European countries' (Temin 1976: 152). As we have seen, Germany partially recovered from its own economic maelstrom in the early 1920s due to the inflow of American money. In part this capital was spent in other European countries, which helped a general recovery in that continent. But by the late 1920s American creditors began to demand their loans back – from over one billion dollars flowing into Germany in 1928 there were just two hundred million by 1929. This may or may not have been limited to a German problem, had a significant percentage of these investors not promptly ploughed their capital into Wall Street. Relatively safe German investments were replaced by reckless gambling.

But these were at least professional investors. The problem was often not only that people were gambling, it was that this gambling could often be so ill-informed. As Peter Rappoport and Eugene White note, 'beginning with General Motors and RCA, the market started to rise with enthusiasm spreading to a larger number of stocks. The increase in prices was not uniform and the larger firms seemed to be more favoured' (Rappoport and White 1994: 2). The Dow Jones index of large firms consistently outperformed weighted measures of smaller companies, the latter of which grew slowly and peaked in February 1929 – several months before the crash. Stocks in big banks and utilities saw major clustering of money, other industries less so. And these trends, as mentioned, were largely the result of new investors. Ordinary workers who had often entered the financial markets relatively recently through the patriotic method of buying Liberty (government) Bonds during the war graduated to private bonds and then finally stocks in the 1920s. As Rappoport and White argue, these investors were strongly influenced by the actions of friends, acquaintances, and a general belief in the wisdom of crowds. This was only compounded by the increased proliferation of investment funds – portfolios of stocks in which the new would-be shareowner could invest en masse. There were many ways for ordinary people to be ensnared by the coming crisis.

Beyond the initial horrors of the crash for anyone who had invested in the stock market, the American banking system began to collapse shortly after. Customers increasingly demanded their deposits to cover their margins and losses, forcing banks to close their doors when they were unable to find the money to pay them. The banks had themselves speculated heavily in the stock market and other investments with their customers' money (a practice that would be made illegal under the Glass–Steagall Act which mandated the separation of retail and investment banking in 1933, only to be made legal again in the late 1990s and arguably contributing to the financial crisis of the late 2000s), subjecting them to heavy losses of their own. As the financial pressure rapidly built, customers began defaulting on their loans, to the extent that 40 per cent of American home mortgages would be in default by the early 1930s. More than 650 banks failed in 1929 alone and another 1,000 the following year. Because there was no government insurance to protect American depositors, if a bank failed the customer simply lost their money if there were no assets from which to pay them (Kyvig 2004: 218–19). Bank runs, in which customers rushed to a bank to withdraw their money if they had heard even the rumour of a failure, became the natural result. 'Had the economy been fundamentally sound in 1929 the effect of the great stock market crash might have been small', Galbraith concluded. Yet the American economy had not been sound, and as a result, 'it was vulnerable to the kind of blow it received from Wall Street' (Galbraith 1961: 192).

In late 1929 and early 1930 the stock market rallied again, but by April it had again wiped out investors, some of whom were now facing ruin for the third or fourth time. Significantly unhelpful in the mind of most economists was the signing of the Smoot–Hawley Tariff Act by President Herbert Hoover in June. The legislation hiked American tariffs on foreign goods, leading to the retaliatory hiking of tariffs by other countries and harming American exports. Unemployment worldwide began to skyrocket. At the time of the 1929 crash, one and a half million Americans were unemployed; a year later that number stood at four million and, in October 1931, 11 million were unemployed. While this rise was shocking, the worst was still to come. The Great Depression had arrived.

The crash beyond the United States

The stock market crash, while dramatic, had of course taken place in the United States. Its effects would naturally play out first in the United States and spread from there. Indeed, for some countries including France, it took more than a year for the onset of the depression to be felt, in part because the country benefitted from a large empire with which it could trade. The stock market crash was all but ignored by the French press, which was more concerned with domestic affairs, and throughout 1929 French economic output grew while unemployment fell. In early November 1929 *The Economist* even wrote approvingly that 'as a result of the Wall Street Crash, lenders in the more unstable centres abroad are now looking not so much for high interest rates as for security. In this respect Paris admittedly occupies a strong position' (*The Economist*, 2 November 1929). Similarly, there was almost no immediate effect of the crash in Italy, where Mussolini's reforms were of far more immediate consequence, nor in Switzerland, renowned for its own banking sector in Geneva and Zurich (Thomas and Morgan-Witts 1979: 406–7). The effects of the crash would only be fully felt by much of the world in the early 1930s. In part this corroborates Peter Temin's theory that 'it is more plausible to believe that the Depression was the result of a drop in autonomous expenditures, particularly consumption, than it was the result of autonomous bank failures' (Temin 1976: 178).

In any event, reflecting on the crash in 1936 in his famous *General Theory*, John Maynard Keynes noted the peculiarly American characteristics that had driven the crisis:

> As the organisation of investment markets improves, the risk of the predominance of speculation does, however, increase. In one of the greatest investment markets in the world, namely, New York, the influence of speculation is enormous … [W]hen he purchases an investment, the American is attaching his hopes, not so much to its prospective yield, as to a favourable change in the conventional basis of valuation, i.e. that he is, in the above sense, a speculator. Speculators may do no harm as bubbles on a steady stream of enterprise. But the position is serious when enterprise becomes the bubble on a whirlpool of

speculation. When the capital development of a country becomes a by-product of the activities of a casino, the job is likely to be ill-done.

(Keynes 1936: 128)

In part, then, this was arguably psychological. The greater optimism of Americans had given way to collective gambling that had imperilled the entire system. But there was a technical and systemic difference too – it simply cost less to trade on Wall Street than it did in the City of London. And as Keynes observed

> it is usually agreed that casinos should, in the public interest, be inaccessible and expensive. And perhaps the same is true of stock exchanges. That the sins of the London Stock Exchange are less than those of Wall Street may be due, not so much to differences in national character, as to the fact that to the average Englishman Throgmorton Street [home of the London Stock Exchange] is, compared with Wall Street to the average American, inaccessible and very expensive. The jobber's 'turn', the high brokerage charges and the heavy transfer tax payable to the Exchequer, which attend dealings on the London Stock Exchange, sufficiently diminish the liquidity of the market (although the practice of fortnightly accounts operates the other way) to rule out a large proportion of the transactions characteristic of Wall Street.
>
> *(Keynes 1936: 129)*

With the transfer tax on US shares sitting at 0.2 per cent since 1914, US traders would have to surrender a five-hundredth of the cost of the purchase of any given share to the government. The equivalent figure in the UK was then 1 per cent, meaning the British trader would lose five times as much to the Exchequer should he wish to buy a share in a British company. This dampened liquidity on the one hand, but it also meant that gambling was simply a more expensive business in London and certain trades just became un-economic. Churning over stocks for a series of micro-profits was not profitable in London, but it might be in New York. For Wall Street, then, Keynes' (unheeded) solution was simple: America should go British: 'the introduction of a substantial government transfer tax on all transactions might prove the most serviceable reform available, with a view to mitigating the pre-dominance of speculation over enterprise in the United States' (Keynes 1936: 129).

Yet despite Keynes' praise, the country most immediately impacted by the crash was indeed his homeland of Britain, which was already in a weakened economic position. In the months prior to the October 1929 US crash, the London Stock Exchange had itself crashed in the wake of a fraud scandal, damaging investor confidence. In addition, Britain was still reeling from the momentous decision taken by Chancellor of the Exchequer Winston Churchill to return Britain to the gold standard in 1925 (Keynes was one of the few to strongly oppose the move, which he viewed as irrational and likely to only harm the working class) (Skidelsky 1995: 188). This decision effectively pegged the British currency to the US dollar at a rate of $4.86 per pound, which was the value it had been fixed at prior to the First World War. The economic reality had changed in the course of the war, however, and the return to the gold standard had simply made the pound too valuable. British goods became expensive for foreign buyers, and company profits began to drop as foreign markets began to dry up. Efforts to increase efficiency (and profits) in British coal mines had helped lead to the 1926 General Strike, and the economy had remained in the doldrums at the same time as the US economy was booming (Galbraith 1961: 14). Despite the crash itself happening in the United States, during the 1930s the American press would frequently cast aspersions on the British for the country's alleged failure to keep the world economy on a stable footing (Moser 1999: 76).

Across the British Empire, crisis gradually unfolded: Australia's economy began to collapse as wheat and wool prices fell; the Canadian stock market plunged with the American market, though the full impact would only be felt when the country's American export market dried up (Thomas and Morgan-Witts 1979: 408–9). In 1931, speculative pressure would force Britain to abandon the gold standard, leading to a rapid decline in the currency's value. Investors who had viewed the British pound as a safe haven were severely hurt, and in the weeks following a number of other countries also abandoned the gold standard. A run on the American gold supply soon began as investors began to demand the gold bullion that backed their dollars, and President Franklin Roosevelt announced that the country would also abandon the gold standard after he was inaugurated in March 1933. The dollar subsequently lost around 40 per cent of its value (Patterson 1965: 192–3). Fearing the instability of American and European markets, some investors flocked to investments in China, which were doing comparatively well until a banking run and a collapse in the Shanghai real estate market in 1934–5 frightened many foreign investors away (Ji 2002: 188–92). The fact that Manchuria had already been invaded and occupied by Japan in 1931 did little to encourage investment as well. Facing an unfolding world crisis, in 1931 President Hoover put a one-year moratorium on the collection of all war debts on the condition that German reparations payments were temporarily suspended to prop up the country's banks, though the idea of simply forgiving the European debt was politically impossible in the face of congressional opposition (Cohrs 2008: 591).

The effect of the crash was felt even more immediately in Germany. Following the renegotiations of First World War reparations, discussed in the previous chapter, the German government had become increasingly dependent on American loans to provide the money to pay the country's bills. Even before the 1929 crash, unemployment had begun to rise in Germany and after the crash stood at more than two million. American investors and financial institutions began to pull back their money to save themselves at home, and the Germany economy began to tailspin further. Desperate banks began offering exorbitant interest rates to account holders who were willing to deposit their money, and interest rates on loans skyrocketed up to 25 per cent for individual borrowers. Despite these measures, the banks still began to fail (Thomas and Morgan-Witts 1979: 405). In 1931, all reparations payments by Germany were suspended in accordance with Hoover's proposal and in 1932 the allies, minus the United States, agreed to abolish them in the face of the unfolding crisis as long as they could negotiate a full end to their debt payments to the United States. Hoover and Congress formally rejected the plan, yet no more reparations would be collected from Germany regardless (Cohrs 2008: 594). The wartime reparations system that had been so controversial throughout the decade had finally collapsed completely.

By the early 1930s, industrial production in Germany had fallen by nearly half. Unemployment skyrocketed further, and the government seemed impotent in the face of a spiralling situation. Extremist parties of both the left and the right saw huge influxes of members, and both the Communist Party and the National Socialists soon had armed gangs that brawled with each other and the police. More than six million Germans were unemployed by early 1932. National Socialist leader Adolf Hitler ran for President that year and lost to war hero Paul von Hindenburg, though he finished in second place with more than 13 million votes (Lamb 1989: 60). The Weimar Republic was increasingly coming apart at the seams, and, in early 1933, Hitler was appointed to the office of Chancellor in the midst of the crisis and soon began consolidating power for the Nazi Party (Evans 2004: 234–7; Cohrs 2008: 578).

Conclusion

The previous chapter began with a quote from Bolshevik leader Vladimir Lenin arguing that capitalism would inevitably result in imperialism and, ultimately, its own destruction when there were no more lands and resources to pillage. For communist thinkers, the crash of 1929 was the inevitable result of capitalism's intrinsic contradictions and the first step in its ultimate destruction. As the world entered the 1930s, this view appeared increasingly plausible to many. From late 1929 through 1930, it appeared that nothing could stop the catastrophic decline that had hit the world's markets. Unemployment skyrocketed worldwide, and in 1932 industrial unemployment stood at 36 per cent in the United States and above 40 per cent in Germany. Britain suffered 22 per cent unemployment, while in Australia it was above 25 per cent. Stock markets had collapsed, with one US stock index falling 85 per cent by 1932 and German stocks falling 69 per cent. Prices in France collapsed, destroying industries throughout the country's vast empire. It was an international catastrophe of unprecedented proportions (Johnson 1997: 21).

As has been seen, there was no single cause of the 1929 stock market crash and the ensuing depression. Indeed, the seeds of the crash had been sown in the immediate aftermath of the First World War. American agriculture was in a slump for nearly the entire decade as the result of low prices, and many farmers had taken on significant amounts of debt just to stay in business. The rich had become exceptionally prosperous, concentrating wealth in the hands of a few and giving them the resources to invest and buy large amounts of luxury goods, on which the economy had become increasingly reliant. As Galbraith observed, 'the rich cannot buy great quantities of bread', and with so much money concentrated in the hands of the wealthy, purely discretionary spending was driving an increasing segment of the economy. This buying could easily be curtailed when the financial screws began to tighten in late 1929 (Galbraith 1961: 182–3). In addition, American banks themselves began speculating in various forms of investments that would later expose them to the risk of failure when their depositors began to demand their money. By early 1930, hundreds of banks had collapsed across the country, meaning that millions of people had lost money, and the worst was still to come.

The fundamental weaknesses of the American economy in the 1920s were largely ignored in the speculative boom that grew to a fever pitch after the inauguration of Herbert Hoover in 1928. The stock market soared, and millions of investors used easy access to credit to invest heavily without actually having the money to do so. The series of crashes that took place in New York in October 1929 were not themselves the sole reason for the onset of the economic downturn, but they did ruin millions of average American investors who had followed their friends and neighbours in using margin to buy stock. A single bad day on the market meant that these individuals were forced to either sell their investments or put up money that they might not have to stay in the market. A series of very bad days, as the market experienced in late 1929, were all but certain to wipe out a large number of investors who were facing this kind of pressure.

The full impact of the crash did not arrive everywhere at once, but the following decade would be consumed by efforts to provide assistance and economic recovery to those who lost everything in its wake. Increasingly desperate governments would begin experimenting with economic policies designed to put their respective countries on the road to recovery. In Germany, Hitler's National Socialist Party would come to power on a combination of resentment toward the Treaty of Versailles, the mass unemployment that resulted from the 1929 crash, and promises to take radical action to rebuild the country. The crisis that began on Wall Street in October 1929 would not come to its complete fruition until the final surrender of Germany and Japan in 1945.

Questions

- What factors helped lead to the crash of the US stock market in 1929?
- Why did the US economy not pull out of the 1929 crash as it had pulled out of previous downturns?
- Why did the impact of the crash arrive more quickly in some countries than others?
- Why were so many people willing to invest heavily in stocks like RCA in the mid-1920s?
- What actions could governments have taken to head off the onset of the Great Depression?

Recommended further reading

Galbraith, J.K. (1961), *The Great Crash*, Boston: Houghton Mifflin Company.
Kyvig, D.E. (2004), *Daily Life in the United States, 1920–1940*, Chicago: Ivan R. Dee.

Patterson, R.T. (1965), *The Great Boom and Panic, 1921–1929*, Chicago: Henry Regnery Company.

Skidelsky, R. (1995), *John Maynard Keynes, Volume 2: The Economist as Saviour, 1920–1937*, New York: Allen Lane.

Temin, P. (1976), *Did Monetary Forces Cause the Great Depression?*, New York: W.W. Norton.

Works cited

Cashman, S.D. (1998), *America Ascendant: From Theodore Roosevelt to FDR in the Century of American Power, 1901–1945*, New York: New York University Press.

Cohrs, P.O. (2008), *The Unfinished Peace after World War I: America, Britain and the Stabilisation of Europe, 1919–1932*, Cambridge: Cambridge University Press.

Evans, R.J. (2004), *The Coming of the Third Reich*, New York: The Penguin Press.

Galbraith, J.K. (1961), *The Great Crash*, Boston: Houghton Mifflin Company.

Ji, Zhaojin (2002), *A History of Modern Shanghai Banking: The Rise and Decline of China's Financial Capitalism*, London: Routledge.

Johnson, H.C. (1997), *Gold, France, and the Great Depression, 1919–1932*, New Haven: Yale University Press.

Keynes, J.M. (1936), *The General Theory of Employment, Interest and Money*, London: Macmillan.

Kyvig, D.E. (2004), *Daily Life in the United States, 1920–1940*, Chicago: Ivan R. Dee.

Lamb, R. (1989), *The Drift to War: 1922–1939*, New York: St Martin's Press.

Moser, J.E. (1999), *Twisting the Lion's Tail: American Anglophobia between the World Wars*, New York: New York University Press.

Patterson, R.T. (1965), *The Great Boom and Panic, 1921–1929*, Chicago: Henry Regnery Company.

Rappoport, P. and White, E.N. (1994), The New York Stock Market in the 1920s and 1930s: Did Stock Prices Move Together Too Much? *NBER Working Paper*, No. 4627.

Skidelsky, R. (1995), *John Maynard Keynes, Volume 2: The Economist as Saviour, 1920–1937*, New York: Allen Lane.

Temin, P. (1976), *Did Monetary Forces Cause the Great Depression?*, New York: W.W. Norton.

Thomas, G. and Morgan-Witts, M. (1979), *The Day the Bubble Burst: A Social History of the Wall Street Crash of 1929*, New York: Doubleday & Company.

12

RESPONSES TO THE CRASH

The stock market crash of 1929 set off a rapid chain of events that careened across the globe. As the previous chapter notes, unemployment began to skyrocket and by 1931 countries had begun to abandon the gold standard. Just as the leadership of the New York Stock Exchange had refused to close the market on the afternoon of 29 October, traditional economic thought held that the depression was part of a business cycle that would be self-correcting if combatted with traditional economic measures (mostly the lowering of interest rates). By 1931, however, the world economy remained in a deep slump.

The figure who would rise to prominence amidst this crisis was the British economist John Maynard Keynes, who had so publicly condemned the Treaty of Versailles and the German reparations plan. By early 1931, Keynes had become convinced that the depression would not be self-correcting and required dramatic action by governments to stimulate investment and generate jobs, though he also rejected the communist view that it represented the final crisis of capitalism from which it could not survive. Instead, he believed, the crisis could be fixed by human intelligence and ingenuity. The wrong approach, however, was to do nothing and let the markets fix themselves (Skidelsky 2009: 439). Initially Keynes' advice fell upon deaf ears. In Britain through the early 1930s his chief political allies would be a Harold Macmillan initially out of Parliament, a David Lloyd George who few trusted, and an Oswald Mosley on the road to adopting the fascist cause in 1932. For all the later praise of his remedies, this chapter will illustrate that countries adopted different approaches to the downturn, some of which involved government deficit spending and others relying more heavily on the market re-adjusting given time.

To analyse the path economies took into the 1930s this chapter first examines the changing ideas of John Maynard Keynes over these crucial years and introduces the theoretical constructs that would increasingly guide world leaders. A note is required here: Keynes was not the only economist reaching such conclusions, but he was certainly the most prominent. Michael Kalecki, a Polish economist of a similar mindset, was given a copy of Keynes' 1936 *The General Theory* when researching in Stockholm. As Joan Robinson later recorded

> He began to read it – it was the book he intended to write. He thought perhaps there would be something different. No, all the way it was his book. [Kalecki] said: 'I confess I was ill. Three days I lay in bed. Then I thought – Keynes is more known than I am. These ideas will get across quicker with him and then we can get on to the interesting question, which is their application. Then I got up'.
>
> *(Robinson 1992: 3–4).*

In a sense, this book takes the Kalecki line. There were other economists working on the same material around the same time – in October 1933, for instance, Kalecki read his paper 'Macro-dynamic Theory of Business Cycles'. But it was Keynes through whom many understood the new economic insights, whose work is most readily and extensively available for readers to access in English, and thus Keynes on whom we concentrate. Readers are of course encouraged to look to the works of thinkers like Gunnar Myrdal, Ernst Wagemann and Knut Wicksell too.

More broadly, whilst too deep an analysis of the 1930s is beyond the purview of this book, it would be equally remiss to draw a line on 31 December 1929 as if history suddenly stopped. The second section therefore traces the actual ways countries responded to the first year of the depression following the crash of 1929. To be sure, the depression had not yet even hit its bottom point at the end of 1930 and these responses were therefore preliminary to what would come later. At the same time, they illustrate the disparate ways in which governments responded to the conditions of the post-crash economy. As will be seen, the decisions made early in the 1930s had a major impact on the speed with which those economies would later begin to recover from the crash, often after adopting Keynesian ideas into their economic strategy.

The emergence of Keynes

We have already encountered John Maynard Keynes several times in the course of this book. Since the 1919 publication of *The Economic Consequences of the Peace*, the Cambridge economist had been publicly known and influential on both sides of the Atlantic, though few policy makers heeded his ideas. He had clashed with Winston Churchill over the disastrous return to the gold standard in the mid-1920s and penned an aggressive follow-up to his previous work, *A Revision of the Treaty*, in which he explicitly defended himself against his critics and reiterated the argument that German reparations were being set unrealistically high.

It was natural that Keynes would weigh in on the developing economic crisis of the early 1930s. In 1930 he published *A Treatise on Money*, a work he had been writing since the early 1920s that examined the relationship between the acts of saving and investing and argued that saving did not necessarily lead to the act of investing (Keynes 1930). Too much saving, or the 'hoarding' of money, could lead to deflation. Traditionally, banks would lower interest rates to encourage increased investment, but Keynes realised that in this scenario the money might simply be sent abroad, where it could generate higher returns, rather than be invested domestically. The solution was therefore to invest more or save less, and the role of central banks was to maintain an equilibrium between saving and investment through its interest rate policies (Skidelsky 2009: 323–5). In a globalised economy there was no natural mechanism that would balance out the two, as classical economists believed.

Keynes did not own shares on Wall Street in October 1929, and therefore his own investments were initially insulated from the crash (his business partner was less fortunate). As unemployment began to grow in Britain, Keynes expanded upon his analysis in *A Treatise on Money* and began to publicly advocate stimulating investment to propel the economy back to recovery. As he told banker Robert H. Brand in 1930:

> The fact that you do not spend that money [that you have saved] means that some business man fails to sell you something he hoped to sell you and has to accept a lower price, and is, therefore, poorer by the exact amount that you are richer ... And very likely, without your knowing it, you yourself as a shareholder find out that you are that much poorer. One of the remedies that eventually comes, is that this process so impoverishes the community that in the end it cannot save at all and so you reach equilibrium.
>
> *(Skidelsky 2009: 351)*

Keynes would eventually codify his economic theories in the 1936 *The General Theory of Employment, Interest and Money*, one of the most significant works of economic theory ever written. As early as 1923, Keynes had expressed the view that the role of economists was not to produce long-term solutions to economic problems per se, but instead to fix the immediate problems presented by economic downturns:

> the long run is a misleading guide to current affairs. In the long run we are all dead. Economists set themselves too easy, too useless a task if in tempestuous seasons they can only tell us that when the storm is past the ocean is flat again.
>
> *(Keynes, 1924: 80)*

This insight was vital because its short-term view deviated greatly from the Hoover Administration in Washington and indeed most governments around the world who, as the next section will note, hoped the depression was simply a matter of a normal economic business cycle and should be allowed to work itself out naturally. In Britain, for one, Oswald Mosley resigned from the Labour government in May 1930 in the belief that the so-called Treasury Orthodoxy – backed by the Bank of

England – was not the solution for an economy from which demand was ebbing away by the day. Cheap money – i.e. lowering interest rates – was broadly the solution pursued by Britain's central bank. Lowering the rate from 6 to 2 per cent over the course of 1932 indeed increased the supply of money by about a third in the four years to 1936. Unemployment remained consistently high across the board until 1933, and in parts of the UK until late in the decade.

Indeed, while classical economists and most others were determined to wait out the recession, Keynes pushed for immediate short-term policies to be put in place, primarily to boost 'aggregate demand' in the economy; that is, the total demand for produced goods and services. Keynes believed there needed to be a combination of monetary and fiscal policies to rescue economies from slumps and to reduce the chances of another one occurring. Here, once again, for clarity it is important to distinguish monetary policy from fiscal policy: monetary policy is a country's ability to control the supply of money through interest rates or the availability of money (a path pursued above by the Bank of England), whereas fiscal policy is raising of taxation and/or the spending of money by the government. Though he believed it could play a part, Keynes was sceptical of monetary policy's ability *alone* to solve the unemployment crisis and argued that the best way to recover from depression, and to boost aggregate demand, would not only be to keep interest rates permanently low to increase credit but also, crucially, to have direct intervention from the government in the form of counter-cyclical spending. By late 1931 he was advocating vast public expenditure on capital projects to put people to work:

> I read a few days ago of a proposal to drive a great new road, a broad boulevard, parallel to the Strand, on the south side of the Thames [in London], as a new thoroughfare joining Westminster to the City. That is the right sort of notion. But I would like to see something bigger still. For example, why not pull down the whole of South London from Westminster to Greenwich, and make a good job of it … Would that employ men? Why, of course it would! Is it better that men should stand idle and miserable, drawing the dole? Of course it is not.
>
> *(Skidelsky 2009: 384)*

Keynes therefore believed the government needed to intervene far more than hitherto for there to be rapid recovery. As private investment in the economy decreased as a result of the downturn, the government should plug this gap and pick up its own investment in order to stimulate the economy. As he noted in his *The General Theory*, 'I expect to see the State … taking an ever greater responsibility for directly organising investment' (Keynes 1936: 216). Through public works programmes, such as the building of railways or roads, government spending would be able to facilitate job creation and economic spending. Accordingly, the policy at the core of *The General Theory* is to combat the high rate of unemployment. The government stimulus would boost aggregate demand and encourage the aggregate spending that is necessary for the economy to function at a healthy level. Since in the long run 'we are all dead', there was every reason to spend money *now*.

In addition, Keynes argued that the traditional economic understandings of risk and speculation were misguided. Most 'classical' economists prior to Keynes believed that risk could be measured in terms of future gains and advocated the idea that individuals acting in the market will be rational, thereby making the market rational. An investment held within the market will increase with time. In contrast, Keynes argued that this was an irrational mindset and behaviour because there is no way to calculate with certainty what the risk, or relative safety, associated with an investment actually is. Thereby, Keynes defined uncertainty in the market to be incalculable. Rather than focusing on risk management like others, he would turn to focus on reducing uncertainty caused by rampant investment speculation. In *The General Theory*, Keynes argued that investment speculation is fundamentally driven by irrationality rather than rational expectation:

> Even apart from the instability due to speculation, there is the instability due to the characteristic of human nature that a large proportion of our positive activities depend on spontaneous optimism rather than on a mathematical expectation, whether moral or hedonistic or economic. Most, probably, of our decisions to do something positive, the full consequences of which will be drawn out over many days to come, can only be taken as a result of animal spirits – of a spontaneous urge to action rather than inaction, and not as the outcome of a weighted average of quantitative benefits multiplied by quantitative probabilities.
>
> *(Keynes 1936: 213)*

One of the ways for uncertainty in the market to be reduced would be through government involvement, which would provide cushioning against the fluctuations that are bound to occur. Keynes argued that it is better to focus on the yield an investment may have over the next few months versus the longer term because events within a market – as New York had so dramatically illustrated – are uncertain. In accordance with the views he had expressed in 1930, the double-edged sword that Keynes noticed throughout the Great Depression was that individuals' perfectly rationale desire to save what dwindling money they had actually would lead to a reduction in total savings across the board. This was because the economy as a whole was dependent on levels of demand, and money saved was a de facto reduction in aggregate demand. And as demand fell, so too would incomes, thus diminishing the proportion of money that could be saved. This so-called 'paradox of thrift' was not a wholly new economic theory, but it was certainly one Keynes re-popularised.

Importantly, Keynes was no socialist – indeed he was a member of Britain's Liberal Party, associated in the nineteenth century with laissez-faire economics, though becoming more interventionist in the early twentieth century – and believed in free market solutions to the challenges of the depression. On the other hand, he believed that it would take the aggressive government intervention he described to spark the level of spending that would be required to pull the economy out of its slump. *The General Theory* was not published until 1936 and Keynes himself remained sidelined by government policy makers until the Great Depression had reached its bottom. In the early 1930s his influence progressively grew, and in 1941 he was appointed as a Director of the Bank of England. In the meantime, however, governments around the world developed different responses to the economic turmoil of the depression that helped determine the speed of their recovery.

Worldwide responses to the crash

Faced with an unforeseen economic collapse, the industrialised nations were presented with the two distinct policy options already described to help guide them back to recovery. One strategy, already referred to as the 'classical' or *laissez-faire* approach, called for limited government intervention and emphasised the importance of balanced fiscal budgets. These classic ideologists advocated for a business-centric approach, holding the belief that the markets would self-correct if left unperturbed. Nations such as Australia, Finland, Norway and the UK adopted this approach as they reduced expenditure levels to match their revenue levels.

As noted, the alternative Keynesian approach argued for an active fiscal policy in which government expenditures would help bolster consumer demand. Supporters of this concept, deemed 'new economics', asserted that a fiscally responsive government would better facilitate economic growth without the volatility risks of a market-centred approach. Countries such as Canada and the United States increasingly embraced the Keynesian approach as the 1930s continued by implementing compensatory policy postures increasing fiscal spending even as revenues were falling.

Despite ideological differences and varying levels of economic hardship, nearly all Western democratic states demonstrated an increase in government expenditures over the first years of the Great Depression. Only Finland and Norway, which both implemented a classical approach, saw their fiscal spending decline from the period 1929–1931 (6 per cent and 4 per cent respectively). While Australia and the UK would begin to reduce their governmental budgets in the mid-1930s, these states exhibited an expansionary fiscal policy trend by increasing spending by 4 and 8 per cent respectively over the two-year period. During this time the United States and Canada increased government expenditures by 14 per cent each, possibly foreshadowing their commitment to the Keynesian approach (Hill 1988: 57). The Hoover Dam, built on the Arizona–Nevada border, was one proto-Rooseveltian project that saw its first foundations laid in this period.

While the majority of these industrialised nations took a similar expansive approach to fiscal policy at the dawn of the depression, it should be noted that government spending patterns began to diverge later in the 1930s. Following the abandonment of the gold standard by many European countries in 1931 (in order, in effect, to devalue their currencies), Western states began to adopt decidedly more rigid approaches to the economic collapse at hand. For nations that adopted the classic fiscal approach, the late 1930s saw expenditure levels that were reduced to better match revenue and thereby balance the books. Following the release of Keynes' *The General Theory*, states that subscribed to the Keynesian school of thought began to increase the rate of fiscal spending in order to help stimulate the reeling domestic economy. However, not all countries followed a distinctly classic or Keynesian approach to their fiscal policy agendas. Sweden's declines in revenue were largely abated by the surpluses collected in the 1920s, and the country made a recovery by 1935 (Hill 1988: 57). Meanwhile, France did not take fiscal policy action in response to the Great Depression until the mid-1930s due largely to its ability to obtain natural resources from its colonial possessions and the fact that the depression's impact was initially more modest there.

Prior to 1931, the monetary policies of most Western democratic nations were shaped largely by the gold standard. As noted previously, this system, designed to settle payment disputes and increase price stability, called for each state's central bank to produce an amount of currency that reflected their bank's gold reserves. This was the primary 'rule of the game', and it was crucial that participating countries uphold this standard at all times. The global retreat from the gold standard happened in multiple rounds, as nations with smaller gold reserves were the first to abandon the system. When the depression caused the global market for primary goods to drop, countries that exported these goods were susceptible to drops in price and demand. Being export-reliant states with low levels of gold reserves, Canada (de facto January 1929, before the crash) and Australia (March 1930) were simply unable to remain on the gold standard. While Australia's currency depreciated by 30 per cent (Hill 1988: 68), many of the countries with larger gold reserves were able to stay afloat for the time being.

Several months after Australia's monetary devaluation, a European banking crisis forced numerous states to leave the gold standard. Bank failures in 1930 caused many investors to liquidate their assets at a rate with which financial institutions could not keep up. In May 1931 Austria's largest bank, *Credit Anstalt*, failed as a result of not being able to meet the demands of clients desiring to liquidate their assets (Hill 1988: 68). This unprecedented collapse caused a banking panic throughout Germany and Eastern Europe, countries to which Britain had made substantial loans. As mentioned, foreign investors now began to withdraw from the UK, forcing this former financial juggernaut to go off the gold standard in September 1931 (Hill 1988: 69). Several nations quickly followed suit, as countries reliant on Britain's exports felt that they too had to devalue their currency in order to prevent a collapse in their export markets. By the end of 1931, 'Sweden, Denmark, Norway, Finland (in that order) had adopted this course', and Canada made its de facto suspension of the gold standard official. In addition, many other states left the gold standard as they were unable to weather the European financial storm of 1931 (Hill 1988: 68). France, Belgium and Italy clung doggedly on into the mid-1930s, but they were a rare breed.

As states retreated from the gold standard, they began to adopt domestically focused monetary policies rather than ones that emphasised international price stability. Many governments implemented a cheap-money approach in which the central bank lowered interest rates in order to increase the money supply and bolster economic activity. This monetary policy was often paired with wage rate reductions and the balancing of fiscal budgets. As noted above, the UK has often been considered the strongest example of this policy, but nearly all Western states lowered their interest rates as a result of the economic depression.

While the gold standard was designed to create a global benchmark for international trade, it proved to be an effort marred by a lack of coordination and regulation. The gold standard system was not run in accordance with the 'rules of the game' and the resulting scheme was 'awkward, qualified, and inherently unstable' as countries did not correctly peg their currency levels to their actual gold reserves (Hill 1988: 67). The standard was clearly not strong enough to withstand the pressure created by the economic collapse of the 1930s. After abandoning the gold standard, countries were 'better able to pursue self-interested domestic monetary policies' as countries who left the gold standard sooner often recovered faster than countries who maintained the standard deeper into the depression (Hill 1988: 67). In the words of former US Federal Reserve Chairman Ben Bernanke, the gold standard proved that 'fixed exchange rate systems, at least those without strong conventions concerning coordination, can be very dangerous and destabilizing' (Bernanke 1993: 266).

Although the Great Depression had profound impacts on Western democratic industrialised nations, it was truly a global crisis and had varying effects on countries with differing governmental and economic systems. One obvious example is the Soviet Union, which experienced an economic situation that was much different from that of other European states. Having pursued a path of autarkic national development and a non-market economy, the Soviet Union witnessed dramatic industrial achievements through strong central planning and repressive government actions. While the state pursued economic policies of state arrangement and self-reliance, it would, however, be erroneous to say that the Soviet Union was unaffected by the Great Depression. In fact, the communist state's isolationist economic policies were caused largely by 'the onset of the global crisis in the capitalist economic system' (Sloin and Sanchez 2014: 8). Once the USSR's export markets began to sputter in the late 1920s, the state decided to restructure its investment priorities to better protect itself from the vulnerability of capitalist markets and their subsequent decline. As a result, the Soviet Union was largely unharmed by the global market collapse – indeed between 1929 and 1932 its economy grew by around 6 per cent – and enjoyed remarkable industrial progress throughout the Great Depression, albeit concurrent with the difficulties we encountered in chapter 8. This – together with the seeming success of right-leaning dictatorships such as Portugal's *Ditadura Nacional* (which presided over a 5 per cent increase in GDP over the same period) – did not speak well to the potential long-term nature of parliamentary democracy on the European continent. Autarky seemed to be the future (Maddison n.d.: passim).

Similarly, China was not as severely affected by the Great Depression initially due to the state's semi-closed economy, condition of perpetual civil war, and adherence to the silver standard. While many countries began to embrace the gold standard in the early 1920s, China's currency remained based on less valuable silver, which greatly harmed its trade balance. Despite this economic burden, China remained on the silver standard throughout the 1920s and when states began to leave the gold standard China was able to maintain price stability. China's price index actually saw 20 per cent growth from 1929 to 1931 when countries began abandoning the gold standard (Gau and Lai 2003: 165). Despite being an initial burden, China's reluctance to accept the gold standard became an asset and prevented the state from experiencing the devastating price deflations of the depression era.

Japan's economic responses to the Great Depression went from disastrous to prodigious over a period of two years. Once a silver-standard-based country, Japan adopted the gold standard in 1930, which was likened to 'opening a window in the middle of a typhoon' (Cha 2003: 127). Following a period of economic downturn, Japanese Prime Minister Wakatsuki Reijiro appointed Takahashi Korekiyo as Finance Minister. This appointment proved crucial for the recovery of the Japanese economy, as Korekiyo implemented a barrage of successful fiscal and monetary policies. Japan quickly abandoned the gold standard, mitigating the overall damage to its economy, and in December 1931 created a system of expansionary economic policies through extensive government spending. Despite Keynes' *The General Theory* not being published until 1936, Japan took a remarkably Keynesian approach to the Great Depression. Its extensive deficit spending, much of which was directed at the military, was crucial in ending the country's recession quickly (Cha 2003: 137). Despite the adoption of the gold standard at an inopportune time, Korekiyo's subsequent abandonment of the gold standard, paired with Keynesian fiscal and monetary policies, allowed Japan to largely avoid the economic troughs that plagued much of the rest of the world.

Aside from the experiences of major nations outlined above, countries as divergent as Poland (a fifth), Nicaragua (a third) and Chile (a staggering 45 per cent) saw their gross domestic products contract by a huge amount between 1929 and 1932 (Maddison n.d.: passim). While the scope and severity of the Great Depression varied with each country, all affected states had to implement economic policies that focused on a domestic recovery. At the dawn of the depression, most countries adopted some limited amount of increased government spending – often, as in the UK, using the accounting trick of bringing forward already-scheduled spending – before adopting either a classical or Keynesian fiscal policy. The global economic collapse also led to the abandoning of the gold standard in favour of policies that could better reform the domestic economy. These afflicted nations established cheap-money monetary policies in which the central bank lowered the interest rates to promote consumer spending and at the same time lower the potential returns on saving. Although Western democratic states were amongst the hardest hit by the depression, countries around the world that were adversely affected had to adapt in many different ways. The Soviet Union was able to largely avoid the economic downturn by enforcing a closed economy and focusing heavily on industrialisation. China's adherence to the silver standard and Japan's hitherto described Keynesian policies allowed them to recover more quickly than most Western countries, although China's economy ultimately relapsed in 1935. The 1920s had seen the emergence of an interconnected global economy in which participating countries grew heavily reliant on one another for certain goods and services. As a result, the Great Depression caused a global chain reaction in which states were forced to retreat from previous economic practices and focus their efforts on the home front.

Conclusion

By the early 1930s, John Maynard Keynes had become the most prominent opposition voice to the economic policies being undertaken by most governments. *The General Theory* in 1936 would mark the full emergence of his views into the public consciousness, but even before that his ideas were gaining increasing acceptance as the status quo had failed to significantly improve the world economic situation. The interconnectedness of the world's economies in the 1920s, particularly the debts that linked them together, meant that the effects of the crash would spread like a contagion between banks and stock markets. With the notable exception of the USSR, which had almost completely withdrawn from the international market economy by 1929, the effects of the crash would be felt by everyone and increasingly demand a solution when the prevailing economic wisdom failed to deliver. It is this gap that Keynes would step into as the 1930s continued.

World responses to the crisis varied dramatically. Britain and the United States clung stubbornly to the gold standard, but the former was dramatically forced off it in the face of declining gold reserves in 1931. In 1933, the United States would do the same. As a general rule, the earlier a country abandoned the gold standard the faster its recovery was likely to be. Japan provides an important counterexample to the United States and Europe: following a failed experiment early in the 1930s, the gold standard was abandoned and the government was willing to embark on massive amounts of deficit spending on the military. While this decision was an obvious reflection of the increasing militarisation of the country and would have significant international ramifications in the 1930s, it also showed the effectiveness of government spending for economic recovery. Capital spending – on roads and weaponry – would increasingly also be adopted by Germany as the decade continued.

The 1920s had started out with a post-war recession and ended with many countries about to fall into depression. In the interim, it had seen explosive economic growth, particularly in the United States, and this expansion of wealth fed the perception of the period as the 'Roaring Twenties'. The cover of this book shows two flappers of the era perilously dancing at a terrifying height: an apt visual metaphor for the decade itself. The jazz, American speakeasies and general decadence of the time all took place on the edge of a cliff from which, once peoples and nations fell off, it would take more than a decade, and a Second World War, for the world to fully recover. To be sure, *Great-Gatsby*-style parties and wealth were not the experience of all, or even most. Yet for those who viewed the 1920s as a sort of golden age before the calamities that were about to beset the globe, the decade would be remembered as the one where the dancing had taken place before the descent over the precipice.

Questions

- Which country responded to the consequences of the 1929 crash most effectively?
- Why did countries adopt different strategies to respond to the crash?
- Eleanor Roosevelt would later remark, 'Refusing to allow people to be paid less than a living wage preserves to us our own market. There is absolutely no use in producing anything if you gradually reduce the number of people able to buy even the cheapest products. The only way to preserve our markets is to pay an adequate wage' (Roosevelt 1933: 140). How does this statement fit in with some of John Maynard Keynes' ideas?
- Why did some countries experience smaller downturns as the result of the 1929 crash?
- How do government responses to the Great Depression compare to responses to the economic downturn of the late 2000s?

Recommended further reading

Hill, K.Q. (1988), *Democracies in Crisis: Public Policy Responses to the Great Depression*, London: Westview Press.

Keynes, J.M. (1936), *The General Theory of Employment, Interest and Money*, London: Macmillan.

Skidelsky, R. (2009). *Keynes: The Return of the Master*, New York: PublicAffairs.

Works cited

Bernanke, B.S. (1993), 'The World on a Cross of Gold: A review of "Golden Fetters: The Gold Standard and the Great Depression"', *Journal of Monetary Economics*, 31/2, 251–267.

Cha, M.S. (2003), 'Did Takahashi Korekiyo Rescue Japan from the Great Depression?' *The Journal of Economic History*, 63/1, 127–144.

Gau, J. and Lai, C. (2003), 'The Chinese Silver Standard Economy and the 1929 Great Depression', *Australian Economic History Review*, 43/2, 155–168.

Hill, K.Q. (1988), *Democracies in Crisis: Public Policy Responses to the Great Depression*, London: Westview Press.

Keynes, J.M. (1924), *A Tract on Monetary Reform*, London: Macmillan.

Keynes, J.M. (1930), 'Monetary Policy Alone Will Not End Depression', *The Nation*, May.

Keynes, J.M. (1936), *The General Theory of Employment, Interest and Money*, London: Macmillan.

Maddison (n.d.), 'Historical GDP data', via www.worldeconomics.com/Data/MadisonHistorical GDP/Madison%20Historical%20GDP%20Data.efp

Robinson, J. (1992), 'Michael Kalecki on the Economics of Capitalism', in Blaug, M. (ed.), *Michael Kalecki*, London: Edward Elgar Ltd, pp. 1–11.

Roosevelt, E. (1933), 'The State's Responsibility for Fair Working Conditions', *Scribner's Magazine*, 93, 140.

Skidelsky, R. (2009), *Keynes: The Return of the Master*, New York: PublicAffairs.

Sloin, A. and Sanchez, O. (2014), 'Economy and Power in the Soviet Union, 1917–1939', *Kritika: Explorations in Russian and Eurasian History*, 15/1, 7–22.

CONCLUSION: A GLOBAL 1920S?

This book has set out to give an introduction to 12 areas which, in one way or another, would all affect citizens across the world throughout the 1920s. But it is worth briefly offering a conclusion on the title of the book itself. Was this, after all, a truly 'global 1920s', and can one speak of any uniform trends given the broad canvas this work operates on?

The first point to note is the clear difference between theory and practice in this period. Of course the gap between rhetoric and reality has always been present, but never before had such high concepts as liberty and self-determination been given so wide a platform through the advance of new media such as cinema and radio. Clearly, this created tensions and contradictions. The image of the flapper and empowered woman was no doubt inspirational for many in the West, but for the woman in areas of Southern Asia likely to be married before her mid-teens it was utterly irrelevant. Likewise, *Great-Gatsby*-type fetishisation of great wealth may have given hope to some of bettering their lot in an America where, as Calvin Coolidge stated, the business of the country was business itself, but great inequalities of class and wealth remained. Charlie Chaplin's tramp continued to go down a storm in part because his anarchic, in some ways anti-capitalist message tapped into the realities of many.

Another key battle lay between the forces of internationalisation and those who wished to preserve what they saw as the greatness of the nation state. Here again the boundaries were fuzzy – Mussolini attempted to woo Italians living in New York or Rio de Janiero to the fascist cause, Lenin and Stalin battled over whether communism meant 'socialism in one country' or a global revolution, and most economic powers bowed down before an international gold standard all the while hoping it would have the most direct benefit for their particular nation. All alternated between the language of 'the global order' or 'the national interest' as and when it suited them.

Symbolising this confusion, the 1920s saw the re-emergence of pre-war debates over free trade versus autarky. Should one engage with the global markets, or go it alone? Here again theory bumped heads with rhetoric – it was no doubt beneficial for the Nigerian consumer to be able to buy cheap Japanese cloth, but if this put his or her fellow countryman out of business this in turn could lead to a downturn that would make the same cloth harder to buy again. In essence, policy makers and ordinary people alike had to deal with the consequences of an increasingly globalised economic system that few yet understood.

But can we see a uniform direction of travel in the 1920s? Can it be seen that, if concepts such as modernisation theory and a capitalist 'End of History' are undeniably simplistic, they contain a modicum of truth? Certainly technology was a big nod in the positive direction here. With radio transmitting messages, and aeroplanes and/ or dirigibles beginning to transport people over vast distances, the connectivity of the globe was vastly, if rather slowly, increased in the 1920s. To the inhabitants of Suva, Fiji who saw a flight from Hawaii touch down for the first time in 1929, it was difficult to convince them that history was not on the march, as it would have been for the Egyptians who witnessed the *Graf Zeppelin* passing over the Great Pyramid. The automobile was perhaps the most visible indicator of technological progress for most people. Before the First World War the automobile had been a relative rarity, particularly outside the United States and Western Europe. By the end of the 1920s, millions owned vehicles of their own and many more were affected by some form of motorised transportation, ranging from public transportation vehicles to tractors. Even the onset of the Great Depression would not turn the world back from the mechanisation and motorisation that began nearly everywhere during the 1920s.

Meanwhile, minds opened too. The link between increased economic prosperity and literacy in parts of Latin America served as evidence that, however imperfect, capitalism was beginning to deliver social results in addition to its economic successes. Generally speaking, debates over equality and its desirability began to shift in a variety of ways. This was partly the result of pressure from the later much-maligned League of Nations and its International Labour Office but also, as Thomas Piketty (2014) has recently noted, the product of the first of the two world wars starting a 60-year-long trend toward increasing economic equality. Convincing the masses to allow a complete reversion to an unredistributive taxation system was just not an option for many democratic politicians until well after the Second World War. The most notable exception to this overall trend was the United States, where Republican administrations kept taxes low to stoke spending and investment. The decadence pilloried in *The Great Gatsby* was one outcome of this, but arguably so too was the explosive growth of American industry at a time when it already had a number of major advantages over its competitors.

On this point, this book slightly goes against those who argue for a de-globalised order in the 1920s – certainly there were attempts, most obviously fascism, to extricate nations from the world order and forge a new path, but not only did these eventually fail, the intellectual roots for their failure were also being sown.

Conservative counterpunches aside, culturally the world was beginning to come together, and unless the pro-autarky nations could win their case both economically *and* militarily, the forces of capitalism ranging from the Bank of England to J.P. Morgan were in a strong position to resist their aims. That is certainly not to say the stranglehold of high finance was a universally positive trend – October 1929 put paid to that – but that it was a formidable foe. For better or worse, we live with its consequences to the present day. In the meantime, much blood would be shed by the adherents of fascism and communism in attempts to derail free market capitalism's progress.

As to what came next, the 1930s of course make any wildly optimistic assessment of the 1920s impossible. Poverty, followed by widespread death and destruction in the form of a second world war, does not suggest the greatest of legacies for the period under consideration here. But if we are to take a longer-term view – and there are difficulties here – then it is possible to view the 1920s more positively. The notion that the 1920s was all jazz, the Charleston and Gin Rickeys is of course nonsense. But after the constricting and dangerous atmosphere of the First World War, and with the unbridled capitalism of the nineteenth century not a distant memory for many, it is at least possible to highlight the good. If the 1950s saw economic growth really begin to benefit the lives of the majority, the 1960s socially conservative norms turned on their head and the 1980s and 1990s the ultimate victory of modern capitalism, then perhaps the 1920s deserves its place as one of the most influential peacetime decades of the twentieth century as well. The economic crash would cast much asunder, and for the not-inconsiderable period of 16 years (1929–1945), but the underlying trends of the 1920s were positive. Economic equality, women's rights, the idea of self-determination, peace as a desirable state of affairs: all were promoted to varying degrees in the 1920s. There were checks and balances here, and given later events it is impossible to assert any inevitability about their eventual triumph, but we can point to a new world becoming nascent at this point. Almost a century later, where that world goes next remains to be determined.

Recommended further reading

Piketty, T. (2014), *Capital in the Twenty-First Century*, Cambridge, MA: Harvard University Press.

INDEX